Lecture Notes in Computer Science 9334

Commenced Publication in 1973
Founding and Former Series Editors:
Gerhard Goos, Juris Hartmanis, and Jan van Leeuwen

More information about this series at http://www.springer.com/series/7409

Nelson Baloian · Yervant Zorian
Perouz Taslakian · Samvel Shoukouryan (Eds.)

Collaboration and Technology

21st International Conference, CRIWG 2015
Yerevan, Armenia, September 22–25, 2015
Proceedings

 Springer

Editors
Nelson Baloian
DCC, Universidad de Chile
Santiago
Chile

Perouz Taslakian
American University of Armenia
Yerevan
Armenia

Yervant Zorian
SYNOPSIS
Santa Clara
USA

Samvel Shoukouryan
Yerevan State University
Yerevan
Armenia

ISSN 0302-9743   ISSN 1611-3349 (electronic)
Lecture Notes in Computer Science
ISBN 978-3-319-22746-7   ISBN 978-3-319-22747-4   (eBook)
DOI 10.1007/978-3-319-22747-4

Library of Congress Control Number: 2015945611

LNCS Sublibrary: SL3 – Information Systems and Applications, incl. Internet/Web, and HCI

Printed on acid-free paper

Springer International Publishing AG Switzerland is part of Springer Science+Business Media
(www.springer.com)

Preface

This volume contains the papers presented at the 21st International Conference on Collaboration Technologies, CRIWG 2015. The conference was held during September 22–25, 2015, in Yerevan, Armenia. The conference is supported and governed by the Collaborative Research International Working Group (CRIWG), an open community of collaboration technology researchers. Since 1995, conferences supported by CRIWG have focused on collaboration technology design, development, and evaluation. The background research is influenced by a number of disciplines, such as computer science, management science, information systems, engineering, psychology, cognitive sciences, and social sciences.

The 26 submitted papers were carefully reviewed through a double-blind review process involving three reviewers appointed by the program chairs. In all, 11 submissions were selected as full papers and eight were selected as work in progress. Thus, this volume presents the most relevant and insightful research papers carefully chosen among the contributions accepted for presentation and discussion at the conference. The papers published in the proceedings of this year's and past CRIWG conferences reflect the trends in collaborative computing research and its evolution. There has been a growing interest in social networks analysis, crowdsourcing, and computer support for large communities in general. As is the tradition at CRIWG, the collaborative learning topic this year was also a prominently represented topic with four papers selected covering this topic in one way or another. This year there was strong participation from Chile and Germany, each having five papers. Also this year we also saw the growing participation of Japan and newcomers like Qatar and of course Armenia. There were also contributions from the USA, Canada, Brazil, and Spain.

As editors, we would like to thank everybody who contributed to the content and production of this book, namely, all the authors and presenters, whose contributions made CRIWG 2015 a success, as well as the Steering Committee, the members of the Program Committee, and the reviewers. Last but not least, we would like to acknowledge the effort of the organizers of the conference, without whom this conference would not have run so effectively. Our thanks also go to Springer, the publisher of the CRIWG proceedings, for their continuous support.

June 2015

Nelson Baloian
Samvel Shoukouryan
Perouz Taslakian
Yervant Zorian

Organization

Program Committee

Pedro Antunes — Victoria University of Wellington, New Zealand
Renata Araujo — UNIRIO, Brazil
Lars Bollen — University of Twente, The Netherlands
Luis Carriço — University of Lisbon, Portugal
Cesar A. Collazos — Universidad del Cauca, Colombia
Marco De Sa — Facebook, USA
Gj De Vreede — University of Nebraska at Omaha, USA
Dominique Decouchant — UAM Cuajimalpa, Mexico, LIG de Grenoble, France
Alicia Diaz — Lifia, UNLP, Argentina
Yannis Dimitriadis — University of Valladolid, Spain
Orlando Erazo — Universidad de Chile, Chile
Jesus Favela — CICESE, Mexico
Benjamim Fonseca — UTAD/INESC TEC
Kimberly Garcia — CINVESTAV-IPN, Mexico
Marco Gerosa — IME - USP, Brazil
Eduardo Guzmán — Universidad de Málaga, Spain
Andreas Harrer — Clausthal University of Technology, Germany
Valeria Herskovic — Pontificia Universidad Católica de Chile, Chile
Heinz Ulrich Hoppe — University of Duisburg-Essen, Germany
Indratmo Indratmo — Grant MacEwan University, Canada
Tomoo Inoue — University of Tsukuba, Japan
Seiji Isotani — University of Sao Paulo, Brazil
Marc Jansen — University of Applied Sciences Ruhr West, Germany
Ralf Klamma — RWTH Aachen University, Germany
Michael Koch — Bundeswehr University of Munich, Germany
David Kocsis — University of Nebraska at Omaha, USA
Thomas Largillier — LORIA, France
Chen-Chung Liu — NCU, USA
Stephan Lukosch — Delft University of Technology, The Netherlands
Wolfram Luther — University of Duisburg-Essen, Germany
Alejandra Martínez — University of Valladolid, Spain
Sonia Mendoza — CINVESTAV-IPN, Mexico
Roc Meseguer — Universitat Politècnica de Catalunya, Spain
Alberto L. Morán — UABC, Mexico
Andres Neyem — Pontificia Universidad Católica de Chile, Chile
Cuong Nguyen — University of Nebraska at Omaha, USA
Sergio Ochoa — Universidad de Chile, Chile

Hiroaki Ogata   Kyushu University, Japan
Hugo Paredes   INESC TEC and UTAD, Portugal
Jose A. Pino   Universidad de Chile, Chile
Christophe Reffay   Institut National de Recherche Pédagogique
Christoph Rensing   Technische Universität Darmstadt, Germany
Ana Respício   University of Lisbon, Portugal
Ana Carolina Salgado   Center for Informatics/UFPE, Brazil
Flavia Santoro   NP2Tec/UNIRIO, Brazil
Marcus Specht   Open University, The Netherlands
Diane Strode   Whitireia Polytechnic, New Zealand
Perouz Taslakian   Universite Libre de Bruxelles, Belgium
Pierre Tchounikine   University of Grenoble, France
Stefan Trausan-Matu   University Politehnica of Bucharest, Romania
Julita Vassileva   University of Saskatchewan, Canada
Vaninha Vieira   Federal University of Bahia (UFBA), Brazil
Benjamin Weyers   RWTH Aachen, Germany
Jürgen Ziegler   University of Duisburg-Essen, Germany
Gustavo Zurita   Universidad de Chile, Chile

Visualization and User Control of Recommender Systems

Julita Vassileva

Department of Computer Science
University of Saskatchewan, Canada
jiv@cs.usask.ca

Abstract. Recommender systems are one of the "hottest" areas for companies that offer items to end users and have a wide scope of applications, from commercial, through entertainment to educational. Most recommender systems are based on implicit or explicit models of user behaviour, including user ratings, click streams or navigation paths, or complex knowledge structures derived through reasoning from user input data. They deploy various personalization algorithms to adapt the recommendation to the user's interest and context. The current recommendation algorithms have advanced to a stage where they offer very high accuracy in predicting which items the user will like.

However, the resulting recommendations are not always accepted well by the users. Sometimes users prefer not to share their data with the system because of privacy concerns, or do not trust the system's recommendations, especially if they do not understand how they were generated. To gain the user's trust, it is important to explain the main principles or mechanism that the recommender system uses; however an explanation would increase the cognitive load of the user and therefore would not be welcome. A visualization of the mechanism or its main principles may be helpful here, since "a picture is worth a thousand words" and it can save users' time and efforts by showing an intuitive and understandable representation of the recommendation mechanism.

This talk will give an overview of some of the existing approaches (both from the speaker's own research lab and from other authors) for visualizing recommendation mechanisms and eventually allowing users to control these mechanisms. Starting with work from the area of open / scrutable learner models in the area of intelligent tutoring systems, through approaches for explaining recommendations to approaches visualizing aspects of collaborative, hybrid and social recommenders, the talk will focus on approaches for visualizing social recommendation in streams of social sites updates.

Contents

Crowdsourcing and Knowledge Co-creation in Virtual Museums   1
Daniel Biella, Daniel Sacher, Benjamin Weyers, Wolfram Luther,
Nelson Baloian, and Tobias Schreck

Using Real-Time Gaze Based Awareness Methods to Enhance
Collaboration   19
Christian Schlösser, Philipp Schlieker-Steens, Andrea Kienle,
and Andreas Harrer

Evaluating Anchored Discussion to Foster Creativity in Online
Collaboration   28
Georg J.P. Link, Dominik Siemon, Gert-Jan de Vreede,
and Susanne Robra-Bissantz

Measuring the Effort Demanded by CSCL Design Processes Supporting
a Consistent Artifact Flow   45
Osmel Bordiés and Yannis Dimitriadis

Supporting Collaborative Decision Making in Geo-Collaboration
Scenarios   63
Nelson Baloian, Jonathan Frez, José A. Pino, and Gustavo Zurita

Analysis of Question and Answering Behavior in Question
Routing Services   72
Zhe Liu and Bernard J. Jansen

An Integrative Tool Chain for Collaborative Virtual Museums in Immersive
Virtual Environments   86
Daniel Sacher, Benjamin Weyers, Torsten W. Kuhlen,
and Wolfram Luther

A Behaviour Awareness Mechanism to Support Collaborative Learning   95
Esunly Medina, Roc Meseguer, Sergio F. Ochoa, and Humberto Medina

Exploiting the Use of Wikis to Support Collaborative Writing:
A Case Study of an Undergraduate Computer Science Class   111
Oluwabunmi Adewoyin, Kewen Wu, and Julita Vassileva

Where to Begin? Using Network Analytics for the Recommendation
of Scientific Papers   124
Laura Steinert, Irene-Angelica Chounta, and H. Ulrich Hoppe

Every Answer Has a Question: Exploring Communication and Knowledge
Exchange in MOOCs Through Learning Analytics   140
Irene-Angelica Chounta, Tobias Hecking, and H. Ulrich Hoppe

Dynamic Credibility Threshold Assignment in Trust and Reputation
Mechanisms Using PID Controller   148
Mohsen Mohkami, Zeinab Noorian, and Julita Vassileva

XCuteKIP: Support for Knowledge Intensive Process Activities   164
Ednilson Veloso Moura, Flávia Maria Santoro,
and Fernanda Araujo Baião

BESIDE: Immersive System to Enhance Learning Within a Museum.   181
Ryuichi Yoshida, Haruya Tamaki, Tsugunosuke Sakai, Ryohei Egusa,
Machi Saito, Shinichi Kamiyama, Miki Namatame, Masanori Sugimoto,
Fusako Kusunoki, Etsuji Yamaguchi, Shigenori Inagaki,
Yoshiaki Takeda, and Hiroshi Mizoguchi

Secure Collaboration in Public Cloud Storages   190
Aram Jivanyan, Roland Yeghiazaryan, Armen Darbinyan,
and Azat Manukyan

Sketchpad: A Learning Tool Supporting Creativity in Collaborative
Learning Activities   198
Gustavo Zurita, Catalina Cárdenas, and Nelson Baloian

A Subscription Overlay Network for Large-Scale and Efficient File Parallel
Downloading   210
Patricio Galdames, Claudio Gutierrez-Soto, and Cristopher Barrientos

Synchronizing Dining Progress in Video-Mediated Time-Shifted Table
Talk Induces More Engagement   219
Tomoo Inoue and Yasuhito Noguchi

Contrasting People's Attitudes Towards Self-disclosure in Online Social
Networks and Face-to-Face Settings   232
Maria L.B. Villela, Simone I.R. Xavier, Raquel O. Prates,
Marcos O. Prates, Frank Shipman, Antônio A.P. Prates,
and Alexandre A. Cardoso

Author Index   249

Crowdsourcing and Knowledge Co-creation in Virtual Museums

Daniel Biella[1], Daniel Sacher[1], Benjamin Weyers[2], Wolfram Luther[1(✉)],
Nelson Baloian[3], and Tobias Schreck[4]

[1] University of Duisburg-Essen, Essen, Germany
{daniel.biella,daniel.sacher,wolfram.luther}@uni-due.de
[2] RWTH Aachen, Aachen, Germany
weyers@vr.rwth-aachen.de
[3] University of Chile, Santiago, Chile
nbaloian@dcc.uchile.cl
[4] Graz University of Technology, Graz, Austria
tobias.schreck@cgv.tugraz.at

Abstract. This paper gives an overview on crowdsourcing practices in virtual museums. Engaged nonprofessionals and specialists support curators in creating digital 2D or 3D exhibits, exhibitions and tour planning and enhancement of metadata using the Virtual Museum and Cultural Object Exchange Format (ViMCOX). ViMCOX provides the semantic structure of exhibitions and complete museums and includes new features, such as room and outdoor design, interactions with artwork, path planning and dissemination and presentation of contents. Application examples show the impact of crowdsourcing in the Museo de Arte Contemporaneo in Santiago de Chile and in the virtual museum depicting the life and work of the Jewish sculptor Leopold Fleischhacker. A further use case is devoted to crowd-based support for restoration of high-quality 3D shapes.

Keywords: Crowdsourcing · Co-creation · Virtual museum · Knowledge creation · Digital 3D exhibits · Standardized metadata · ViMEDEAS · ViMCOX

1 Introduction and Motivation

Crowdsourcing and co-creation are major players in an emerging field of research on collaborative systems. The technologies available nowadays, such as smartphones and social networks, enable people to provide and consume information in ways that were never possible before. But to what extent can these emerging technologies and changes in everyday life positively influence the fields of information systems and technology research? In this paper, we explore how crowdsourcing can be used in virtual museums (VMs) by creating and visiting virtual exhibits in various use cases. The main goal of this proposed extension of virtual museums is the enrichment of the virtual environment with information from engaged users (such as their preferred viewpoints, comments and search histories) and the generation of additional input for the curation of new museums and exhibits.

© Springer International Publishing Switzerland 2015
N. Baloian et al. (Eds.): CRIWG 2015, LNCS 9334, pp. 1–18, 2015.
DOI: 10.1007/978-3-319-22747-4_1

Biella [1] provides a comprehensive literature review that describes various kinds of VMs as digital heritage content, including virtual exhibits of replicated historical laboratories for the purpose of study, education and leisure. VMs and exhibits need digital reconstruction and interpretation of existing or lost artwork and their metadata, which can be deduced from existing items, photos, drawings or descriptions in books, oral tradition, expert knowledge or available metadata and recorded in a standardized metadata format. The digital representations of the artwork are then placed into a spatio-temporal context realized as indoor or outdoor exhibition space and hyperlinked to context-related information that will help visitors comprehend the digital interpretation [2]. Furthermore, through interaction with objects, displayed or spoken texts, thematic tours and electronic catalogues or tour movies, visitors can convey ideas and concepts.

In addition to the properties listed above, a VM metadata standard is also expected to support the following features [3]:

- Description of requirements concerning the presentation of exhibits and an adequate context (carrier, wall, room, lighting and so on);
- Specification of interaction methods with exhibits via adequate interfaces and reversibility to the original state after user interaction;
- Modification of exhibits with regard to position, form and content, even with the aim of creating new enhanced instances of one or more cultural objects;
- Simulation of a kind defined by a discrete or continuous process model.

In an earlier paper [2], we described the framework Replicave, developed by Biella [1] in 2006, which provides a cost-efficient way to create virtual exhibits by reusing 3D models and generating additional digital content dynamically. Its successor, Replicave2, developed by Sacher [3], uses X3D and X3DOM as rendering platforms and Java EE and the Tomcat servlet container to present exhibits online. The virtual environments can be created using customizable exhibition area templates, such as entrance halls, galleries, various media-rooms and additional interactive experiments. Replicave2 allows dynamic generation of arbitrary room designs, depending on given parameters and metadata designs specified in the VM modeling language ViMCOX. The main contribution of this paper is to present a concept that focuses on content development and enhancement realized by participatory practices and crowdsourcing, especially for Web-based museums and virtual science centers.

The paper is structured as follows. Section 2 introduces related work and focuses on the role of crowdsourcing approaches in various contexts. The discussion will show how these evolving techniques can be embedded into the creation and visiting process of VMs. Then we introduce several new approaches for the use of crowdsourcing concepts in creating (Sect. 3) and visiting (Sect. 4) VMs. Section 5 shows the feasibility of these concepts by examining three case studies. Section 6 develops a research agenda, and Sect. 7 discusses our conclusions and presents future work.

2   Related Work

Crowdsourcing on social platforms affecting social interaction is an emerging form of knowledge generation and problem solving that complements well-known practices of collaboration and co-creation. Nguyen et al. [4] define crowdsourcing as an online strategy in which an organization proposes defined task(s) to the members of the crowd via a flexible open call in order to harness their work, knowledge, skills and/or experience. They go on to provide a structured literature review, describing how to decide when to use crowdsourcing. Platforms enabling crowdsourcing offer calls to the crowd, asking for them to provide information in a meaningful way that supports the creation and use of a VM.

Many websites, including Wikipedia, Open Street Map and Second Life, illustrate important examples of crowdsourcing. We will not enter into a deep discussion about the differences between crowdsourcing and collaboration and will summarize only some of the opinions found on the web. Often, crowdsourcing and the evaluation of requested data go hand in hand with statistical evaluation. If the most probable solutions or averaging is needed, crowdsourcing seems to be a good choice since those involved work mostly independently and individually. Crowdsourcing can also bring new ideas, special knowledge and innovation into a community, whereas collaboration seeks to solve a specific problem or complete a specific task by integrating mutually complementary competences and experiences—a goal which demands qualified project management. But perhaps the best results can be achieved through a good mix of the two. As Benson [5] observes, "co-creation is a collaborative initiative which operates like crowdsourcing by seeking information and ideas from a group of people. There is, however, one crucial difference. The call for contributions is not put to an open forum or platform but to a smaller group of individuals with specialized skills and talents."

Uden and Zipf's [6] Volunteered Geographic Information (VGI)-based approach to 3D city modeling seems promising and expands the options for crowdsourcing 3D city models. They present a concept for a new Web platform called OpenBuildingModels, which allows the models to be linked to Open Street Map objects and displayed by a dedicated 3D viewer.

Colfi [7] provides an overview of key issues that are related to social and cooperative interactions—particularly around the design and use of technology—at heritage sites that have emerged in CSCW and that involve the conduct and the activities of visitors, the design and evaluation of interactive installations for guidance and access, and the creation of novel artistic performances and interactions with exhibits.

These areas of interest are defined in greater detail by Baloian and Zurita [8], who suggest using guidelines in the knowledge creation process that will also apply in modified form within the crowdsourcing and co-creation scenario in VMs: (a) it is necessary to consider a knowledge creation model based on crowdsourcing to organize human resources, knowledge creation and the task-completion process; (b) in complex contexts like 3D virtual environments, content and metadata creation and enhancement require crowd selection and motivation and the exploitation, validation and dissemination of knowledge; (c) knowledge creation in mobile scenarios visiting indoor and outdoor expositions demands an appropriate hardware and software platform, as well as new types of interaction support and guidance and metadata collection using current standards.

Using content produced by crowdsourcing requires an appropriate online platform that eases the transformation of 3D models and metadata into the right formats. The Virtual Museum and Cultural Object Exchange Format ViMCOX [9] has been developed in order to provide a semantic structure for exhibits and complete museums. The standard supports the hierarchical description of VMs and provides stylistic devices for sophisticated and lifelike exhibit design, interactive exhibits, assets, and outdoor areas. ViMCOX is based on international metadata standards and uses LIDO version 1.0 as its interchange and harvesting format for cultural objects.

Simon [10] lists five stages of social participation in a VM, where each stage has something special to offer to visitors. Stage one equips them with access to the content they seek. Stage two provides an opportunity for inquiry, in which visitors can take action and ask questions. Stage three allows them to see where their interests and actions fit in the wider community of visitors to the institution. Stage four helps them connect with particular people—staff members and other visitors—who share their content and activity interests. Stage five makes the entire institution feel like a social place, full of potentially interesting, challenging, and enriching encounters with other people.

In contrast, our focus is to ask what visitors have to offer the VM during the five stages when they are accessing content, interacting with artwork, asking questions, taking their own tour and communicating with other people.

An example of this is described by Rodriguez Echavarria et al. [11]. People in local communities were invited to take photographs of the objects in the collection of public monuments and sculptures in the city of Brighton and Hove in the United Kingdom and upload them to a website along with provenance information. In this way, the same object was photographed at different times and from different perspectives, increasing the amount of data and thus helping to produce a quality 3D shape using computer vision techniques. In this way, crowdsourcing enables the generation of several 3D shapes representing the same object at different times.

Morin [12] discusses how crowdsourcing improves Web3D user navigation. User interactions are collected in order to detect meaningful elements in a 3D object and to simplify 3D navigation. Recommended views are computed and suggested to subsequent users. A similar approach is described by Nghiem [13], who proposes a new paradigm based on crowdsourcing to facilitate online 3D interactions that consists of analyzing 3D user interactions to identify regions of interest (ROIs) and generating recommendations to subsequent users. The paradigm also includes crowdsourcing activities for building semantic associations between text and 3D visualizations. The links produced are suggested to upcoming users so they can easily locate 3D visualizations associated with particular textual content.

Dallas [14] suggests a guestbook presented as a separate section of the virtual exhibition website and accessible through a link labelled "Reflections" in the permanent navigation bar of the exhibit. It is organized in sections, mirroring the internal structure of the actual exhibit, and visitors are asked to contribute to discussions by responding to a predefined question for each individual section. Admittedly, a guestbook is meant to address a public audience, not to open up interaction between communities of active participants. There are, however, some instances where visitors interact.

In Carletti et al. [15], a web survey was carried out on 36 crowdsourcing projects promoted by galleries, libraries, archives, museums and educational institutions. The authors provide classification for crowdsource tasks akin to common curator tasks (selecting, classifying, describing, maintaining) and public participation models:

- Classification—gathering descriptive metadata related to an object in a collection;
- Contextualization—adding contextual knowledge to objects;
- Collection integration/completion;
- Co-curation—using the inspiration/expertise of non-professional curators to create (web exhibitions);
- Crowdfunding—collective cooperation to support efforts initiated by others.

In conclusion, there are several proposals in the literature that support the construction and operation of VMs and exhibits by crowdsourcing; however what is missing is a complete taxonomy of such activities and a coherent architectural approach that offers tools providing feedback information from crowdsourcing to the creation process of virtual museums.

Now we want to redefine the activity of digital curation: *Digital curation* (e.g., Digital Curation Center: (http://www.dcc.ac.uk/) is the maintenance of digital research data throughout its lifecycle: re-usability of metadata, surrogates and other media or digital assets. This includes the development of digital repositories and, more importantly, the definition of guidelines and workflows for purposes such as digitization, documentation, presentation, transfer and preservation (interoperability, encoding/formats, standards, vocabularies, tool chains, services) as well as the transformation and combination of artworks to create new instances. Challenges in co-curation and digital curation include documenting provenance and applying digital rights management (DRM), for example, transfer of ownership.

Next, we focus on the generation of knowledge regarding the co-curation of museums and exhibits. The following factors are key in the crowdsourcing approach:

- There are three important stages of supporting curators in building expositions and visitors in exploring VMs through crowdsourcing:
  - Co-curating: Online creation or enhancement of digital 2/3D exhibits and contributing metadata;
  - Supporting visitors as they select and publish tours on the museum's platform, navigate in the 3D environment and interact with exhibits;
  - Discussing additional content and creating appropriate context using the electronic guestbook. Visitors are invited to use their smartphones to take photos and comment on the exhibit. This material can be used to enhance the exhibit.
- Two types of human capital are involved:
  - People in the crowd are motivated and have appropriate knowledge to contribute;
  - People working in house gather material, execute quality control and integrate exhibits and metadata into the VM using a VM metadata standard like ViMCOX and applying a DRM strategy.
- An adequate communication platform is needed, including interfaces that make collection of information and transformation to standardized datatypes accessible to the crowd.

In most cases, the artwork is copyrighted and curators are requested to adopt a high quality DRM. Thus, building and operating a VM requires the cooperation of several stakeholders. The owners of the artwork must grant permission for the creation of digital 3D representations and their dissemination via the Internet or a standalone system under certain conditions, such as watermarking the exhibit and displaying copyright information concerning limitation of use and propagation. The curator provides metadata and exposition layout, which are part of the copyright agreement. The software engineer organizes the creation of digital representations together with their metadata, installs protection and builds a VM, which is hosted on a server, kiosk system or other appropriate platform. Volunteers and visitors are invited and encouraged to contribute to the exhibition and must sign off on copyright agreements prohibiting abusive use and distribution of digital artwork.

As an alternative, leading museums abstain from watermarking and use the Open Archives Initiative Protocol for Metadata Harvesting (OAI-PMH). The OAI is an organization that develops and applies technical interoperability standards that allow archives to share catalog information (metadata). It attempts to build a low-barrier interoperability framework for archives (institutional repositories) containing digital content (digital libraries) and allows people (service providers) to harvest metadata (from data providers). Open data collections such as Europeana, 3D Icons, Web Gallery of Arts and Wikipedia, together with cultural heritage institutional (OAI-PMH) repositories include metadata records, knowledge bases and corresponding interfaces for re-use of assets and artworks. The Rijksmuseum OAI application program interface collection (https://www.rijksmuseum.nl/en/api/), for example, is a set of more than 110,000 descriptions of objects (metadata) and digital images. Through suitable APIs, the museum provides a state-of-the-art service for application developers that makes collections available for use in web applications. As mentioned in [16], the Yale Center for British Art (YCBA) and the Rijksmuseum release high resolution images, thumbnails and metadata of their collections and artworks licensed under creative commons and public domain licenses using OAI-PMH. The Rijksmuseum releases metadata records as Dublin Core data sets, and the YCBA collection metadata is available in the LIDO format. This allows the combination of artwork surrogates and sophisticated metadata elaborated by domain experts with generative VMs to let the public curate individual exhibits.

3   Supporting Curators Through Crowdsourcing: Building Exhibits

As discussed in the introduction and literature review, crowdsourcing can have various benefits for the generation and curation of VMs and their exhibits. It can offer concepts and ideas, 3D models, metadata and work contexts. One of the most cogent arguments for crowdsourcing digital 3D models is that generating them involves high costs; with crowdsourcing, these models can be visualized and stored or exported together with appropriate textures to modern 3D printers. Similarly, an appropriate DRM can be used to combine community contributions to administrative and descriptive metadata with technical and use metadata provided by the institution.

Although high-quality 3D modeling is a task for specialists, involving engaged volunteers can help reduce costs. Volunteer involvement can be supported with software based on game consoles and open-source modeling software (e.g., low-cost 3D scanning and modeling with MS Kinect and ReconstructMe) and contribute metadata by respecting XML-based standards. However, in the museum community there are no simple solutions for both because a lot of pre- and post-processing is needed and comfortable interfaces are lacking. Generally, reconstructing software includes a viewer or editor that allows for inspecting or repairing and annotating the 3D shapes, which are afterwards stored in the exhibition repository and can be searched and selected within their local and temporal context using keywords from descriptive metadata.

Typically, one of two scanning principles is implemented: cameras or lasers moving around the object or a fixed camera setup with objects revolving on a turning table. Other image-based approaches are the Arc 3D web service (www.arc3d.be/) and the proprietary 123D Catch from Autodesk (www.123dapp.com/catch), which allows 3D digitization using modern smartphones. A comparative overview on existing models is provided in [17], which discusses multiple applications for 3D scanning, modeling and printing and provides an overview of future directions for this technology, such as 3D video capture. To create the 3D model from the image data, several software packages can be utilized to produce a triangulated surface or a mesh object and to process the color information of the object being scanned.

To mention only one system we cite MeshLab as an open source, portable, extensible system for the editing and processing, subdividing, converting, repairing and coloring of unstructured 3D triangular meshes (http://meshlab.sourceforge.net/).

The Fraunhofer IGD also provides a service for the preparation of 3D models for Web-based presentations utilizing X3DOM (http://publica.Fraunhofer.de/documents/N-264523.html). This service was tailored for the cultural heritage domain to ease the use of scanned and complex 3D models in VM applications.

Let us come back to the impact of the crowd in the generation phase. Volunteers use (1) an open source software tool for capturing 3D data from real objects using (2) an affordable 3D scanner, such as the Kinect, (3) reconstruction software that produces textured 2D or 3D models and (4) a Web-based interface for checking and transferring the model, rights and metadata. In general, the process should be completely runnable on mobile devices, especially content capture.

On the curator's side, post-processing is done by the VM staff on workstations or in a reduced form on mobile devices. An enhanced platform provides automatic post-processing facilities together with a Web-based interface for entering the 2D/3D content, metadata and copyright information.

It is important to define a versatile hardware environment to host the exhibition, for instance, a kiosk system with a modified operation mode prohibiting unauthorized user actions and an adequate user interface supporting user navigation, interaction, text input and multilingual text and speech output and logging functionalities.

Clear software requirements and standardized data formats facilitate seamless integration of contributed content. An extensive test program must include verification of software stability in accordance with the ISO/IEC/IEEE 29119 norm, stress tests for fluent navigation and display, and confirmation of complete and correct realization of the curator's content specifications and failure-free system operation over a specified time. Further recommendations are given in the next section and the use cases.

4   Enhancing Exhibitions Through Crowdsourcing: Collaborative Knowledge Creation and Management

There are several ways to collect knowledge or information during or after a user's visit by using communication or voting tools and interaction interfaces, which may be integrated into the VM or accessed separately. Important means are input forms for entering text or formatted metadata, special purpose interfaces for interacting with the exhibit or an electronic guestbook where users can comment on the exhibit or ask questions about particular items. Typical information concerns the personal data which help to define user groups and their interests: (virtual) museums, categories of exhibits, artists and their epochs, user comments concerning the museum and exposition design, presentation of the exhibits and complementary information, quality of digital exhibit and metadata, reports of erroneous or missing information or technical flaws, system handling and usability, free navigation and guided tours, facilities to communicate with the curator, technical staff or other visitors, degree of immersion, modern multi-touch interfaces.

An example how the analysis of user input allows for adapting user interfaces is shown in [18]. Here, input is used to identify input errors through modeled error automata. These error automata can also be used to generate reconfiguration rules for formal reconfiguration of a user interface on its logical layer together with reconfiguration patterns derived from psychological guidelines. In the context of VMs, this approach can be used to identify certain visitor interaction patterns to trigger changes in the interface, the content and the exposition layout. Furthermore, other visitors can profit from this type of adaption.

In the following list, we summarize the most relevant activities in correlation with visitors' input. Most visitors' contributions concerning modifications of the exhibit and exhibition design via interaction are relevant to Sect. 3 much as the spiral model is applied in software engineering.

- *Correcting/enhancing or completing exhibits, metadata or the technical platform.*
  Visitors are invited to ask questions and to provide information via various communication channels like an electronic guestbook or writing an email;
- *Identifying areas of interest.*
  User actions, such as approaching an exhibit, turning objects, and zooming in on certain features, are recorded and evaluated to inform further enhancement of the digitized 3D object and facilitate users' navigation in these areas, to determine user groups and navigation behavior and to assess important/interesting exhibition areas or most frequently targeted areas using heat maps that display the results of a cluster analysis. They are also used to determine which exhibition areas are less frequently visited and detect design flaws. This information can be used directly to support the curator in exhibition planning;
- *Modifying the exhibit when interaction is provided.*

As described in [3], visual objects can be inspected and scrutinized from different vantage points, and the user can modify an object's position, exposition and appearance. Geometric objects can be moved or rotated, superposed, scaled or modified, cloned, or made invisible. Scene graph–based languages support the deconstruction of an object into its various parts and, in a different way, even its reconstruction from its parts. Thus, visitors become creators of various new representations of an artwork;

- *Creating appropriate context/placing objects in a context.*
Visitors navigate within the exposition by moving through different viewpoints or clicking inside an exhibit area, watch metadata activating information frames, look at collections of similar items, comment on the exhibit in a virtual guestbook, make annotations, and cite related work;
- *Building their own exposition, publishing tours / storytelling / disseminating information.*

As proposed in [19] as a structured task, in order to record a sequence of ideas and adapt it to the VM context, users can

- objectify: mentally represent ideas as (an existing) pictorial artwork and their context as a museum;
- organize: (conceive a tour) and order the pictures in the sequence required to produce a story;
- associate and aggregate: distribute parts of the story to separate rooms or a proposed tour;
- place or displace: hang or move each item on a wall;
- access and enter: visit the museum (sometime later);
- move: walk through the rooms;
- perceive: see the items hanging on the walls, placed in the room or outside area;
- discover: find each item along the way;
- recognize and interpret: remember what each item represents;
- *Recommending and voting.*

To elaborate valuable recommendations, information about users is needed. This information can be collected before, during or after visits.

To support the visitor or user, the VM or exhibit should be hosted on a versatile technical platform and displayed via high-performance software tools. Unfortunately, most web browser plugins that visualize virtual environments do not provide meaningful server logs or data to reconstruct visitors' tours and point-and-click navigation. A visitor moving in a HTML5/X3DOM scenario facilitates logging the position, determining proximity to an exhibit, orientation and walk direction as well as jumping to another room via a door connector or a tele-porter to produce a sort of camera replay. Also, the dwell time in front of the exhibit and clicks to access to metadata and further material can be recorded. At the entrance, during the visit or before leaving, visitors can provide information about themselves and their interests, comment or access the exhibit or parts of it. A statistical evaluation of specific user group walks makes available transition matrices, averaged dwell time and engagement. These data can help identify areas of interest (cf. list of visitors' contributions above), develop favorite tours, and publish series of pictures together with context and stories surrounding tour highlights. However, using a solution with a browser plugin requires additional effort to collect user input, record viewpoints and sojourn time, measure engagement and support tour publishing or storytelling in accordance with DRM.

One interesting question is how museum staff can encourage visitors to participate. We propose awarding participation by providing users with extra features; these might include electronic catalogues, opportunities to assess the exhibit or upload additional material, or ways to publish on the museum platform or recommend their tour. Nevertheless, which instruments are most suitable has to be further evaluated in one of our use cases.

For the first use case, which is presented in the next section, we opted for the kiosk system solution based on the European legislation that allows collection material to be made digitally available to individual members of the public through a closed network and within a special exhibition context for the purpose of research or private study [20].

5   Use Cases

5.1   The Virtual Leopold Fleischhacker Museum

The Virtual Leopold Fleischhacker Museum consists primarily of annotated photographs and reconstructed tombstones. We decided to develop the museum using X3D and Java/PHP technology and the powerful BS contact X3D plugin to display the virtual environment at http://mw2013.museumsandtheweb.com/paper/the-virtual-leopold-fleischhacker-museum/ (cf. Fig. 1).

Unfortunately, current X3D plugins neither support a multiuser perspective nor generate group awareness; however, an individual user may interact with the items and retrieve further information via an avatar, and Java-capable X3D browsers can be used in shared workspaces to walk, navigate and work together in complex collective tasks. It was decided by the curator that no interaction and animation should be included as stylistic devices in the free walking and guided tours.

Fig. 1. Welcome page of the Leopold Fleischhacker Museum with access to free and guided tours

Therefore, we will also present a digital 2D/3D object browser similar to familiar examples where visitors have the opportunity to browse and search for 2D/3D exhibit items and their corresponding metadata as well as rotating, zooming and panning the 3D reconstructions or watching predefined animations. (cf. http://examples.x3dom.org/v-must/ipad_metadata_expert/)

Additional support for annotating objects could be implemented as well to focus on crowdsource and co-knowledge creation.

Fig. 2. Tombstone in the outside area

An alternative method is to use WebGL and display X3D files using X3DOM. X3DOM is developed and maintained by Fraunhofer IGD and proposes a new HTML profile that is an extension of X3D's interchange profile. However, at the start of the Fleischhacker project, tests showed that this solution performed worse than the one ultimately selected.

The virtual Fleischhacker museum hosts about 200 pictorial exhibits; 3D assets like plants, pillars, glass vitrines, benches and information tableaux; and 29 tombstones reconstructed by the crowd using photographs, Blender and X3D export and carefully placed outside in a virtual Jewish cemetery (cf. Fig. 2). Several masks (cf. Fig.3) were reconstructed together with one greatly enlarged seal presented in the entrance hall of the VM (cf. Fig. 4).

Most of this work was provided by volunteers and submitted online. Among others, Dr. Michael Brocke, director of the Solomon Ludwig Steinheim Institute for

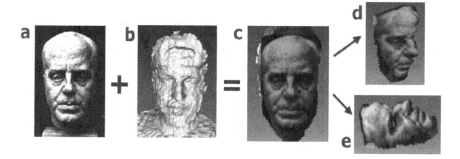

Fig. 3. 3D reconstruction of a mask by S. Yaslar

German-Jewish history in Essen has done significant, extensive research on Leopold Fleischhacker and allowed the museum to incorporate his archive.

The exhibition design, texts and room arrangements were contributed by the curator, Dr. Barbara Kaufhold, and thematically arranged in 15 exhibition rooms in a star-shaped museum and a forest landscape. At the end of this year, the VM and selected tours will be presented in a traditional museum environment together with a few physical artworks in several displays.

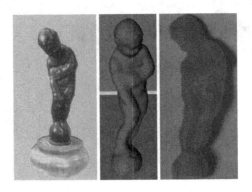

Fig. 4. Seal and digital 3D reconstruction by S. Yaslar, 3D print out by K.-Michael Köhler (http://mw2013.museumsandtheweb.com/paper/the-virtual-leopold-fleischhacker-museum/)

It has been proven that the impact of the crowd was significant and indispensable. Volunteers contributed work to the extent of about three man-years in different categories of tasks:

- Creating and enhancing digital 3D exhibits and context, mostly tombstones and medals, setup of rooms and outdoor areas, physical support for information, navigation aid etc.;
- Developing and completing the metadata standard, checking new sorts of metadata and room and landscape design;
- Defining tours, acting as test persons, and contributing to information material and catalogues.

5.2   Cooperation with the Museo de Arte Contemporaneo at Santiago de Chile

In January 2010 and September 2014, we digitized nine rooms presenting paintings and sculptures in permanent and temporary exhibits with the help and support of the Museo de Arte Contemporaneo (MAC) staff.

The results are partially described in [3], where we developed a new taxonomy of interactivity types inspired by certain elements of the actual learning object metadata standard LOM, such as interactivity type, intended end user role and entries measuring occupation time. Whereas geometric objects can be moved or rotated, superposed, scaled or modified, cloned, or made invisible, visual objects were inspected and scrutinized from different vantages, regions of interest annotated, and position, exposition and appearance modified.

Fig. 5. Animated spring experiment

Lingemann [3] has developed a framework that enables the user to manipulate objects described in a scene graph–based language like X3D via input frames and special dialogues. Configurations of an animated object and its interactive deconstruction into its various parts are recorded in X3D, correspond to the given metadata standard and can be visualized, exported or reconstituted at any time. Furthermore, the deconstruction of parts of a house consisting of cutouts of two adjacent fronts and a roof is discussed. Lingemann also implemented a virtual instance of the spring installation created by the artist Pablo Langlois in 1995 and displayed in the MAC (cf. Fig. 5).

The virtual exhibit is constructed using five textured black cylinders showing human faces. At the lower end, identical springs are attached to small picture frames. The springs can be extended and animated by the visitor.

These examples show the feasibility of collecting visitors' modified artwork and user-generated animations that can be recorded and published. During the work on this use case, it was mostly volunteers who contributed to the development of a VM performance standard and to the interaction design, including implementation of prototypical realizations, such as exposition and room editors and mobile capture tools for the digitization of exposition rooms.

5.3 Crowd-Based Support for Shape Restoration

Reconstruction of high-quality 3D shapes is a difficult problem, yet high-quality shapes are needed for scientific exploration (e.g., taking measurements of buildings and comparing details) or providing high-quality visualization results. As discussed in Sect. 3, existing methods of 3D crowd acquisition, like ARC3D or PHOTOSYNTH, allow 3D reconstruction from crowd-provided images. However, depending on the availability of images, the reconstructions may still be flawed, with incomplete or inaccurate geometry. While this might be improved by adding more images of the target object, the problem becomes even more severe when the original artifact has been chipped, eroded or even destroyed. Recently, a comprehensive workflow for the restoration of chipped, eroded or otherwise damaged 3D objects from the Cultural Heritage domain has been proposed [21]. This workflow comprises the following steps: (a) digitization, (b) reassembly, (c) shape completion, and (d) missing object export.

Fig. 6. Successful restoration of an incomplete 3D shape using automatic, symmetry-based completion (left). Symmetry-based shape completion may fail if the missing section extends across a candidate symmetry plane (e.g., the tombstone on the right).

Clearly, crowd-sourced approaches can help with (a). Fragment reassembly (b) can be done automatically if certain assumptions hold, as recent results on real Cultural Heritage object data show [21]. A problem which typically cannot be solved completely independently of application domain, or involvement of users, is the completion of missing sections of 3D shapes (step (c) in the workflow). For certain types of shapes, symmetry-based completion may be possible, and recently, robust symmetry detection in incomplete and noisy shapes has been supported using interest-point analysis [22] (see also Fig. 6 left). However, for non-symmetric shapes, and shapes where the missing elements coincide with candidate symmetry planes, the method will not provide best results (see Fig. 6, right). Especially in the latter cases, crowd involvement could be extremely useful in helping restore plausible, high-quality 3D shapes. Specifically, a simple Web-based query form can be designed, in which voluntary users can flag automatically created candidate reconstructions as successful or unsuccessful. In the latter case, a lightweight 3D interface could be created to allow a user to adjust the symmetry plane (if it has not been successfully detected) or to complete a missing section manually.

6   Recent Progress and Open Problems in the Field

In recent years, the authors and their collaborators have concentrated their research on the development of a viable VM standard, ViMCOX, in the context of existing standards like LIDO, the realization of the multipurpose system ViMEDEAS and smaller editors to design and generate virtual 3D and 2D museum environments or to publish and archive virtual exhibition layouts. The software *Mobile Object Catcher* was created to support curators and volunteers in digitizing existing museum rooms using a smartphone and its camera to measure the room photogrammetrically, to reconstruct doors, windows and walls along with the exhibit and to generate the corresponding ViMCOX metadata [23]. This also includes various ways to design and realize outdoor areas with typical landscape characteristics. Furthermore, the authors have developed an application for use by the 3D museum designer as a management tool for editing 3D objects within a graphical user interface, including real-time adjustment of their size, location and orientation as well as the creation of 3D light sources for the scene; this information can be saved in a standardized document file format. Allahbakhsh et al. [24] and Wienecke's PhD thesis [25] show evidence that a substantial effort remains to be done in automatizing the process chain to request, collect, assess and integrate crowd contributions to virtual museums.

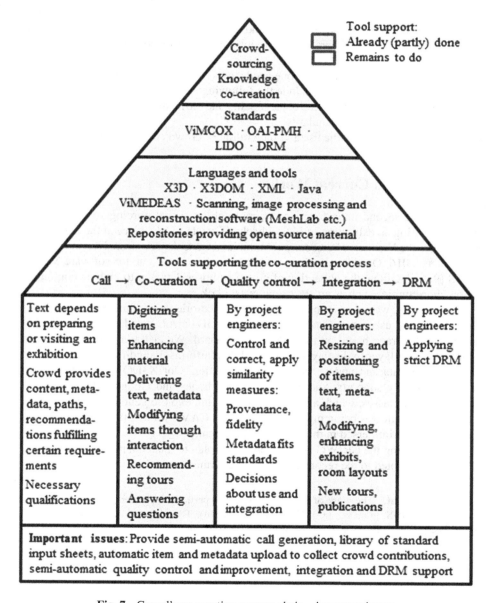

Fig. 7. Crowd's co-curation process chain – important issues

Figure 7 summarizes the various tasks and roles within the co-curation process. This process starts by first preparing, then visiting the exhibit and, finally, identifying already completed work and important issues yet to be dealt with. The main challenges in this process include the automatic generation of

- a specific call defining the task, the qualifications necessary to address the task, and the provision of input sheets to collect text, data and metadata along with an object to be uploaded;
- access to special purpose digitizing and modeling software and communication facilities (e.g., chats) where questions may be asked or comments collected and saved;
  On the software engineers' side, one needs tools to control, correct and integrate the content created. These tools include the following:
- Special similarity criteria to rate object fidelity and the means to clarify its provenance
- Metadata that meets the standards
- Decision support about the use and integration of crowd contributions

7   Outlook and Current Work

Aspects of the second main focus in our research on crowdsourcing support will be examined during an exhibition of Fleischhacker's estate to take place at the Düsseldorf Memorial to the Victims of Persecution (Mahn- und Gedenkstätte) from November 2015 to February 2016. On this occasion, we plan to enhance our curator software ViME-DEAS [9] to facilitate the collection of crowd and user data and to include communication opportunities such as an electronic guest book.

Furthermore, we propose to implement a service-oriented architecture including a server to host the user profiles and WebServices for 3D object, metadata and tour content creation and storage based on the ViMCOX standard. We also plan to implement an X3DOM render layer to display VMs on mobile platforms, including a sensor layer to gather sensor data and update the VM representation. Our X3DOM virtual museum generator already supports Android-based smartphones and Google's DIY low-cost Cardboard VR glasses, which allow users to visit and explore generated VM environments. Further effort is being made to implement a CAVE version that allows multiple users to become immersed in the virtual environment.

Finally, during the CRIWG 2015 meeting, we plan to launch a new crowdsourcing VM project devoted to the reconstruction of the Armenian ecclesiastical heritage.

Acknowledgement. The work of Tobias Schreck was partially supported by EC FP7 STREP Project PRESIOUS, grant no. 600533 (www.presious.eu). The 3D restoration result of Fig. 6 (right) is courtesy of Dr. Ivan Sipiran, University of Konstanz.

References

1. Biella, D.: Replication of Classical Psychological Experiments in Virtual Environments. University of Duisburg-Essen, Berlin (2006). Ph.D.-Thesis
2. Biella, D., Luther, W.: A general framework for replicated experiments in virtual 3D environments. In: Proceedings of the 4th International Conference on Web Information Systems and Technologies (WEBIST2008), vol. 1, pp. 316–323, INSTICC Press (2008)
3. Biella, D., Luther, W., Baloian, N.: Virtual museum exhibition designer using enhanced ARCO standard. In: XXIX International Conference of the Chilean Computer Science Society (SCCC) 2010, 15–19 November, pp. 226–235. IEEE Press (2010)
4. Thuan, N.H., Antunes, P., Johnstone, D.: Factors influencing the decision to crowdsource. In: Antunes, P., Gerosa, M.A., Sylvester, A., Vassileva, J., de Vreede, G.-J. (eds.) CRIWG 2013. LNCS, vol. 8224, pp. 110–125. Springer, Heidelberg (2013).http://staff.sim.vuw.ac.nz/pedro-antunes/wp-content/uploads/criwg-13-cs.pdf
5. Benson, S.: Co-creation 101: How to Use the Crowd as an Innovation Partner to Add Value to your Brand. (Web log comment). VisionCritical, 21 October 2013. https://www.visioncritical.com/cocreation-101/
6. Uden, M., Zipf, A.: OpenBuildingModels: towards a platform for crowdsourcing virtual 3D cities. In: 7th 3D GeoInfo Conference. Quebec City, QC, Canada (2012)
7. Ciolfi, L.: The collaborative work of heritage: open challenges for CSCW. In: Bertelsen, O.,W., Ciolfi, L., Grasso, M.A., Papadopoulos, G.A. (eds.) Proceedings of the 13th European Conference on Computer Supported Cooperative Work, pp. 83–101, Springer, London (2013)
8. Zurita, G., Baloian, N.: Mobile, collaborative situated knowledge creation for urban planning. Sensors **12**(5), 6218–6243 (2012)
9. Biella, D., Luther, W., Sacher, D.: Schema migration into a web-based framework for generating virtual museums and laboratories. In: 18th International Conference on Virtual Systems and Multimedia (VSMM) 2012, pp. 307–314, IEEE Press, Milan (2012)
10. Simon, N.: The Participatory Museum. http://www.participatorymuseum.org/chapter1/
11. Rodriguez Echavarria, K., Theodoridou, M., Georgis Ch., Arnold, D., Doerr, M., Stork, A., Peña Serna, S.: Semantically Rich 3D Documentation for the Preservation of Tangible Heritage. In: Arnold, D., Kaminski, J., Niccolucci, F., and Stork, A. (Editors): The 13th International Symposium on Virtual Reality, Archaeology and Cultural Heritage VAST, the Eurographics Association (2012)
12. Morin, G.: 3D Models for…. Habilitation à Diriger les Recherches in Computer Sciences. Institut National Polytechnique de Toulouse, Université de Toulouse (2014)
13. Nghiem, T.P.: Enhancing the Use of Online 3D Multimedia Content through the Analysis of User Interactions. Doctoral Thesis, INP Toulouse (2014)
14. Dallas, C.: The Presence of Visitors in Virtual Museum Exhibitions. Paper Presented to the Numérisation, Lien Social, Lectures Colloquium, University of Crete, Rethymnon, 3–4 June 2004
15. Carletti, L., McAuley, D., Price, D., Giannachi, G., Benford, S.: Digital humanities and crowdsourcing: an exploration. In: MW2013: Museums and the Web 2013, The Annual Conference of Museums and the Web, April 17–20, 2013, Portland, OR, USA. http://mw2013.museumsandtheweb.com/paper/digital-humanities-and-crowdsourcing-an-exploration-4/
16. Sacher, D., Biella, D., Luther, W.: Towards a versatile metadata exchange format for digital museum collections. In: IEEE Proceedings 2013 Digital Heritage International Congress
17. Straub, J., Kerlin, S.: Development of a large, low-cost, instant 3D scanner. Technologies **2**, 76–95 (2014)

18. Weyers, B., Luther, W.: Formal modelling and identification of operating errors for formal user interface reconfiguration. In: 7th Vienna International Conference on Mathematical Modelling (MATHMOD 2012), vol. 7 (1), pp. 487–492, Elsevier (2012)
19. Kuhn, W., Blumenthal, B.: Spatialization: Spatial Metaphors for User Interfaces, Tutorial CHI 96. http://www.ncgia.buffalo.edu/i21/papers/kuhn.html
20. Dierickx, B., Tsolis, D.: Overview of Collective Licensing Models and of DRM Systems and Technologies Used for IPR Protection and Management. eContentplus (2005). www.athenaeurope.org/getFile.php?id=665
21. Gregor, R., Sipiran, I., Papaioannou, G., Schreck, T., Andreadis, A., Mavridis, P.: Towards automated 3D reconstruction of cultural heritage objects. In: Proceedings of the EUROGRAPHICS Workshop on Graphics and Cultural Heritage, pp. 135–144, Eurographics Association (2014)
22. Sipiran, I., Gregor, R., Schreck, T.: Approximate symmetry detection in partial 3D meshes. Comput. Graph. Forum 33(7), 131–140 (2014)
23. Hopmann, D.: Room Measurement Using Photogrammetric Methods and Mobile Phones for Exhibition Planning and Archiving. Diploma thesis (in German), University of Duisburg-Essen (2013)
24. Allahbakhsh, M., Benatallah, B., Ignjatovic, A., Motahari-Nezhad, H.R., Bertino, E., Dustdar, S.: Quality control in crowdsourcing systems: issues and directions. IEEE Internet Comput. 17(2), 76–81 (2013)
25. Wienecke, L.: An Analysis of Productive User Contributions in Digital Media Applications for Museums and Cultural Heritage. Ph.D. Thesis. Bauhaus-University, Weimar (2010)

Using Real-Time Gaze Based Awareness Methods to Enhance Collaboration

Christian Schlösser[1(✉)], Philipp Schlieker-Steens[1], Andrea Kienle[1],
and Andreas Harrer[2]

[1] University of Applied Sciences and Arts Dortmund, Dortmund, Germany
{christian.schloesser,philipp.schlieker-steens,
andrea.kienle}@fh-dortmund.de
[2] Clausthal University of Technology, Clausthal-Zellerfeld, Germany
andreas.harrer@tu-clausthal.de

Abstract. Using eye-tracking in applications can be used to identify which areas are looked at by their users. In collaborative software this information can be transmitted to partners in real-time to provide an additional information channel. This paper compares different types of real-time gaze data visualizations. For this purpose, a study with three groups is conducted, who have to solve a collaborative puzzle. In every group the gaze data from each participant is recorded and visualized in a different way depending on the specific group condition. The aim is to evaluate a new context-based visualization to be able to make use of the known advantages of coordinate-based gaze data visualization outside of the domain of What-You-See-Is-What-I-See (WYSIWIS) interfaces.

1 Introduction

Working in groups is increasingly mediated by computers. The spatial distance is bridged by distributed applications. Those collaborative applications serve as mediators and help to support the collaboration itself [1]. This support is a key factor and is done in different ways in the specific applications. Awareness tools help the user to give their respective partners the knowledge about their current context, so they can adjust their own actions accordingly [2]. In order to integrate such an awareness support in a collaborative application, eye-tracking can be used as an interactive method.

Efficient collaboration is highly dependent on the so-called joint attention, which denotes a common focus on an object by two or more persons [3, 4]. The concept is very general and represented in various fields of research. Shared Gaze is considered to be the weakest form of joint attention, which describes at least two individuals viewing at the same object. Pietinen et al. [5] assume that only the number and duration of shared gaze events may indicate the intensity of collaboration, even if it is explicitly stated that collaboration takes place outside of the sensor eye-tracker as well. In the personal interaction Shared Gaze can be achieved by keeping track of each other's gaze. Because this method is missing in computer-mediated interaction, an obvious solution is the transfer of the current gaze coordinates (gaze cursor) to each other. This method is known as Gaze Sharing [4, 6]. Prerequisite for gaze cursor sharing are What-You-See-Is-What-I-See (WYSIWIS)

© Springer International Publishing Switzerland 2015
N. Baloian et al. (Eds.): CRIWG 2015, LNCS 9334, pp. 19–27, 2015.
DOI: 10.1007/978-3-319-22747-4_2

interfaces [7], where all users see the same content. This is necessary because otherwise there is no correlation between the gaze data of the partner and the own screen content, which is why, for example, the aspect ratio of the monitor and its screen resolution must be taken into account. Since these identical environments are usually not present outside of laboratory conditions and the WYSIWIS principle is not applicable to all types of software, a more flexible approach to gaze sharing, without the constraint to use WYSIWIS interfaces is required. To achieve this, a transition from coordinate-based (Where?) gaze sharing to a context-based (What?) gaze sharing must be made. This is also supported by the results of [8] that information on the attentional processes can indeed be relevant, but are rarely needed in the detail of the exact gaze coordinates. She assumes, that the knowledge, that a partner is focusing a particular object is sufficient. The aim of this paper is to evaluate a new context-based gaze sharing method in comparison to the coordinate-based gaze cursor sharing. The question is, if the context-based method has similar positive effects and can thus be used outside of the WYSIWIS domain.

2 Experiment

To answer this question, the two types of gaze sharing visualization mentioned above were compared to a no gaze sharing control group. For this purpose, a between-subjects design with three groups was used. In the following, the term Gaze Awareness is used for the group with context-based gaze sharing, the term Gaze Cursor for the group with coordinate-based gaze sharing and the No Gaze for the group with no gaze support. A total of 60 college-level participants were acquired to record ten dyads per group. The average age was 23.2 with a standard deviation of 3.4. The gender ratio was 14 females to 46 males.

Material: The application used in this study was a collaborative puzzle, which was developed with reference to the turtle puzzle from Mühlenbrock [9]. In order to achieve an acceptable solving time, the pieces, in contrast to a real world puzzle, could not be rotated. As shown in Fig. 1, there were nine drop zones for solving the puzzle, as well as nine stack zones, which initially held the puzzle pieces.

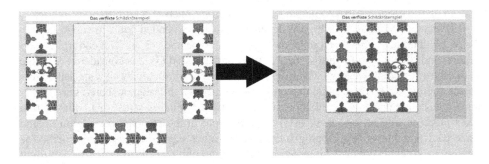

Fig. 1. Turtle puzzle from the initial piece distribution to the solved puzzle. Screenshots taken from the experimenters view with included gaze visualizations.

Every dyad had the same initial piece distribution. Pieces could not be stacked, doing so, led to the system swapping the involved pieces. It was implemented as a WYSIWIS real-time web application, which transmitted every drag and drop with a minimal delay of 1–5 ms to other clients. Conflicts like dragging the same piece or using the same drop zone was prevented by the system.

Participants were assigned to a color, which was used to highlight drop zones and gaze indicators. Figure 2 shows the support of gaze for each group mentioned above. The No Gaze group had no gaze support at all, the second group was supported by a mutual gaze cursor and the third group used a gaze enabled application, which highlighted the visible elements on the screen while fixating it.

Fig. 2. The gaze visualizations used in each conditions: no gaze, gaze cursor and gaze awareness

Procedure: Each trial included two participants that were briefed about the procedure in general and told they had to collaboratively solve an online puzzle, each participant in a separate room, connected via audio chat. They were informed that the experimenter would join the audio chat for announcements. After that they were presented a description of the puzzle and its game mechanics, as well as condition specific features. The experimenter used a third client computer to observe the puzzle, each participant's eye-tracking status and the audio chat. Irrespective of the current condition, this experimenter's client displayed all gaze related features. The puzzle was started from the experimenters' computer after making sure that the task was understood and the participants were ready. The maximum duration was 20 min, without the participants actually knowing about this time-limit. If close to completion, up to two additional minutes were granted. The experimenter used the voice chat for start and stop signals, as well as required corrections of the participants seating position regarding eye-tracking data quality.

Eye-Tracking Setup: We used two desktop-based Tobii eye-trackers. One TX300 running at 300 Hz as well as one x 120 running at 120 Hz. The user specific eye-tracker calibration was performed using a five-point calibration at the beginning of the experiment. Due to 24 in displays and large areas of interest (puzzle parts and stack zones), no correction for gaze deviation was needed. An in-house server was used to synchronize and capture all gaze data.

Captured Data: During the experiment, various data from different channels were captured. Irrespective of the current condition, the same data was saved. On the one hand, raw interaction data that belongs to game mechanics like drags and drops were saved, as well as computed data like solution status after each drop. On the other hand, raw and computed data associated to gaze were captured, such as raw and denoised gaze data, fixations and pupil diameter. Fixations were complemented by information about underlying elements such as puzzle parts or stack zones. For an in depth retrospective analysis of each session, a video from the shared workspace complemented by the participant's voices and gaze data was recorded.

Hypotheses: To examine the research question three hypotheses were formulated. These hypotheses assume the effectiveness of context-based gaze sharing from different perspectives. The aim is to determine whether it is possible to apply the positive effects of coordinate-based to context-based gaze sharing mechanisms outside of a WYSIWIS interface.

1. The quality of a collaboration in the Gaze Awareness group is on the same level as the Gaze Cursor group and higher than in the No Gaze group.
2. The frequency of Shared Gaze events in the gaze sharing groups is on a comparable level but higher than in the No Gaze group.
3. While using both gaze sharing methods the cognitive load amount is lower than using No Gaze sharing.

3   Methods

For the evaluation of the three hypotheses mentioned above, the following methods were used:

Method 1 - Rating Scheme for Collaboration Quality: The quality of computer-supported collaboration has been quantified and measured by means of a multi-dimensional rating approach in the literature. In the original work [10] a rating scheme was presented for medical diagnosis tasks mediated by video-conferencing; the scheme consists of nine dimensions derived by a combination of bottom-up (empirically induced categories) and top-down (theoretically justified aspects) analyses. This rating scheme has been adapted to synchronous collaborative problem solving tasks and applied to shared workspace scenarios [11]. For our study two dimensions of the original rating scheme have been left out because they were not applicable in our scenario: Time management was not considered because there was no time limit known by the partic-ipants a priori, thus there was no need for the participants for timekeeping and scheduling (the used time limit of 20 min was because of practical purposes on the experimenter's side to schedule the dyads on proper intervals). Technical coordination was not relevant because additional tools were not used besides using a mouse and gaze information of the peer (if applicable for the condition). Because of the nature of our problem-solving task some of the dimensions have been adapted based on reformulation via the setting's specific constraints and expected/detected positive and negative behaviors for the adapted dimensions (following closely the approach in [11]). Dimension "Task division" was reformulated as "task coordination" because in the synchronously shared workspace an explicit division of labor and decomposition into sub-tasks is limited, but the coordination of accesses to cards and moves of these is relevant to coordinate the peers' efforts. The dimension of "individual task orientation" was replaced with a score that represents the balance of actions between the peers, because in contrast to the original scheme we didn't have any asymmetries in competence that require individual efforts on specific sub-tasks; in contrast, each participant engaged equally in problem-solving would result ideally in a balance between the contributions, thus we measured the substitute dimension "contribution balance".

A rating handbook was created by the two raters after watching three previously recorded videos with each rater taking notes for all dimensions. Afterwards the two raters discussed their individual perception of how a dimension should be evaluated. Due to the task of solving a puzzle and missing asymmetries in competence between the participants a concise handbook was sufficient. For each dimension requirements for a very good or very bad rating were formulated. If possible examples of communication and action were given. All videos were watched and rated in random order without the raters being aware about the current experimental condition of the dyad. In some cases participants mentioned the gaze visualization so that the rater could conclude the specific group.

Method 2 - Shared Gaze Occurrences: Within a collaboration a high frequency of Shared Gaze events can be an indicator for the efficiency of collaboration [5]. The closer the partners work together, the more often their gazes meet on the same elements which are in the current context of interest. The collision of the partners gaze on elements (puzzle parts and stacks) was automatically captured by the system, using a real-time distance-based hit detection [6]. Therefore no algorithm based on the spatial distance was needed. Accidental collisions were filtered afterwards by using the average fixation duration of all participants as a minimum length for a single Shared Gaze event. As there are no known numbers for high or low Shared Gaze frequencies, which are presumably strongly dependent on the scenario, a comparison with the No Gaze control group was made.

Method 3 – Pupillometry: The method for measuring the pupil diameter is referred to as pupillometry. Holmqvist [12] says that the pupil diameter can be used for inter-pretations of cognitive load and the recognition of emotions, because the pupil diameter varies depending on the mental workload. Linking that information to the current action of the participant, the mental workload could give information about the complexity of the current exercise. But he emphasizes, that there are many external factors which influence the pupil diameter. The most influencing factor are light conditions. During the experiment only artificial light was used. The puzzle did not cause any noticeable changes to the screen brightness and can be considered constant. To avoid measuring errors due to different eye characteristics of the partic-ipants, the lowest values were removed. Because we were interested in the overall cognitive load during a trial in each condition we divided each measure by the total number of data points for each participant.

4   Results

In total more than six hours of footage was recorded. The eye-tracking brings certain restrictions to the participant's movements, because otherwise false or No Gaze data can be recorded. For this reason, some of the participants had to be occasionally reminded to maintain a proper posture, whereby three of the thirty dyads had to be discarded, because no reliable gaze data was recorded. That led to a population for each group as follows: No Gaze n = 10; Gaze Cursor n = 9; Gaze Awareness n = 8. In evaluations where No Gaze data was needed, all 30 dyads were analyzed.

Hypothesis 1: To investigate the quality of collaboration the evaluation scheme described above was used. We evaluated the validity of the rating scheme for our research by checking for the robustness of inter-rater results, using the ICC (intra-class correlation coefficient) on the results of two independent raters on the whole dataset. The result with a mean value of 0.7 is an acceptable match (M = 0,701; SD = 0,035). The application of the adapted rating scheme with the original scale ranging between -2 (very bad) and +2 (very good) by the two independent raters brought the results in Table 1. The leftmost column refers to the numbering in the original rating scheme, the two reformulated dimensions are marked with an asterisk.

Table 1.   Results of the adapted rating scheme for quality of collaboration

#	Dimension	No gaze		Gaze cursor		Gaze awareness		$F_{(2,27)}$	p	n^2
		M	SD	M	SD	M	SD			
1	Sustaining mutual understanding	0,35	1,25	0,40	0,94	0,70	0,75	0,32	0,73	0,02
2	Dialogue management	0,95	1,01	1,10	0,83	0,75	0,51	0,42	0,66	0,03
3	Information pooling	-0,15	1,18	0,40	1,07	1,00	0,63	3,04	0,06	0,18
4	Reaching consensus	-0,65	0,74	0,35	1,07	0,75	0,72	6,33	0,01	0,32
5	Task coordination*	0,30	1,10	0,65	0,71	0,55	0,82	0,37	0,70	0,03
8	Reciprocal interaction	1,00	0,89	1,20	0,46	1,20	0,60	0,26	0,77	0,02
9	Contribution balance*	1,20	0,60	0,30	0,64	0,40	0,92	4,08	0,03	0,23
Sum of points		3,00		4,40		5,35				

In an overall comparison the groups with gaze sharing support achieve better results in terms of collaboration quality in comparison to the No Gaze group. The collaboration quality is therefore to be conditionally considered higher. Likewise, it can be seen that the Gaze Awareness group's collaboration quality is higher than the Gaze Cursor group.

The analysis of variance reflects the results of the dimensions in the comparison group. It can be seen that only the dimensions of Reaching consensus and Contribution balance vary significantly. The dimension of information pooling is almost significantly different with p = 0.06. Comparing the sums of the dimensions among the groups, it can be seen that the Gaze Awareness group performs best. However, this result is not to be interpreted as statistically significant ($F(2,18) = 0.90$; p = 0.42, $\eta2 = 0.09$), which is due to the small number of participants.

Hypothesis 2: To measure the frequency of Shared Gaze events in each group we used the computational data as described in Method 2. As Fig. 3 shows, the gaze sharing groups generated at least one more Shared Gaze event per minute compared to the No Gaze group. The average Shared Gaze event duration is nearly identical in all groups (No Gaze: 0,44 s; Gaze Cursor: 0,46 s; Gaze Awareness: 0,44 s).

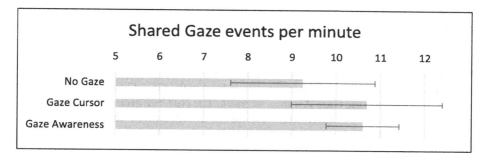

Fig. 3. Average shared gaze events per minute for each condition with standard deviation. The minimum length for each event was set to the mean fixation duration of all participants.

Hypothesis 3: The pupillometry described in Method 3 was used to estimate the cognitive load. Figure 4 shows the comparison of the mean pupil diameter of all participants grouped by the three conditions.

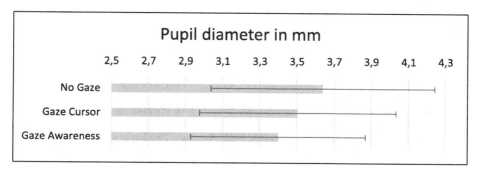

Fig. 4. Estimation of cognitive load by pupil diameter in mm with standard deviation.

The Gaze Awareness group shows a lower amount of cognitive load compared to the Gaze Cursor and No Gaze group ($F(2,27) = 26,53$; p = 4,6E-12; $\eta2 = 0,032$).

5   Discussion and Conclusion

Hypothesis 1: The quality of collaboration increases with the aid of mutual gaze data transmission. It is not important whether the participants are supported by the Gaze Cursor or the Gaze Awareness. Both visualizations achieve better results compared to the No Gaze group.

Hypothesis 2: The analysis of Shared Gaze events showed that the gaze sharing groups had a slightly higher Shared Gaze frequency as the No Gaze group which confirms the hypothesis. The gaze sharing groups generated more short Shared Gaze events in the beginning of the trials which were also sorted out by the minimum threshold of the mean fixation duration which was initially introduced to filter accidental gaze collisions. This is probably due to the fact, that all of the participants never used an eye-tracker prior to the study and had to get used to the gaze cursor and gaze awareness feature. We assume that those short Shared Gaze events are not part of the problem solving process and could be safely removed.

Hypothesis 3: Due to the constant movements of the Gaze Cursor, which reflexively draws attention to itself, an increased cognitive load in the Gaze Cursor group is measured in comparison to the Gaze Awareness group. The No Gaze group has, as expected, the highest amount of cognitive load because the coordination effort is probably the highest due to the lack of the additional information channel.

In summary, it should be noted that all three hypotheses have been confirmed. The context-based gaze sharing method achieved comparable positive effects on the collaboration as the coordinate-based gaze sharing, with the advantage of a slightly less cognitive load. Thus, a use of gaze sharing outside of the WYSIWIS domain is possible. Due to the limited scenario as well as the relatively small amount of participants no generalization should be made here. However, the results are promising and should be elaborated on in larger studies.

References

1. Reinmann-Rothmeier, G., Mandl, H.: Analyse und Förderung kooperativen Lernens in netzbasierten Umgebungen. Zeitschrift für Entwicklungspsychologie und Pädagogische Psychol. **34**(1), 44–57 (2002)
2. Dillenbourg, P., Järvelä, S., Fischer, F.: The evolution of research on computer-supported collaborative learning. In: Balacheff, N., Ludvigsen, S., de Jong, T., Lazonder, A., Barnes, S. (eds.) Technology-Enhanced Learning, pp. 3–19. Springer, Dordrecht (2009)
3. Richardson, D.C., Dale, R.: Looking to understand: the coupling between speakers' and listeners' eye movements and its relationship to discourse comprehension. Cogn. Sci. **29**(6), 1045–1060 (2005)
4. Schneider, B., Pea, R.: Real-time mutual gaze perception enhances collaborative learning and collaboration quality. Int. J. Comput. Support. Collab. Learn. **8**(4), 375–397 (2013)

5. Pietinen, S., Bednarik, R., Tukiainen, M.: Shared visual attention in collaborative programming: a descriptive analysis. In: Proceedings of the 2010 ICSE Workshop on Cooperative and Human Aspects of Software Engineering, pp. 21–24. ACM, New York (2010)
6. Nüssli, M.-A.: Dual Eye-Tracking Methods for the Study of Remote Collaborative Problem Solving. École Polytechnique Fédérale de Lausanne (EPFL), Lausanne (2011)
7. Stefik, M., Bobrow, D.G., Foster, G., Lanning, S., Tatar, D.: WYSIWIS revised: early experiences with multiuser interfaces. ACM Trans. Inf. Syst. (TOIS) 5(2), 147–167 (1987)
8. Müller, R.: Blickbewegungen in der computermediierten Kooperation. Chancen und Schwierigkeiten in der Verwendung einer weniger expliziten Kommunikationstechnologie. unveröffentlichte Dissertation, Technische Universität Dresden (2012)
9. Mühlenbrock, M., Hoppe, U.: Computer supported interaction analysis of group problem solving. In: Proceedings of the 1999 Conference on Computer Support for Collaborative Learning, p. 50 (1999)
10. Meier, A., Spada, H., Rummel, N.: A rating scheme for assessing the quality of computer-supported collaboration processes. Int. J. Comput. Support. Collab. Learn. 2(1), 63–86 (2007)
11. Kahrimanis, G., Meier, A., Chounta, I.-A., Voyiatzaki, E., Spada, H., Rummel, N., Avouris, N.: Assessing collaboration quality in synchronous CSCL problem-solving activities: adaptation and empirical evaluation of a rating scheme. In: Cress, U., Dimitrova, V., Specht, M. (eds.) EC-TEL 2009. LNCS, vol. 5794, pp. 267–272. Springer, Heidelberg (2009)
12. Holmqvist, K.: Eye Tracking: A Comprehensive Guide to Methods and Measures. Oxford University Press, Oxford (2011)

Evaluating Anchored Discussion to Foster Creativity in Online Collaboration

Georg J.P. Link[1], Dominik Siemon[1(✉)], Gert-Jan de Vreede[2], and Susanne Robra-Bissantz[1]

[1] Technische Universität Braunschweig, Braunschweig, Germany
{g.link,d.siemon,s.robra-bissantz}@tu-bs.de
[2] University of Nebraska at Omaha, Omaha, NE, USA
gdevreede@unomaha.edu

Abstract. Open innovation and crowdsourcing ideas rely on people to be creative through an online collaboration system. Creativity in online groups depends heavily on the interaction between group members. Anchored discussion was evaluated in a preliminary laboratory experiment as a new mode for creative interaction. In anchored discussion every comment is tied to some aspect of the idea. This first exploration generated novel insights for additional and refined research. Results indicate that anchored discussion leads to a more structured discussion amongst group members. For the same level of creativity, groups using anchored discussion needed less interaction and less discussion than the control groups. In a post session survey, participants made several suggestions on how to improve anchored discussion. We conclude that anchored discussion is promising as a new tool to aid online groups in creative collaboration.

Keywords: Anchored discussion · Idea generation · Ideation · Creativity · Online collaboration · Creativity support systems

1 Introduction

Companies constantly struggle in a competitive and ever changing environment. New solutions are needed to meet the new paradigm of global competitiveness, which requires rapid innovation [31]. The innovation process relies on the ability to generate, evaluate and refine ideas. Therefore companies are constantly searching to find ways to develop innovative ideas.

One such search for innovative ideas is evident in open innovation, which is the purposeful usage of internal and external sources for ideas [6]. More generally speaking, ideas can originate from a company's employees, suppliers, partners, customers, etc. One way to encourage these people to generate ideas and make the ideas accessible to the organization is the usage of online collaboration systems. These systems have the potential to evoke and enhance the creativity of a diverse set of participants [28].

© Springer International Publishing Switzerland 2015
N. Baloian et al. (Eds.): CRIWG 2015, LNCS 9334, pp. 28–44, 2015.
DOI: 10.1007/978-3-319-22747-4_3

However, there are many factors influencing the creativity of individuals and groups [3, 44]. Organizations that design and deploy online collaboration systems should be aware of these factors so that they stimulate rather than discourage the creative process. This is, for example, evident in the area of small group brainstorming. Early research demonstrated that blocking effects significantly reduced group productivity and creativity in traditional brainstorming groups where only one person can talk at a time [13]. Information System researchers developed collaboration systems where group members can generate ideas simultaneously leading to higher levels of creativity and productivity [15].

To enhance organizational innovation processes, open innovation and crowd-sourcing approaches have received more attention in recent years. A key challenge in these approaches is to enable online groups to generate creative ideas. Many open innovation systems have features for idea competitions or for collecting ideas straightforwardly, yet little support is offered to evaluate and refine ideas as a group effort [19]. Traditionally, companies would take the ideas from open innovation platforms and continue the innovation process internally. However, when people collaborate and improve each other's ideas, the resulting ideas tend to be more creative [4, 45] and thus can be more beneficial for companies.

We propose that new tools for online collaboration that are grounded in creativity and ideation theory have the potential to foster group creativity. Specifically, we follow the Design Science approach to design a tool that enables us to evaluate online anchored discussions as a mechanism to stimulate creative idea development. Anchored discussion originates from the field of education where it is used for students to collaboratively understand academic literature [30]. Students see a split screen with an academic text on one side and students' comments on the other side. Comments are tied to specific sections of the academic text. This design has increased collaboration, knowledge sharing, and engagement of the students [1]. We propose to replace the academic text with a shared idea editor. Generated ideas can then be the center of an anchored discussion, which has the potential to stimulate a more structured collaboration process for elaborating and evaluating ideas.

The remainder of this paper is structured as follows. First, the theoretical background is discussed and hypotheses are stated. Second, a prototype and its evaluation in a lab experiment are described. Results are briefly stated. Then the results are discussed. Last, a critical conclusion is provided.

2   Background

2.1   Creativity in Groups

According to Amabile [3] "a product or response will be judged as creative to the extent that it is (a) both a novel and appropriate, useful, correct, or valuable response to the task at hand, and (b) the task is heuristic rather than algorithmic in nature." This implies that some process is required which will result in a creative outcome. Different people can collaborate in this creative process. The term distributed creativity refers to situations in which collaborating groups create shared creative products [38].

Research on creativity can be grouped into the Four P's of Creativity: person, process, product, and press [34]. Early creativity research focused on describing attributes of creative people. Furthermore, creativity tests, like the widely used Torrance Test of Creative Thinking (TTCT), were conceived to evaluate the creative potential of individual people [23]. More recent research focuses on the creative process and its products. Amabile [3] describes the creative process to be heuristic in nature. Mumford et al. [26] provide a model of the creative process which distinguishes eight core processes: (a) problem definition, (b) information gathering, (c) information organization, (d) conceptual combination, (e) idea generation, (f) idea evaluation, (g) implementation planning, and (h) solution monitoring. These eight core processes, which we will refer to as phases, can occur in different order, due to the heuristic nature of the creative process. Even loopbacks are possible. Especially within a group it can be assumed that several of these phases occur simultaneously in different people. As stated in the introduction we focus on the idea generation phase of groups collaborating online.

A creative product is "a product or response [that] will be judged as creative" [2]. This definition assumes that a creative product is tangible and can be evaluated. Many researchers use an evaluation of the creative product as a proxy to assess the quality of the creative process [9]. However, there is no objective measurement for what would make something a creative outcome. Amabile [2] suggested to use subjective measurements by asking judges to rate the creativity based on provided dimensions. She found that judges reliably agree on what can be considered as creative, even without prior training. The dimensions to be rated by the judges can be tailored to the task that the creative outcome resulted from, but certain elements are predominantly present: novelty and quality [9]. Dean et al. [9] reported high inter-judge reliability on different problems when using their developed ordinal scales on eight different dimensions, such as Originality, Implementability, and Effectiveness.

Researchers have studied different factors influencing the creative process in groups. For example, Sawyer and DeZutter [38] found that the interaction among group members can be a substantial source of creativity. This is evident in the reported case of a theatre play in which actors construct the narrative in taking turns. One actor can make a new proposal for a development but the actual development of the narrative depends on how the next actors chooses to respond and what parts of the proposal they choose to continue. Sonnenburg [40] specifically views creativity as something that results from the interaction of many factors. He developed the 1-5P-Model which describes the creative potential to be influenced by the factors: person, place, process, problem, and (proto-)prototype. From this point of view the group members represent one factor (person) that influences the potential for creativity. Sonnenburg recognized that only people can start the creative process, but the interaction is influenced by much more than just the group members.

Interaction amongst group members is a key source of creative potential. This is for example demonstrated by the Team Creativity Model, which was the result from an exploratory field study [44]. According to the Team Creativity Model the two main antecedents to group creativity are individual creativity and shared mental model. Especially the shared mental model is a direct result from the interaction of the group members. A shared mental model represents the extent to which group members have a shared understanding of the group situation and the task [8]. In the Team Creativity Model shared mental model acts as a mediator between knowledge sharing, which is a form of interaction, and group creativity. More generally speaking, higher levels of group performance have been linked to higher levels of mental model similarity [25]. Thus, supporting diversity and independence to evoke creativity with different participants is important [28,42], and equally essential are interaction and knowledge sharing between the participants to enhance the shared mental model. In summary, these findings apply to groups in general and we assume that they hold true in online groups:

Hypothesis 1a: Group members reporting more similar shared mental models will have more creative products.

Hypothesis 1b: Groups with a more structured and goal oriented interaction will report higher similarity in their shared mental model.

Hypothesis 1c: Shared mental model mediates the relationship between group member interaction and group product creativity.

2.2 Individual Creativity and Group Creativity

According to the Team Creativity Model, individual creativity is the second antecedent to group creativity and is also influenced by the interaction of the group members. This can be explained with the search for ideas in associative memory (SIAM) model [27]. SIAM assumes that links between ideas in people's memory exist and that usually only ideas with a strong link to current thoughts are activated. A creative thought is characterized by two distinct, simultaneously active ideas that were not or only loosely linked before. This activation can result from the interaction within the group or other outside stimulation, such as from a group facilitator.

A common form of stimulation is to change perspective, which can occur in one of three ways [24]: (a) by searching for similar situations (analogy) and generating ideas for those situations; (b) by challenging assumptions (provocation) and using resulting situations for idea generation; and (c) by using random elements and knowledge about them to generate ideas. However, due to the social norm of not changing the subject and the tendency of building on other ideas, people have the tendency of voicing similar ideas [37] and not explore changes of perspective. The term paradigm preserving is used to describe, that an idea is similar to previous ideas, while paradigm modifying ideas introduce new elements or explore different relationships.

The goal is to gain paradigm modifying ideas. Groups can be stimulated to explore a wider variety of ideas when giving diverse stimuli, for example from a computer algorithm [39] or from a facilitator [7,35]. The latter intervention method was informed by the Cognitive Network Model of Creativity, which draws a connection between the stimuli, cognitive load, and resulting creative thoughts [36]. Simply put, the model posits that creative thought results from the combination of previously unlinked ideas, which is aided by a variety of stimuli, but impeded if the individual has a high cognitive load. Cognitive load increases when many different ideas are active at once but cannot be combined into a chunk. Santanen et al. [35] conclude that providing stimuli increases group creativity provided the prompts are well dosed.

The research by Santanen and colleagues applies to real groups that have access to dedicated facilitation support. We want to know how online groups can be supported that are not facilitated.

When a group uses an electronic system to generate ideas without having a facilitator to provide additional stimuli, then only ideas that the group generated earlier can serve as stimuli [37]. The way in which the system displays previous ideas can influence the creative process. Javadi et al. [21] recognized that attention diversion and lack of attention to other people's ideas can both be the result of excessive exposure to other people's ideas. Following the logic of the Cognitive Network Model of Creativity, this is due to the increase in cognitive load among the group members. Javadi et al. propose to limit the number of displayed ideas based on a ranking derived from user votes. A differently designed user interface could separate different aspects of a problem into different dialogs (similar to different pages of a book) and thus separating the discussion [10,11]. Dennis et al. [11] found that splitting idea generation on a problem into subcategories resulted in the generation of more ideas, more high-quality ideas, and more novel ideas. However, if a complex problem has multiple areas that could be subdivided but have a high interdependence, then the dependencies might not be considered if the problem is only viewed in subcategories and never as a whole.

In summary, it can be argued that the way a group interacts will impact individual creativity and group creativity. The interaction is a stimulus for individual creativity. As a result individuals share their ideas and thereby stimulate creative thoughts in other individuals and overall impact group creativity. A better structured and more goal oriented interaction can reduce cognitive load and stimulate more diverse ideas. We formulate the following hypotheses:

Hypothesis 2a: The higher the creativity of individual group member, the higher the group creativity.

Hypothesis 2b: The more structured and goal oriented the interaction among group members, the higher the individual creativity.

Hypothesis 2c: Individual creativity mediates the relationship between group interaction and group creativity.

2.3   Anchored Discussion in Online Groups

When a group uses an electronic system to collaborate, the design of the system shapes their interaction. Early electronic brainstorming research demonstrated that the negative effects of face-to-face groups, such as production blocking and evaluation apprehension [13,14], could be mitigated. Evaluation apprehension was reduced by making all contributions anonymous. Production blocking was reduced by allowing every individual to contribute as they are able, to review other's ideas at their own pace, and never have to wait for a turn to speak. Using electronic brainstorming can also enable larger groups to still be productive, especially because they need not wait for each other to finish voicing an idea [12,16].

Recently, Voigt and Bergener [43] conducted a literature review to compile an integrated framework for designing group creativity support systems. To aid the development of group creativity support systems the framework provides 12 design principles and six components with different tasks within one system. For our research focus, the two components that are tasked to allow users to collaboratively generate ideas are relevant: shared idea editor and communication component. The related design principles are as following: (a) Provide the possibility to share ideas to foster mutual inspiration, (b) provide session histories and dialogue mapping, to support idea reflection and information storage to build trust within the group, and (c) support group awareness to avoid coordination problems and foster reciprocal inspiration. Additional design principles can be derived from other literature: (d) Limit the number of displayed ideas to reduce cognitive load [21], (e) allow discussion and idea generation for different aspects of a problem to be separated [11], and (f) provide a way to maintain the big picture, to allow groups to consider the relationships between different aspects of the problem.

Based on these design principles, we think that anchored discussion represents a viable system and user interface design. Anchored discussion originates from the education research literature and aims to allow students to collaboratively process academic literature [30]. The user interface for an anchored discussion displays the article that students discuss on one side and the discussion on the other. "Anchoring is a process of creating reference points between parts of a document and comments in the discussion space to help prevent drifting within the context" [1].

The advantages of anchored discussion are argued to include more meaning-oriented discussion, more frequent referring to content, fewer self-clarifications, fewer words needed to express ideas, increased sharing of ideas, enhanced participation, and improved engagement [1,30]. Anchored discussion is often compared to a forum discussion, which typically has participants focussing more on establishing social relationships and regulating the collaborative process. Also in forums there are more argumentations and confirmations. While the actual level of shared understanding (shared mental model) may not be increased through anchored discussion researchers claim that less effort is required to reach the same level of shared understanding [30].

To the best of our knowledge, there is no prior research on anchored discussions to stimulate creativity in problem solving tasks. We suggest to replace the discussed academic literature frame in an anchored discussion tool with a shared idea editor. The original idea would always be present in the shared idea editor, so that the big picture is not lost. At the same time, using anchored discussion, separate subcategories of the overall problem can be discussed without interference of discussion of other subcategories. In other words, an anchored discussion for online idea generation will consist of a text editor and an area for comments. In the comments area only comments related to the currently selected text in the editor would be displayed. Thus, in-depth discussions can occur separately for each aspect of the whole idea. The group would make changes to the original idea, based on the discussion. All comments should remain accessible, regardless of changes to the text in the shared idea editor.

We propose that anchored discussion is well suited to enable an online group to better structure discussions of a larger idea. Especially the promise that anchored discussion requires less interaction to achieve the same level of shared mental model can benefit crowdsourcing settings where participation fluctuates.

Hypothesis 3a: Groups that use anchored discussion will report about equal shared mental model similarity than groups that do not.

We propose that anchored discussion reduces cognitive load because it limits the displayed comments to only those relevant to the subcategory a user is currently focussing on. Thus we hypothesize that:

Hypothesis 3b: Groups that use anchored discussion will produce higher levels of individual creativity than groups that do not.

In Hypotheses 1c and 2c we propose that shared mental model and individual creativity mediate between group interaction and group creativity. Consequently, if anchored discussion improves the group interaction, we hypothesize that group creativity will be improved as well:

Hypothesis 3c: Groups that use anchored discussion will produce higher levels of group creativity than groups that do not.

3   Method

Following the principles of design science research, we designed and developed an artefact to evaluate our hypotheses [17,18,29]. Our artefact approaches a defined problem based on the theoretical foundations described above and provides a solution in terms of adding the functionality of anchored discussion to a shared idea editor [29]. Our web-based artefact is a real-time synchronised editor with functionality that allows a group to work on the same text with all changes immediately visible to all members. In addition, we implemented anchored discussion, which provides the users with the ability to add comments to certain aspects of the idea. In our case comments were tied to a specific line of the text, to keep previous comments accessible after changes have been made. Based on where a user currently has his cursor, the comments for this line would be visible. The actual idea is written within the shared idea editor and the comments are arranged in a separate area to the right. The idea and the comments are real-time synchronised so that everyone in the group can see changes and new comments immediately (Fig. 1).

The prototype was implemented by altering the open source software Firepad, which provided the real-time synchronized text editor. Firepad is a reference implementation for the Firebase database by Firebase Inc. The MIT License allowed us to use and change Firepad without restrictions. The main feature of

Firepad is real-time collaborative text editing. The technical challenge is that users are allowed to make any changes to the text, but that all changes need to be replicated for all other users despite using an internet connection with non-deterministic latency [20]. Firepad solves this issue by implementing operational transformation. Operational transformation (OT) is a technique to achieve system consistency without imposing restrictions on users [41]. The architecture is replicated for each user locally, where changes are applied immediately. Then, changes are propagated through the database to be replicated for distant users [20]. We used the Firebase database which stores and syncs data in real-time. The Firebase database is provided as a cloud service by Firebase Inc. A free account, The Hacker Plan, provided enough resources for the experiment. Firebase is available for many platforms, including iOS, Android, and Web; We used the API provided by a JavaScript library for web applications. To support an empirical test of our hypotheses, we designed two different versions of the artefact. For our control groups we modified the prototype by disabling the functionality of anchored discussion and implemented a discussion function, which is equivalent to a normal chat. Therefore, the control groups had no ties between comments and idea, but still had a way of interacting and communicating.

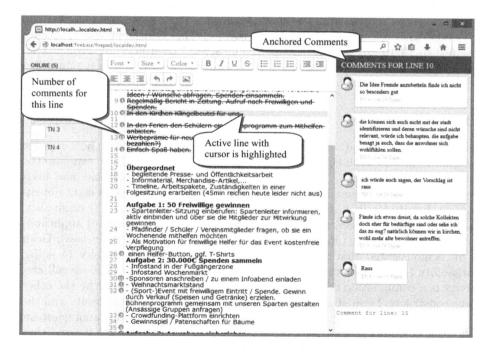

Fig. 1. Screenshot of the prototype with Anchored Discussion. Clarify that it is the prototype for the AD-groups.

3.1 Experiment Structure

We conducted a laboratory experiment with a total of 98 participants (64 male and 32 female). The participants were between the ages of 18 and 30 (M = 24.09, SD = 2.87). All participants were German university students. They were undergraduate (44), graduate (52), and post-graduate (2) students with majors in different fields (48 management of information systems, 32 industrial engineering, 9 computer science, and 9 others). Students were assigned to one of 26 groups of 3 to 5 participants each.

The task for all groups was to use the prototype to collaborate as board members of a fictitious organization that wants to redesign the city parks. The city council requires of the organization to organize volunteers, to collect enough donations, and to ask the people in the neighboring houses for their ideas on the park redesign. The group was provided with a few initial ideas of an absent board member, had to refine these ideas, and develop further ideas.

The experiment sessions were structured in three phases. During the introduction phase the participants were randomly assigned to groups and received an introduction into the prototype and the task. The second phase of the experiment was the collaboration phase which lasted for 45 min. In the final phase a survey was issued to capture additional information and feedback.

We had two treatments. The first treatment, Treatment AD, included the prototype with the anchored discussion feature. This treatment was randomly assigned to 13 groups (48 participants). The second treatment, Treatment CD, was our control group and included the prototype with chat discussion. This treatment was also randomly assigned to 13 groups (50 participants).

3.2 Measures

For our measure of creativity, we evaluate group creativity based on how creative the group outcome is judged. We asked four independent judges to evaluate the creativity of each group. To aid the judges we used the scales that had been created in previous research [9]. The creative outcome was rated on eight dimensions (1-4 scale for first six dimensions, 1-3 scale for last two): (a) originality, (b) paradigm relatedness, (c) acceptability, (d) implementability, (e) applicability, (f) effectiveness, (g) implicational explicitness, and (g) completeness. Dean et al. demonstrated that these dimensions reliably measure novelty (a + b), workability (c + d), relevance (e + f), and specificity (g + h). The overall creativity is a combination of novelty and quality, which is measured by the other three constructs. Dean et al. [9] recommend using thresholds on novelty and the three dimensions of quality, because a strength in one dimension cannot compensate for a weakness in another area. Our goal is to compare creativity and thus we created thresholds based on the respective means so that we separate the group outcomes into two groups on each dimension. Only when the creative outcome is in the higher rated group on at least three of the four dimensions, did we consider the group to have created a creative outcome.

The judges also rated how well structured and goal oriented the discussion within the group was. The dimensions were informed by the benefits that anchored discussion offers. The means of the dimensions formed what we called an anchored discussion score (AD-score).

A standard survey instrument, based on Johnson et al. [22], was used to capture the shared mental model (SMM). After each session, every participant was asked to rate 26 items (1 = strongly agree, 5 = strongly disagree). For each participant we calculated the mean of all answers to arrive at a SMM-score. Using the mean within each group we arrived at a SMM-score on a group level.

In the post-experiment survey we also assessed participants' perceptions of effectiveness and satisfaction. These measures were adapted from previous research [10].

The last construct we want to measure is individual creativity. A common way to measure creativity is the good-idea count, by rating every submitted idea [32] like we did with the group outcome. However, the shared idea editor captures entries from every person in a way that does not allow us to determine who entered what idea or changed another idea. Until we extend our prototype, individual creativity cannot be measured reliably. For preliminary results, we assume that individual creativity can be expressed by proxy as the number of ideas presented to the group and assuming that this is related to the amount of text a participant enters into the prototype [5]. We count contributions in terms of the number of characters added to the idea editor, the number of changes in formatting and the number of characters sent in comments.

4   Preliminary Results

The results in Table 1 show that groups using anchored discussion produced more creative outcomes. For each group a dimension was counted, if the rating was above the dimension mean over all groups. Groups that reached at least the mean on three dimensions are considered to be more creative. 8 AD groups and 5 CD groups meet this criteria. The inter-judge reliability on group creativity was okay, given the Cronbach's alpha for the dimensions novelty (.56), workability (.60), relevance (.51), and specificity (.74). Only on workability we excluded the ratings of one judge because they showed a clearly different rating scheme.

The group creativity mean rating on all four dimensions do not significantly differ between the anchored discussion groups and the control groups. Novelty is within the total range of 2–8 more on the lower end (AD: $M = 4.19$, $SD = .76$;

Table 1. AD groups were rated on more dimensions above means

	Creative		Not creative		
Dimensions rated above means	4	3	2	1	0
Anchored discussion groups	1	7	2	3	
Control groups		5	4	3	1

CD: M = 4.15, SD = .76). Workability (AD: M = 7.54, SD = .29; CD: M = 7.23, SD = .55)) and Relevance (AD: M = 6.50, SD = .53; CD: M = 6.38, SD = .56) are on the same range on the upper end, but slightly higher for anchored discussion groups. Specificity is within a different total range of 2-6 fairly high for all groups.

The anchored discussion score (AD-score) captures how well structured and goal oriented the discussion within a group was (from 1 = unstructured to 4 = well structured). Inter-judge reliability is high on four items (Cronbach's alpha: .89). The AD-factor is the mean of the four items and is much higher (M = 3.32, SD = .60) for anchored discussion groups than the control groups (M = 2.84, SD = .35).

Shared mental model (Cronbach's alpha: .93) is on a reversed scale (1 = most similar, 4 = different) with a better score for the control groups (M = 1.74, SD = .42) than the anchored discussion groups (M = 2.08, SD = .35). Perceived satisfaction (Cronbach's alpha: .82) and effectivity (Cronbach's alpha: .75) are on the same scale and also better for the control groups (M = 2.36, SD = .57; M = 2.13, SD = .41) than the anchored discussion groups (M = 2.76, SD = .61; M = 2.49, SD = .45).

Contribution counts average 2081 (SD = 659) characters for participants in anchored discussion groups and 2426 (SD = 563) characters for participant in control groups. Table 2 gives a summary of all results.

Table 2. Summary of the results

	Anchored discussion (AD)		Chat discussion (CD)	
	M	SD	M	SD
Group creativity: novelty	4.19	.76	4.15	.76
Group creativity: workability	7.54	.29	7.23	.55
Group creativity: relevance	6.50	.53	6.38	.56
Group creativity: specificity	4.36	.77	4.38	.91
AD-factor	3.32	.60	2.84	.35
SMM-score	2.08	.35	1.74	.42
Perceived satisfaction	2.76	.61	2.36	.57
Perceived effectivity	2.49	.45	2.13	.41
Contribution count	2081	659	2426	563

5 Discussion

We set out to increase group creativity in an online environment and implemented a first version of a tool with anchored discussion. At first, the preliminary results seem to not support our hypotheses. Below we will explore possible explanations. Groups using anchored discussions produced a few more creative outcomes in the sense that they were above the mean on at least three of the four creativity dimensions. But within each dimension there appears to be no difference between the treatments.

Considering our hypotheses 1a and 2a, we proposed that the group creativity would be influenced by the shared mental model (SMM) of the group and the individual creativity (estimated by contributions as a proxy) of the group members. We based this on the Team Creativity Model [44], which stated a relationship between SMM and individual creativity to group creativity. Both antecedents differed in their results between the treatments; the control group had the more favorable results. However, group creativity appears to be unaffected by this. This could indicate that some other factor was involved and that the relationship as stated in the Team Creativity Model is different from how we tested it. Furthermore, de Vreede et al. [44] mentioned that a less similar SMM could be beneficial to group creativity, which might partly explain why the anchored discussion groups had a lower SMM-score but had slightly more creative outcomes.

In theory, a more structured and goal oriented group interaction was supposed to positively influence SMM and individual creativity, as stated in hypotheses 1b and 2b. The results did not support these hypotheses. The same discussion from the previous paragraph applies.

Anchored discussion did enable the groups to have a more structured and goal oriented discussion with less needs to create references to the text and as a result require less discussion. The AD-score clearly indicates that anchored discussion produced a more efficient interaction amongst the group members. However, hypotheses 3a and 3b are not supported by the results.

Interestingly, the groups using anchored discussion had a more structured interaction, but SMM, individual creativity, satisfaction, and perceived effectiveness were lower than in the control group. However, in support of hypothesis 3c, but contrary to our hypotheses 1a and 2a, the group creativity was slightly better with anchored discussion. One possible explanation could be that our measurements are faulty, however we used tested methods for group creativity, SMM, satisfaction, and perceived effectiveness. Using the contribution count as a proxy for individual creativity is arguably not preferable, and results in not being able to reliably support or refute hypotheses 2a, 2b, 2c, and 3b.

Comments from participants can aid the search for explanations. In the post-session survey participants were asked to comment on the experiment. A reoccurring theme was that participants were overwhelmed by anchored discussion and did not intuitively understand how to use it. Many participants commented that they would have preferred a more detailed explanation of how to use anchored discussion and maybe even have an additional training before the actual creative task was assigned. It can be concluded that the unknown workings of anchored discussion caused a cognitive load that impeded on the collaboration task. However, giving an introduction on how to use the anchored discussion tool effectively could influence the reported levels of perceived effectiveness and thereby interfere with the measured results.

The negative effect of our prototype on satisfaction and perceived effectiveness could be explained by some unexpected behavior. One anchored discussion group noticed early, that deleting a line in the shared idea editor results in the attached comments to be combined with the next line and thus diluting that other discussion. The group's solution was to write into a line "[deleted]" and thereby maintaining all the comments. We conclude that a software design in which comments are moved to a different space if they become orphaned due to a deleted anchor would be better. Also participants asked for comments to be tied to the text and thus be moved with the text, if the text is rearranged. One group left the lines with comments in the original order to maintain all comments and compiled the fully developed plan below in new lines. In summary, this unintuitive behavior also appeared to increase cognitive load and reduce perceived effectiveness and satisfaction. The effect was strongest on the antecedents, but the more structured discussion compensated for this and as a result the group creativity was slightly above the control group.

Continuing with participants' suggestions for improvements, the most requested feature was a visual indication that an unread comment existed. In our prototype the number of comments were displayed next to the line number, and when this number increased no visual cue was provided. We had not implemented this feature to avoid distraction to not disrupt a creative thought. However, it seems that a non-obtrusive change of color for the comment count could aid the collaboration of the group members by reducing the time in search for changes.

Only participants in the control groups argued that they would have liked additional support to structure their collaboration process. The suggestions for more support included to-do-lists and voting features. The communication was described in some comments as unstructured, having too many conflicts, and not being goal oriented. One feedback described in detailed how the constant stream of comments in the chat area caused attention diversion and prevented creative work in the shared idea editor.

Four of the 13 control groups helped themselves and created an anchored discussion within the text editor. Comments directly related to a specific text were added into the shared idea editor, often marked as a comment by putting "->" in between text and comment. This was unique to the control group, thus we can see how anchored discussion is a solution for structuring text related discussions. The effectiveness is supported by the fact, that three of the four groups were rated as having created a creative outcome. If we had counted the groups with self-build anchored discussion to the AD group, then 11 AD and 2 CD groups are rated as creative. This strongly supports hypothesis 3c and indicates the benefit of anchored discussion to increase creativity.

6   Conclusions

Our research has several limitations. First, the standard limitations of a lab experiment apply. For example, students were encouraged to participate but may not have had any intrinsic motivation to do so. When anchored discussion is used on social media platforms where people collaborate only voluntarily, different motivations and incentives may apply so a field evaluation of anchored discussions is recommended. Also, the fictitious experiment task may not have stimulated creativity and participation equally for all students.

Additional limitations are related to the prototype. Many participants complained about the performance and attributed slower collaboration to this aspect. Additionally, as argued above, the functionality of anchored discussion was unknown to the subjects. Prior training might have aided performance and yielded different results. Better results might have also been achieved if the participants' suggestions were implemented and the stability was improved.

The design of our prototype did not allow us to perform personalized idea counts, which would be a preferred measurement for creativity [33]. Using number of characters typed as a proxy for individual creativity has several drawbacks. Contribution counts could be high for other reasons, like correcting spelling mistakes, or communicating unrelated messages. We argued that this can all contribute to a creative process. However, using the count of good-ideas would be a more correct measurement, especially since the ratio of good-ideas to total ideas can serve as an indicator for cognitive inertia experienced by the group [5], which anchored discussion should reduce. Thus, comparing contribution counts has no value in comparing individual creativity between control groups and anchored discussion groups.

The judges for the group creativity criticized the tool we used. The dimensions from Dean et al. [9] appear to be better fit for evaluating many ideas that are created after another, and not so much for evaluating the overall creative outcome. This can be demonstrated on the dimensions originality and paradigm relatedness, which both are better judged in comparison to previously created ideas, but are tough to judge without reference points. Another limitation in our evaluation of the creative group outcome is that we did a short training with the judges and not as extensive as was suggested [9].

There are several promising avenues for future research. To date, anchored discussion has not been evaluated for creative tasks. Our first prototype was positively received by participants, who made some suggestions for a more optimized design. Further research could incorporate and improve the usage of anchored discussion in creativity support tools and other group support tools. Comprehensive tasks and problems can be separated into different aspects to reduce cognitive load, while still maintaining the big picture. Our research results can therefore be seen as a design guideline, on how to implement anchored discussion into group support systems.

In social media, people are more likely to contribute when a task is enjoyable, easy to understand, rewarding, and when it creates a state of flow. Further research could evaluate the effect of anchored discussion on these dimensions.

We evaluated anchored discussion as a standalone prototype. Further research could evaluate how it is best incorporated into a larger group creativity support systems. We think that anchored discussion could be best used for the shared idea editor within the framework by Voigt and Bergener [43].

To summarize our findings, anchored discussion seems promising. From the experiment we had expected a better support for our hypotheses, but this was the first prototype evaluating anchored discussion for creativity in online groups. We have gained a better understanding of what can be improved. Our contribution is to advise future research on how to build better prototypes using anchored discussion to increase the creative quality of online group ideation. In conclusion, anchored discussion is a promising avenue to be explored further.

Acknowledgements. Funding for the first author's contributions was provided through a scholarship from the Hanns-Seidel-Foundation as part of its efforts to support highly talented students with financial support from the German Federal Ministry of Education and Research (BMBF).

Funding for the third author's contribution to this research was provided by the National Science Foundation Grant #1322285.

References

1. Alrushiedat, N., Olfman, L.: Anchored asynchronous online discussions: facilitating participation and engagement in a blended environment. In: Proceedings of the 45th Hawaii International Conference on System Science (2012)
2. Amabile, T.M.: Social psychology of creativity: a consensual assessment technique. J. Pers. Soc. Psychol. **43**(5), 997–1013 (1982)
3. Amabile, T.M.: The Social Psychology of Creativity. Springer, Heidelberg (1983)
4. Blohm, I., Bretschneider, U., Leimeister, J.M., and Krcmar, H.: Does collaboration among participants lead to better ideas in IT-based idea competitions? an empirical investigation. In: Proceedings of the 43rd Hawaii International Converence on System Science (2010)
5. Briggs, R.O., Reinig, B.A.: Bounded ideation theory: a new model of the relationship between idea-quantity and idea-quality during Ideation. In: Proceedings of the 40th Annual Hawaii International Conference on System Sciences (2007)
6. Chesbrough, H., Vanhaverbeke, W., West, J.: Open Innovation: Researching a New Paradigm. Oxford University Press, New York (2006)
7. Connolly, T., Routhieaux, R.L., Schneider, S.K.: On the effectiveness of group brainstorming: test of one underlying cognitive mechanism. Small Group Res. **24**(4), 490–503 (1993)
8. Cooke, N.J., Salas, E., Cannon-Bowers, J.A., Stout, R.J.: Measuring team knowledge. Hum. Factors **42**(1), 151–173 (2000)
9. Dean, D.L., Hender, J.M., Rodgers, T.L., Santanen, E.L.: Identifying quality, novel, and creative ideas: constructs and scales for idea evaluation. J. Assoc. Inf. Syst. **7**(10), 646–699 (2006)
10. Dennis, A.R., Valacich, J.S., Connolly, T., Wynne, B.E.: Process structuring in electronic brainstorming. Inf. Syst. Res. **7**(2), 268–277 (1996)
11. Dennis, A.R., Valacich, J.S., Carte, T.A., Garfield, M.J., Haley, B.J., Aronson, J.E.: Research report: the effectiveness of multiple dialogues in electronic brainstorming. Inf. Syst. Res. **8**(2), 203–211 (1997)
12. Dennis, A.R., Valacich, J.S.: Computer brainstorms: more heads are better than one. J. Appl. Psychol. **78**(4), 531–537 (1993)

13. Diehl, M., Stroebe, W.: Productivity loss in brainstorming groups: toward the solution of a riddle. J. Pers. Soc. Psychol. **53**(3), 497–509 (1987)
14. Diehl, M., Stroebe, W.: Productivity loss in idea-generating groups: tracking down the blocking effect. J. Pers. Soc. Psychol. **61**(3), 392–403 (1991)
15. Fjermestad, J., Hiltz, S.R.: An assessment of group support systems experimental research: methodology and results. J. Manag. Inf. Syst. **15**(3), 7–149 (1998)
16. Gallupe, R.B., Dennis, A.R., Cooper, W.H., Valacich, J.S., Bastianutti, L.M., Nunamaker, J.F.: Electronic brainstorming and group size. Acad. Manag. J. **35**(2), 350–369 (1992)
17. Gregor, S., Hevner, A.R.: Positioning and presenting design science research for maximum impact. MIS Q. **37**(2), 337–355 (2013)
18. Hevner, A.R., March, S.T., Park, J., Ram, S.: Design science in information systems research. MIS Q. **28**(1), 75–105 (2004)
19. Hrastinski, S., Kviselius, N. Z., Ozan, H., Edenius, M.: A review of technologies for open innovation: characteristics and future trends. In: Proceedings of the 43rd Hawaii International Conference on System Sciences (2010)
20. Imine, A., Rusinowitch, M., Oster, G., Molli, P.: Formal design and verification of operational transformation algorithms for copies convergence. Theor. Comput. Sci. **351**(2), 167–183 (2006)
21. Javadi, E., Mahoney, J., Gebauer, J.: The impact of user interface design on idea integration in electronic brainstorming: an attention-based view. J. Assoc. Inf. Syst. **14**(1), 1–21 (2013)
22. Johnson, T.E., Lee, Y., Lee, M., O'Connor, D.L., Khalil, M.K., Huang, X.: Measuring sharedness of team-related knowledge: design and validation of a shared mental model instrument. Hum. Resour. Dev. Int. **10**(4), 437–454 (2007)
23. Kim, K.H.: Can we trust creativity tests? a review of the Torrance Tests of Creative Thinking (TTCT). Creat. Res. J. **18**(1), 3–14 (2006)
24. Knoll, S.W., Horton, G.: Changing the Perspective: Improving Generate thinklets for ideation. In: Proceedings of the 43rd Hawaii International Conference on System Sciences (2010)
25. Lim, B.-C., Klein, K.J.: Team mental models and team performance: a field study of the effects of team mental model similarity and accuracy. J. Organ. Behav. **27**(4), 403–418 (2006)
26. Mumford, M.D., Medeiros, K.E., Partlow, P.J.: Creative thinking: processes, strategies, and knowledge. J. Creat. Behav. **46**(1), 30–47 (2012)
27. Nijstad, B.A., Stroebe, W.: How the group affects the mind: a cognitive model of idea generation in groups. Pers. Soc. Psychol. Rev. **10**(3), 186–213 (2006)
28. Van Osch, W., Avital, M.: Collective generativity: the emergence of IT-induced mass innovation. In: All Sprouts Content (2009)
29. Peffers, K., et al.: A design science research methodology for information systems research. J. Manag. Inf. Syst. **24**(3), 45–77 (2007)
30. Van der Pol, J., Admiraal, W., Simons, P.R.-J.: The affordance of anchored discussion for the collaborative processing of academic texts. Int. J. Comput. Support. Collab. Learn. **1**(3), 339–357 (2006)
31. Porter, M.E., Van der Linde, C.: Green and competitive: ending the stalemate. Harvard Business Review **73**(5), 120–134 (1995)
32. Reinig, B.A., Briggs, R.O.: Measuring the quality of ideation technology and techniques. In: Proceedings of the 39th Annual Hawaii International Conference on System Sciences (2006)
33. Reinig, B.A., Briggs, R.O., Nunamaker Jr, J.F.: On the measurement of ideation quality. J. Manag. Inf. Syst. **23**(4), 143–161 (2007)

34. Rhodes, M.: An analysis of creativity. Phi Delta Kappan **42**(7), 305–310 (1961)
35. Santanen, E.L., Briggs, R.O., de Vreede, G.-J.: Causal relationships in creative problem solving: comparing facilitation interventions for ideation. J. Manag. Inf. Syst. **20**(4), 167–198 (2004)
36. Santanen, E.L., Briggs, R.O., de Vreede, G.-J.: The cognitive network model of creativity: a new causal model of creativity and a new brainstorming technique. In: Proceedings of the 33rd Annual Hawaii International Conference on System Sciences (2000)
37. Satzinger, J.W., Garfield, M.J., Nagasundaram, M.: The creative process: the effects of group memory on individual idea generation. J. Manag. Inf. Syst. **15**(4), 143–160 (1999)
38. Sawyer, R.K., DeZutter, S.: Distributed creativity: how collective creations emerge from collaboration. Psychol. Aesthetics Creat. Arts **3**(2), 81–92 (2009)
39. Siemon, D., Robra-Bissantz, S.: Integration of information retrieval in creativity support: a prototype to support divergent thinking. In: Tremblay, M.C., Vander-Meer, D., Rothenberger, M., Gupta, A., Yoon, V. (eds.) DESRIST 2014. LNCS, vol. 8463, pp. 388–392. Springer, Heidelberg (2014)
40. Sonnenburg, S.: Kooperative Kreativität: Theoretische Basisentwürfe und organisationale Erfolgsfaktoren, 1st edn. Deutscher Universitäts-Verlag, Wiesbaden (2007)
41. Sun, D., Xia, S., Sun, C., Chen, D.: Operational transformation for collaborative word processing. In: Proceedings of the ACM Conference on Computer Supported Cooperative Work, vol. 6, pp. 437–446. ACM (2004)
42. Surowiecki, J.: The Wisdom of Crowds: Why the Many Are Smarter Than the Few and How Collective Wisdom Shapes Business. Doubleday, New York (2004)
43. Voigt, M., Bergener, K.: Enhancing creativity in groups - proposition of an integrated framework for designing group creativity support systems. In: Proceedings of the 46th Hawaii International Conference on System Sciences (2013)
44. De Vreede, T., Boughzala, I., de Vreede, G.-J., Reiter-Palmon, R.: A model and exploratory field study on team creativity. In: Proceedings of the 45th Hawaii International Conference on System Science (2012)
45. Yu, L., Nickerson, J.V.: Generating creative ideas through crowds: an experimental study of combination. In: Thirty Second International Conference on Information Systems (2011)

Measuring the Effort Demanded by CSCL Design Processes Supporting a Consistent Artifact Flow

Osmel Bordiés$^{(\boxtimes)}$ and Yannis Dimitriadis

Universidad de Valladolid, 47011 Valladolid, Spain
obordies@gsic.uva.es, yannis@tel.uva.es
http://gsic.tel.uva.es

Abstract. Artifact flow represents an important aspect of teaching / learning processes, especially in CSCL situations in which complex relationships may be found. However, consistent modeling of CSCL processes with artifact flow may increase the cognitive load and associated effort of the teachers-designers and therefore decrease the efficiency of the design process. The empirical study, reported in this paper and grounded on mixed methods, provides evidence of the effort overload when teachers are involved in designing CSCL situations in a controlled environment. The results of the study illustrate the problem through the subjective perception of the participating teachers, complemented with objective parameters, such as time consumed or errors committed, and objective complexity metrics.

Keywords: CSCL · Learning design · Artifact flow · Effort subjective measurement

1 Introduction

The consistent artifact flow definition has been found to be important in the field of Learning Design and especially in collaborative learning processes. This coordination mechanism helps managing the dependencies (e.g. time, documents, etc.) among the individual or group activities in particular CSCL scenarios. For instances, in a basic PEER REVIEW activity the criticizing task should start once two conditions are fulfilled: the reporting specific task is completed and delivered reports (e.g. documents or other products types) are available for specific group or individual tasks [11]. Satisfying these conditions or dependencies in design-time may lead to an effective implementation of best practices but at the same time, such definition process may be highly demanding and error-prone even for typical situations. In run-time, misunderstandings or omissions on processing artifacts created individually or in group may jeopardize the completion of the whole activity [22] and teachers or facilitators need to be aware about how the learning process should be or is conducted [24].

© Springer International Publishing Switzerland 2015
N. Baloian et al. (Eds.): CRIWG 2015, LNCS 9334, pp. 45–62, 2015.
DOI: 10.1007/978-3-319-22747-4_4

Nevertheless, the definition of these dependencies is considered as a complex and effort demanding task for teacher-designers becoming cumbersome even for typical CSCL situations [2]. Specifically, the PEER REVIEW pattern may be customized in several different and complex instances depending on the decisions made with respect to the number of composing elements and the interconnection among them. The overload issue is aggravated given the limitations exhibited by current authoring tools to support such a process. Thus we should aim to achieve explicit, consistent and reusable definitions of the artifact flow for CSCL situations, which may be beneficial for teacher-designers in design effectiveness by reducing the modeling and cognitive effort. However, although the overload using objective measures has been already analyzed, the subjective perspective has not been sufficiently studied.

Findings [2] illustrated the effort overload issue in terms of (a) effort demanded; (b) information content with respect to models without a consistent artifact flow definition; (c) additional editing steps for mapping one model to another; and (d) the effect of incorporating additional pedagogical setting options in cognitive terms. Moreover, measurements were performed when several pedagogical parameters were modified as the basis upon which their influence on size complexity was assessed. This study illustrated the overloading issue but had several limitations such as: only one type of activity was considered (PEER REVIEW) and the set of particular models analyzed was created as a result of a controlled modification of specific parameters: number of individual or group participants, artifacts enrolled, the artifact assignment or the way in which the artifacts are accessed by the learners. Thus our main research questions can be formulated as [RQ1] "Do the teachers perceive the effort expended in defining the flow of artifacts for particular CSCL scenarios, as significant?" Moreover, we may argue also that [RQ2]: "A relation exists between structural complexity and modeling effort perceived", as predicted in previous works using objective measures.

In order to explore these questions, we have conducted a study with university teachers from different disciplines with some prior experience on Computer Supported Collaborative Learning (CSCL), given their participation in professional development workshops or in research experiences in this field. The goal of the Art-FlowDER study (Artifact Flow Design-Effort-Redesign) described in this paper was to assess the effort perceived by real teachers on designing realistic and functional CSCL scenarios in two different design situations. Firstly, they customized a high-level CSCL scenario, in which constraints were imposed by the use of specific collaboration strategies. Secondly, the teachers reused their previous ideas and the initial learning design in order to set a new scenario with a different class size. The effort perceived is estimated by combining the teacher's subjective assessment, the measurement of time consumed, the number of errors committed, and the structural complexity of the artifact created, as well as findings derived from observations. Thus, in order to reach some conclusions, through this study we gather and analyze data about the effort devoted by the participant teachers and aim to suggest factors that may explain the phenomenon.

The structure of the paper is as follows: in the next section works related with the modeling effort measurements and model complexity metrics are presented and analyzed, including those related with CSCL modeling. Section 3 describes the ArtFlowDER study, i.e. its context, the methodology adopted, the interventions that were made and the associated data gathering techniques. In the following section, the results of the study are presented and discussed, while the last section resumes the conclusions and provides pointers for future work.

2 Effort Estimation in CSCL Design Processes

The Learning Design approach and tools attracted the interest of the research community during the last decade, due to their benefits in supporting teacher-designers during the design process of learning activities [7]. Collaborative learning is especially challenging in terms of learning design, since the incorporation of social interaction for group knowledge building is made at expense of making learning designs necessarily more complex. Despite of such benefits, the adoption of the learning design approach in CSCL by the teacher community is still low [23]. Several studies assessed the teacher perception regarding available learning design approaches and multiple authoring tools; nevertheless the design effort perception is an issue that has not been sufficiently studied as a way of explaining the low adoption issue.

Teachers are frequently involved in learning design processes as designers [6]. In most higher education institutions teachers are called to act as designers and deployers of learning scenarios allowing to express their own pedagogical decisions [9]. From the technical-professional perspective they may build ready-to-use learning activities design from scratch, redesign their own products doing cosmetic adaptations, redesign products created by other stakeholders and also cooperating with other colleagues. Teachers also learn through the process of designing but typically they lack time to develop their instructional design expertise and the available authoring tools present usability issues [17]. For instance, Webcollage [15] is limited on managing the artifact flow dependency among the activities during the particularization process. Others do not contemplate the possibility of efficiently modeling the flow of artifacts. Therefore, it deems necessary to evaluate the effort perceived by teacher when they are designing CSCL scenarios with explicit artifact flow definition considering the limitations of the authoring tools and the inherent complexity of plausible CSCL scenarios, and show evidences regarding the importance of the artifact flow definition in this perception.

This paper pays attention to advanced designs, which complement the definition of learning activity flows with consistent artifact flow definition. This coordination mechanism aims to satisfy the dependencies among group or individual activities involved the teaching and learning process [20,22]. Theoretically such learning designs are more complex because the artifact flow components are deeply grounded in context [16]. According to a previous work [2], PEER REVIEW scenarios with explicit/consistent artifact flow definition incorporate approximately 3 times more information content, demand 10 times more of effort and generate about 2 times of uncertainty when facing the design process, as compared to learning designs without artifact flow definition. From this analytical study, parameters such as the access mode, the number of artifacts involved, and the number of learners participants were identified as the most influencing factors in terms of complexity.

The measurement of effort in the field of workflow process modeling has been addressed mainly through the proposal of objective complexity metrics [4,19,30]. Currently most of these metrics are not empirically validated [21,25] and there is not enough evidence that the can serve as predictors of assessing the effort perceived by human designers, when such perception is affected by several factors in a specific modeling context. For instance, in the field of process modeling Cardoso et al. validates the correlation between control flow complexity and perceived complexity [5], or Mendling et al. related the proneness of error situations during the modeling process with the model structural complexity [19]. However, in the field of CSCL design, there is still need for studies in which the modeling effort should be measures and related and complemented with objective metrics.

3   The ArtFlowDER Study

The study has been carried out in order to illuminate both research questions, which were exposed in the introductory section. The rest of this section will describe the study context, the methodology adopted, as well as the interventions that were carried out. Such information is necessary in order to be able to interpret adequately the results that are included in the following section.

3.1   Context

The ArtFlowDER study was conducted within a laboratory research context in working sessions that took place between December, 2014 and February, 2015. Each session took approximately 2 hours of work. A total of 5 university teachers from different teaching areas (Computer and Telecommunication engineering, Nursing, Education, and Geography) and profiles were enrolled in these sessions. Three of them are teachers that had participated in previous professional development workshops on collaboration strategies and CSCL design. The other two teachers have experience researching on CSCL design and ICT. Each face-to-face session was composed of two main tasks where the participant teachers were invited to customize (DESIGN) a high-level CSCL scenario (named MOSAIC) provided in a document. They followed the orientations incorporated therein related with contextual characteristic such as the class size and the available educative ICT tools. During the second task, they reused the initial design in order to adapt it to a different class size (REDESIGN).

The MOSAIC scenario is an enriched version of a similar scenario employed in [22], and it is composed of 6 phases involving several collaboration strategies (PUZZLE, SNOWBALL, PEER REVIEW and GROUP FORMATION) [12,14]. As depicted in Table 1, the SNOWBALL is composed of 3 levels, the first level integrates a PUZZLE structure whose phases are interwoven with PEER REVIEW situations. The high level CSCL scenario description also incorporated four artifact flow dependency constructs or *variability facets* [3] (in bold and tagged as [VF1][VF2][VF3] and [VF4]) where two or more activities are

Table 1. MOSAIC pattern-based scenario description

No	Mosaic phases description
p1	Initial subphase of PUZZLE: students create an initial version of a concept map. To do so individuals or groups involved in the first phase study 3 supporting documents (one on each "dimension" of the problem in question). **At the end, each individual/group should review the concept maps generated by peers who have studied the same initial documents [VF1]** (PEER REVIEW)
p2	Expert subphase of PUZZLE: students-experts, who have studied the same "dimension" problem, group together in order to discuss and generate a new version of the concept map. **Again, students review the concept maps created by other expert groups and provide appropriate feedback [VF2]** (PEER REVIEW)
p3	Final subphase of PUZZLE: student-experts of different "dimensions" of the problem are incorporated in puzzle groups to generate a new conceptual map. **Once generated, the students individually reflect on the maps generated by other puzzle groups [VF3]** (PEER REVIEW). Complementarily, **the teachers supporting the activity read and analyze the maps created by the various puzzle groups [VF4].** This support task allows teachers to decide on the most suitable combination of groups of the second phase of the SNOWBALL
p4	Phase 2 of SNOWBALL: students are grouped according to the decision made by the teaching staff (GROUP FORMATION). The new groups now produce a fourth reconciled version of the concept map
p5	Phase 3 of SNOWBALL: Students, as a whole class, generate the final version of the concept map based on the maps of the previous phase

involved. In these constructs the relationships among the activities are expressed as setting constraints or rules in terms of the coordination components (Goal, Activity, Actors and Dependencies), thus allowing to configure the particular design according to several different pedagogical settings.

In the first task (DESIGN) of the sessions the teachers are encouraged to customize the CSCL scenario described in the document and follow the orientations provided to them a few days before. This way the teachers came to participate with some previous knowledge of what to do, thus saving time and avoiding a "cold start" effect at the beginning of the sessions, just as they would do in real situations. To achieve the first task teachers-participants are also provided with a worksheet which consists in a dot matrix, where the Y-axis represents the phases sequence and the colored dots on X-axis represent the organization of individuals or groups in each phase (Fig. 1 shows a participant together with the worksheet). The worksheet approach was adopted as instrumental tool instead of working with more demanding learning design authoring tools, such as Web Collage/GLUE!-PS [15], edit2 [27], or directly using the target virtual learning environments, such as LAMS or Moodle. The artifact flow sequencing is represented by interconnecting clustered or single dots of different phases with

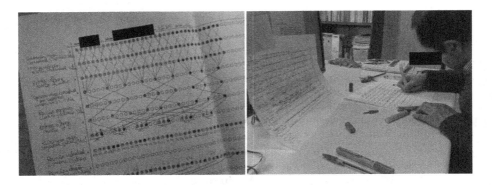

Fig. 1. Participant working with the worksheet provided.

Table 2. Structure of sessions

Session tasks	Teacher participant actions	Facilitator Actions
Pre-session task (online)	- Read the provided CSCL scenario description - Answer the profiling questionnaire	- Read the questionnaire answers as a basis to prepare the session
DESIGN task	- Configure the CSCL scenario taking into account the information provided and applying the functionality criteria	- Introduce the experience - Guide on how to work with the worksheet - Observe the process and eventually intervene
REDESIGN task	- Configure the CSCL scenario regarding the new requirement.	- Inform about the second task of the session, which has not been previously introduced - Observe the process and eventually intervene
Post-session activity	- Answer a post-session questionnaire about the perception of the effort demanded, influencing factors and procedures followed	- Observe, orientate and formulate questions about events that emerged during the session. - Process the gathered data and present the analysis results

colored lines or arrows. With regards to the second task (REDESIGN), the teachers-participants are invited to rethink their initial design, considering a new requirement, i.e. that the class size has been reduced by a 20 %). The fact that both design and REDESIGN tasks were performed in the same session allowed participants to reflect and perceive better the differences between the requirements and the proposals that they made. The global sessions structure is depicted in Table 2.

3.2   Methodology

The study followed a mixed-methods approach [8], attending the complexity of the issue under study and the multiple perspectives involved [29]. Specifically, quantitative and qualitative evidences are analyzed and triangulated, using on the one hand quantitative evidence such as the complexity metrics, in order to confirm or not the hypothesis initially formulated, and data extracted from the questionnaire answers provided by the teachers. On the other hand, qualitative data extracted from observations are employed. Our interpretation of the data does not pursue the generalization of results but to provide an in-depth analysis of the phenomenon under study, i.e. the artifact flow modeling in CSCL design and redesign.

Regarding the data analysis, our evidences have been structured according to the main issue of our study ("how do the teachers-participants perceive the effort demanded by the process of modeling CSCL scenarios with consistent artifact flow definition") regarding (a) the decision making process associated with the design problem; (b) the modeling process; and (c) the model structural complexity [28]. The decision making process is analyzed based on the answers provided by the teachers in the questionnaires or in response to specific interventions of the researcher, when decisions are made on the alternative settings that were considered. The modeling process analysis also uses data from the questionnaires as well as errors committed, gestures adopted, comments emitted and time consumed in reflection or mapping actions. Finally, the resulting design artifacts (see completed worksheets depicted in Fig. 1) are processed using the aforementioned objective metrics comparing the changes in the complexity measures and the effort ratings considering the DESIGN and REDESIGN tasks. All interventions will be explained in detail in the following section.

For this reason we performed an open coding of all available qualitative data (open responses, observation notes, semi-transcriptions of audio-video recordings), as well as a descriptive analysis of the quantitative data gathered from questionnaires, the time measured or the estimation of objective metrics [1] on the model artifacts created by the teachers-participants. A graphical representation of the data gathering and analysis techniques and their timing is shown in Fig. 2.

3.3 Description of the Interventions

The ArtFlowDER sessions are preceded by filling a profile questionnaire [Q0] (see tags in Fig. 2). The sessions are carried out with the intention to intervene as less as possible during the execution of DESIGN [I1] and REDESIGN [I2] tasks. As explained before the participants were invited to customize the MOSAIC scenario considering both intrinsic or extrinsic restrictions [10] (see Fig. 2). The former are related with characteristics of the collaborative strategies involved. The latter are inferred from parameters such as the size of the class (initially 48 students) and the ICT tools available (BSCW or Google Documents) and the fulfillment of a functional setting as requirement. Nevertheless, when initiating the face-to-face sessions, the participants were made aware about the degrees of freedom available to modify the sequences of activities, incorporate different alternatives, etc. [I1]. The activity was completed once all groups are formed for

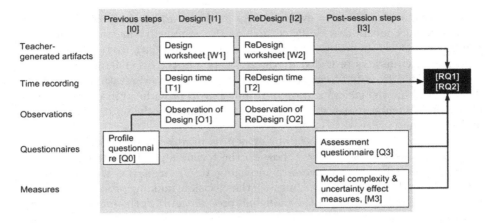

Fig. 2. Data gathering and analysis techniques used during the mixed methods study. Data source labels (between brackets) are used in the result section.

each phase of the scenarios, tools and delivery times are assigned, and dependencies among individual or group activities have been satisfied [W1][W2]. During the process the researcher observes [O1][O2], measures time consumed for each task [T1][T2], (1) takes notes about the happenings and intervenes, (2) clarifying the doubts posed by the participants, (3) intervening to know about which are the setting options that have been considered in the process, and (4) remarking the need of representing all the particular dependencies in the same way, as they would do when using authoring tools they are eventually familiar with.

In the end of the session an assessment questionnaire [Q3][1] is filled out by the participants, while design and redesign worksheets [W1] and [W2] are also processed by the researcher using process model metrics [M3].

4   Results and Discussion

This section summarizes the main results obtained in the ArtFlowDER study. Results are organized according to the topics defined to analyze our research questions [RQ1] and [RQ2], i.e. (a) modeling effort perception and the connection-triangulation with the presence of errors committed, signs of fatigue or overwhelm and responses from the questionnaires; (b) the effect of the epistemic uncertainty on the effort perception; and (c) the relation of the aforementioned aspects with the model structural complexity. Finding are supported on quantitative and qualitative data.

---

[1] The original questionnaires used in the study can be accessed at http://goo.gl/gS0Mxp [Q0] and http://goo.gl/vdOZCp [Q3].

Table 3. Summary of results relating design product and design process measures with teachers profiles

Parameters measured	Teacher 1		Teacher 2		Teacher 3		Teacher 4		Teacher 5	
	E1	E2	E1	E2	E1	E2	E1	E2	E1	E2
Agreement on that the modeling of artifacts flow has demanded lot of effort [Q3]	5	2	5	4	5	3	3	2	2	2
Particular Structural complexity [M3]	221	194	187	174	129	117	157	146	171	160
Time intervals (Reflection /Mapping) [T1] [T2]	24/19	9/17	32/30	15/18	12/11	9/9	30/18	8/2	45/23	9/14
Errors committed [O1] [O2]	0	0	5	1	2	1	2	0	3	0
Years of teaching experience [Q0]	11		18		5		4		16	
I use regularly collaborative learning techniques in my teaching [Q0]	4		3		5		4		4	
I have modeled before flow artifacts in my designs [Q3]	5		1		5		4		5	
I often use ICT to support collaborative work [Q0]	3		3		5		4		4	

4.1 Perception of the Artifact Flow Design Effort

As depicted in Table 3, the five teachers-participants found the scenario provided as plausible [Q0] and they responded directly to a question on whether the modeling process demanded a lot of effort or not in the DESIGN task using a 5 point-Likert scale [Q3].

Three of the teachers (1, 2 and 3 in Table 3) agreed completely that *"the modeling of artifacts flows has demanded a lot of effort"* [Q3], while these scores were further reinforced through other data. On one hand, [teacher 2] pointed out that the complexity of the task itself effect when perceiving the effort has a greater effect than the design tools that are employed (*"the design tool employed is not a decisive factor, the task is really difficult"*, or *"the task required to have a picture of a large group featuring complementary tasks and it was not always easy to allocate actions or artifacts without getting the students bored"*). Moreover, fatigue or overwhelm expressions were observed when repetitive actions were realized during sessions (*"phew, this is a pain..."*, *"he/she sighed, settled in his chair as a sign of discomfort and complain scribbling the worksheet due to the excessive number of [data flow] interconnections"* [O1]). Also, 4, 3 or 2 errors were committed per teacher during sessions when they were mapping their setting solutions to the worksheet model representations, as expected since the model complexity is high [18] and concentrated in design sessions, which lasted between 30 and 60 min.

A more in-depth analysis of the times devoted for reflection and mapping for DESIGN and REDESIGN task is made. The completion of the definition of each artifact flow situation ([VFs] in Table 1) requires time for reflection (decision making) and mapping actions (drawing the solution at the worksheet).

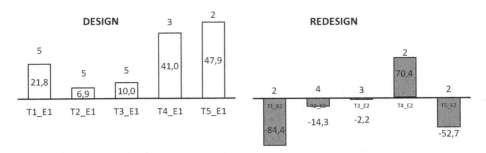

Fig. 3. Relationship between the assessments, and the percentage of time differential (reflection-mapping) for DESIGN (left) and REDESIGN (right) tasks.

In the analysis, ratings given by the teacher-participants are related to the percent difference between the time intervals of reflection and mapping for the DESIGN and REDESIGN tasks (see Table 3). The Fig. 3 depicts that the effort rating bears some relation with the percent difference between the time intervals of reflection and mapping. Teacher 1, 2 & 3 which agreed completely that *"the modeling of artifacts flows has demanded a lot of effort"* [DESIGN] show smaller differences between reflection and mapping time intervals comparing with Teachers 4 & 5 who hesitated or they did not agree to consider that artifact flow modeling was an effort demanding task and differences between reflection and mapping time intervals get double or higher. Similarly, the analysis of the [REDESIGN] task show that smaller differences coincide with higher effort ratings, while bigger time interval differences are lower rated. Presumably some degree of similarity between reflection and mapping intervals bears some relation to the perception of effort rated by teachers, emphasizing the mapping actions, while these cases in which the difference between the reflection and mapping intervals is higher show that the greatest emphasis is on the reflection actions. The low ratings are ultimately be related to the experience of those particular teachers (e.g. Teacher 5) in the design and configuration of CSCL scenarios. Exceptionally [Teacher 4] in the [REDESIGN] task shows a positive difference because he declined to represent the rest of interactions assuming the reuse of all prior settings and just representing minors in changes in worksheet.

On the other hand, all teachers-participants considered to some degree that the artifact assignment is a repetitive and an error-prone process (*"the* [artifact-assignment] *pattern is repetitively applied for all [the participants]"*), an aspect, not well addressed by current authoring tools. In fact, several errors were committed when groups were formed and artifact dependencies were satisfied [O1]. Although tools such as WebCollage (the teacher took previous contact with this tool) was positively valued regarding the visual appeal (*"it is useful to work visually with the represented groups"* [Teacher 1]), further suggestions were made (*"An artifact [assignment] pattern functionality should be implemented"*). In contrast, [teacher 4] hesitated to consider that artifact flow modeling was an effort demanding task (*"It is demanding mainly when trying to create balanced groups [with respect to the number of learners]"*). Additionally, [teacher 5] considered that the task was not effort demanding, due to her prior experience in modeling collaborative scenarios (*"I'm used to model flows and it wasn't difficult to me"*).

The structural complexity can provide hints about the rating of perceived modeling effort, but it must be supplemented by other measures in order to have a more reliable picture of what actually occurs in the design processes. For example while [Teacher 3] rates the DESIGN task as one demanding significant effort given the 129 units of measured structural complexity, [Teacher 5] considers the creation of her model, which is 32 % more complex, as a not demanding task. Thus we can clearly see the effect of other contributing factors which are not considered in the complexity metric employed. Teachers 1, 2 and 3 attribute the effort overload to the complexity of the process and models (amount of elements handled or editing steps made in the modeling process), while teacher 4 and 5 pay more attention on the complexity of the decision-making process (setting elements or design variables to be considered and the available setting options).

4.2 The Effect of the Epistemic Uncertainty

As discussed in Sect. 3.1, the artifact flow of the scenario is described in terms of four high level dependency constructs. These constructs express in terms of rules or constraints the variability on setting elements associated with (a) group formation; (b) artifacts generated; (c) artifact assignment; and (d) tool types for different pedagogical contexts. Thus the design problem be considered as a collection of several setting element whose values are decided throughout the design process. Nevertheless, this decision making process may generate certain degree of uncertainty on teachers without experience as designers and enactors of CSCL scenarios, thus increasing the perceived effort. Two perspectives of epistemic uncertainty can be considered. The first perspective expresses the lack of information by the teacher regarding the setting elements involved in the particularization process. The other perspective is related with their setting options available (possible values) once the setting elements are known and how each setting option contributes to fulfill the functional requirements.

The number of reasonable setting options of our CSCL scenario depends on one hand, on the intrinsic features of the collaborative patterns involved and on the relation between these patterns. On the other hand, the number of options is determined by the design requirements (i.e. class size, tool types, effectiveness, etc.) and the aforementioned designer experience. The higher the number of possible setting options (i.e., the search space) with similar probabilities of being chosen, the higher is the epistemic uncertainty [13, 26]. An interpretation for such a relation is that the designer does not have enough information to efficiently discriminate which is the best candidate options set able to fulfill the design requirement (in our case: a functional setting). The analysis of the MOSAIC high-level description, and the particular solutions in both Design, and REDESIGN tasks, has shown the existing gap between the *expected* theoretical options in the search space and the number of options actually considered by the teachers in order to fulfill the functional setting requirement (see Table 4).

Table 4. Artifact flow dependencies constructs (VF) analysis in which the options considered by the teachers are compared with those theoretically expected. E1 and E2 means DESIGN and REDESIGN tasks respectively. "Idem" acronym means that during the REDESIGN task the [initial] DESIGN setting was directly reused.

Dependency description		Observed options/Expected options									
		Teacher 1		Teacher 2		Teacher 3		Teacher 4		Teacher 5	
		E1	E2	E1	E2	E1	E2	E1	E2	E1	E2
[VF1]	Each individual or group reviews concept maps generated by peers who have studied the same initial documents (Individual JIGSAW)	1/15	idem	1/15	2/12	1/15	1/12	2/15	idem	1/15	1/10
[VF2]	Students review the concept maps created by other expert groups (Expert JIGSAW)	1/11	idem	2/9	1/9	1/5	1/2	2/9	idem	2/22	idem
[VF3]	Students individually reflect on maps generated by other puzzle groups (Puzzle JIGSAW)	2/4	idem	2/8	idem	1/4	1/4	2/4	idem	1/4	idem
[VF4]	Teachers supporting the activity review the maps created by groups Puzzle (Puzzle JIGSAW)	1/1	1/1	1/1	1/1	1/1	1/1	1/1	1/1	1/1	1/1

The expected theoretical options correspond to the search space [26] associated with each situation described by the dependency constructs [VF1, 2, 3 & 4], and they depend on the constraints of the collaboration patterns enrolled (i.e. PYRAMID, PEER REVIEW, JIGSAW), but also on the cascading effect of the already made decisions. The expected theoretical options set were calculated [M3] by analyzing and processing each design artifact created [W1][W2], the video recordings [O1][O2], and finally applying documented collaboration setting guidelines. The observed options are those which were considered and expressed by teachers as the set of candidates to be adopted in their designs.

Noticeably, the number of observed options is, in most of the cases, significantly less than the number of expected options [M3], resulting in the reduction of the perceived uncertainty. The low number of observed options may be explained by that fact that only one functionality requirement was posed in the task description without including additional domain information. Aspects defining the "common knowledge" related with the design problem [28], such as realistic group size, or individual profiles or domain involved in the concept maps were not specified a priori and remained open. The conditions described above enable the richness of a wide range of possible designs. The explanation of such criteria is beyond the scope of this paper. However, as a consequence, teachers could consider freely the aspects of number and size of groups, which became much more relevant in their decision process. Then, ranking of options was much easier and therefore less options were considered by the teachers and observed during the study (*"all this [the scenario description] is generic and there are no arguments to make a special selection of students or settings"* [Teacher 2], *"Large groups lose quality but are more feasible for teacher"* [teacher 4] [O1]).

Aligned with this reasoning, teachers 1, 3 and 4 chose the simplest situations, assigning only one artifact for reading and analyzing, in order to probably make the scenario more feasible ("the simpler the better"). These choices were reused later in the REDESIGN task. Exceptionally, [Teacher 2] configured the situation associated with the variability facet [VF1] as an individual review of the concept maps generated by the three peers in the subgroup. This teacher considered two different setting options for each artifact flow situation [VF1], [VF2] and [VF3], but new options were considered to reconfigure [VF2] regarding the new conditions. Similarly, [Teacher 4] also considered two setting options for [VF2] and [VF3], but as [Teacher 1] did, the choices made for the DESIGN task were directly reused. [Teacher 5] considered one or two options at the DESIGN task for customizing the artifact flow situations, and reused two artifact assignment settings. On the contrary [Teacher 5] enriched the situation associated with [VF3] by incorporating a new artifact flow situation in which each group "puzzle" group examines three conceptual maps created by expert groups, adding the individual reviews made previously by their peers from other jigsaw groups using Google Forms. From the above analysis we can highlight two emerging groups: first, the teachers facing the REDESIGN task by reusing setting strategies as they were conceived in the DESIGN task. (i.e. [Teacher 1] [Teacher 4]), and then those who faced the task of redesigning, proposing new settings which they considered better suited to the new requirements (i.e. [Teacher 2][Teacher 3][Teacher 5]).

4.3   Perception of the Artifact Flow Redesign Effort

As depicted in Table 3, four teachers out of 5 hesitated to agree in considering that the REDESIGN task model the new scenario (E2) on the basis of the first scenario (E1) as demanded a significant effort, or directly disagreed. The reduction of the effort assessment rating [Q3] is aligned with the reduction of 8,6 % in terms of structural complexity of the models [M3], while the effect of reusing setting and representation strategies from the previous DESIGN task (E1) is larger. Additional data supporting the fact that the perceived effort was reduced in the REDESIGN task as compared to the DESIGN task are presented in Table 5. Noticeably, in general there is a significant difference between the number of observed options and expected options as shown the Table 4.

The reduction of the effort demanded in the REDESIGN task is confirmed in terms of time consumed (an average of 30 min instead of 45 min consumed in the previous DESIGN task). In this case the change of ratings of perceived modeling effort from (E1) to (E2) is observable in objective terms regarding the reduction in time consumed [T2] and complexity of the reuse-based particular model [W2][M3], but also the reduction of the number of setting options considered for configuring the new artifacts flow situations. Globally, only two errors were

Table 5. Analysis of changes on rating effort from design (E1) to DESIGN tasks (E2)

Teacher	Rating change	Argumentation
Teacher 1	5-3	"The scenario E2 has taken more effort than scenario E1" [Q3]
Teacher 2	5-4	"Starting [REDESIGN] on the basis of previous experience (E1) facilitates the task. However, we must devote extra effort to adjust the design to the new requirement of the class size feature. In this case, the new group size implies that the setting is more complex than the scenario (E1)" [Q3], "I had no idea how to do it" [O2]
Teacher 3	5-2	"I was able to take advantage of all the effort made in DESIGN task (E1) and the modifications made were very simple (size and number of groups)" [Q3]
Teacher 4	3-2	"I would apply the same logic but with fewer students" [O2] "I left it distributed the same way, more balanced regarding the new number of students" [Q3]
Teacher 5	2-2	"I normally use a strategy that usually works in these cases, i.e., to play with the number of students in each group. It is true that in this way I have go back to fit the design according to the new class size. I faced more trouble setting the upper pyramid phases" [Q3]

committed during the realization of this REDESIGN task. Nevertheless, when the REDESIGN task was carried out, fatigue or overwhelm were also present with continuous sighs, or expressions such as "several things [actions] are repetitive" [O2]. The willing to represent only fragments of the particular solution satisfying the artifact flow dependencies was evident, declining to represent the rest of interactions [Teacher 4].

Moreover, as explained in the previous subsection, the uncertainty of the REDESIGN situation (E2) is lower than the one in the DESIGN scenario (E1). As depicted in Table 4, four out of the five teachers-participants reused at least one artifact flow setting just as they built it in the previous DESIGN task (E1), thus reducing the effort employed. However, the REDESIGN task (E2) implied rethinking some prior settings or even forced teachers to consider new options (Teachers 2, 4 and 5).

[Teacher 1] represents a singular case in which several contradictions were observed. As shown in Table 5, contrary to his oral statement, he rated DESIGN as more demanding task than REDESIGN (5 vs. 3). Such comment is also contradictory considering the reduction on the model structural complexity (221 vs. 194 units), time consumed (38 vs. 30 min), the fact that no errors were committed during all session (see Table 3), and that all artifact flow setting strategies were directly reused from the DESIGN task (Table 4).

5   Conclusions and Future Work

In this paper we have explored two research questions, i.e. (a) [RQ1] "how significant is the effort perceived by teacher designers facing the design and redesign of particular CSCL scenarios which incorporate consistently and explicitly the artifact flow dependencies", and (b) [RQ2] "which is the relation of the perceived effort with the objective complexity of the design". The consistent definition of the artifact flow is perceived as an effort overloading task but, depending on the skills of the teacher as process designer.

In this line, the ArtFlowDER study presented in this paper highlights two main aspects referring to [RQ1] and [RQ2]. The effort perceived by teachers may be high [RQ1] considering the number of repetitive or redundant editing tasks associated with the artifact flow definition. On one hand, this effort is expressed in terms of concentration, the occurrence of error-prone situations and time consumed on reflection or mapping actions for both DESIGN and REDESIGN tasks. Certain tendency was observed between the ratings given by the teacher-participants and the percentage difference between reflection and mapping times: the higher difference, the lower effort perception rating. Moreover, is also observed that DESIGN task demand more time and effort for reflection and conversely REDESIGN task demand more time for mapping actions assuming that most of decisions are already made and four out the five teachers reused at least one setting as they were conceived at the DESIGN task.

On the other hand, the effort load is expressed in terms of the epistemic uncertainty faced in the process of figuring out which setting solution fits better with the functional requirements (e.g. manageability, tools available, class size). In our study, the uncertainty was moderate comparing the number of setting options considered by teachers to apply in their designs, to the number of setting options that were actually available. In most cases they were not sure about the feasibility of the options adopted, especially the teachers with less experience on modeling and deployment of collaborative processes. It is noticeable, that none of the teachers-participants considered the influence of the tool functionality on the way the learners can access the artifacts, nor how the scenario model complexity is affected. Intentionally, they were not advised of this aspect to know the importance they give to this aspect. The lack of this setting element makes designs simpler and reduces the epistemic uncertainty associated with the selection of setting options for each variable and its effects on the range of options in other design elements.

Regarding [RQ2], the effort perceived bears some relation with the structural complexity of the design models. However, the findings are not homogeneous because the number of participants so far collected in the initial phase of the study is limited as to identify tendencies, and the perception of effort has not been clear and consistent within the five participants. Differences among teachers with respect to their experience in modeling scenarios CSCL with artifact flow may explain the aforementioned rating inconsistency. Thus the results reported in this paper cannot be considered as a sufficiently valid test of the metrics used to characterize CSCL scenario design with flow artifacts. However, this finding is clearly interwoven with both contextual factors such as the methodological design of the study and subjective factors such as the experience in process modeling or the characteristics of the specific domains the teachers adopted to customize the scenario provided.

Our study allows us to better comprehend the design process of CSCL scenarios, identify underlying factors and assess their degree of influence. This understanding would be useful allowing the proposal of alternative design models that reduce the effort demanded for teachers-designers and contribute to promote the wider adoption of the learning design approach and tooling. In the near future we plan to extend this study with a larger number of teachers-participants, aiming to understand better the relation between subjective perception of effort demanded and the objectives metrics of complexity and uncertainty. Finally, we are currently working towards the proposal of a new design process that takes into account the consistent artifact flow definition, while keeping the effort overload low enough. Such proposal will be supported through the adaptation of existing authoring and deployment tools.

Acknowledgments. This research has been partially funded by the Autonomous Government of Castilla and León, Spain (ORDEN EDU/346/2013), the Spanish Ministry of Economy and Competitiveness (Project TIN2011-28308-C03-02) and the European Education, Audiovisual and Culture Executive Agency Project 531262-LLP-2012-ES-KA3-KA3MP. The authors would like to thank the rest of the GSIC/EMIC research team, for their effort and contributions to the ideas expressed in this paper.

References

1. Ameri, F., Summers, J., Mocko, G., Porter, M.: Engineering design complexity: an investigation of methods and measures. Res. Eng. Des. **19**(2–3), 161–179 (2008)
2. Bordiés, O., Dimitriadis, Y.: Using objective metrics to measure the effort overload in CSCL design processes that support artifact flow. In: 2014 IEEE 14th International Conference on Advanced Learning Technologies (ICALT). IEEE, Athens, Greece (2014)
3. Bordiés, O., Papasalouros, A., Dimitriadis, Y.: Estimating the gap between informal descriptions and formal models of artifact flows in CSCL. In: de Freitas, S., Rensing, C., Ley, T., Muñoz-Merino, P.J. (eds.) EC-TEL 2014. LNCS, vol. 8719, pp. 554–555. Springer, Heidelberg (2014)
4. Braha, D., Maimon, O.: The measurement of a design structural and functional complexity. Syst. Man Cybern. Part A: Syst. Humans **28**(4), 527–535 (1998)
5. Cardoso, J.: Process control-flow complexity metric: an empirical validation. In: IEEE International Conference on Services Computing, 2006. SCC 2006, pp. 167–173. SCC 2006. IEEE Computer Society, Washington, DC, USA (2006)
6. Casey, J., Brosnan, K., Greller, W., Masson, A., MacNeill, A., Murphy, C.: Designing for change: visual design tools to support process change in education. Handbook of Visual Languages in Instructional Design: Theories and Practices, pp. 413–438 (2008)
7. Conole, G.: Designing for Learning in an Open World. Explorations in the Learning Sciences, Instructional Systems and Performance Technologies, vol. 4. Springer, New York (2012)

8. Creswell, J.W.: Research Design: Qualitative, Quantitative, and Mixed Methods approaches. Sage publications, Los Angeles (2013)
9. Derntl, M., Neumann, S., Griffiths, D., Oberhuemer, P.: The conceptual structure of ims learning design does not impede its use for authoring. IEEE Trans. Learn. Technol. **5**(1), 74–86 (2012)
10. Dillenbourg, P., Tchounikine, P.: Flexibility in macro-scripts for computer-supported collaborative learning. J. Comput. Assist. Learn. **23**(1), 1–13 (2007)
11. Dochy, F., Segers, M., Sluijsmans, D.: The use of self-, peer and co-assessment in higher education: a review. Stud. High. Educ. **24**(3), 331–350 (1999)
12. Hernández-Leo, D., Villasclaras-Fernandez, E., Asensio-Perez, J., Dimitriadis, Y., Retalis, S.: CSCL scripting patterns: hierarchical relationships and applicability. In: Sixth International Conference on Advanced Learning Technologies, 2006, pp. 388–392. ICALT 2006. IEEE Computer Society, Washington, DC, USA (2006)
13. Jung, J.Y., Chin, C.H., Cardoso, J.: An entropy-based uncertainty measure of process models. Inf. Process. Lett. **111**(3), 135–141 (2011)
14. Karakostas, A., Demetriadis, S.: Adaptation patterns as a conceptual tool for designing the adaptive operation of CSCL systems. Educ. Technol. Res. Dev. **59**(3), 327–349 (2011)
15. Karakostas, A., Prieto, L.P., Dimitriadis, Y.: Opportunities and challenges for adaptive collaborative support in distributed learning environments: evaluating the GLUE! suite of tools. In: 2012 IEEE 12th International Conference on Advanced Learning Technologies (ICALT), pp. 446–450. IEEE (2012)
16. Malone, T.W., Crowston, K.: The interdisciplinary study of coordination. ACM Comput. Surv. **26**(1), 87–119 (1994)
17. McKenney, S., Kali, Y., Markauskaite, L., Voogt, J.: Teacher design knowledge for technology enhanced learning: an ecological framework for investigating assets and needs. Instr. Sci. **43**(2), 181–202 (2015)
18. Mendling, J.: Metrics for Process Models: Empirical Foundations of Verification, Error Prediction, and Guidelines for Correctness. Lectures Notes in Business Information Processing. Springer, Heidelberg (2008)
19. Mendling, J.: Metrics for business process models. In: Aalst, W., Mylopoulos, J., Rosemann, M., Shaw, M.J., Szyperski, C. (eds.) Metrics for Process Models. Lecture Notes in Business Information Processing, vol. 6, pp. 103–133. Springer, Heidelberg (2009). Chapter 4
20. Miao, Y., Burgos, D., Griffiths, D., Koper, R.: Representation of coordination mechanisms in IMS learning design to support group-based learning. In: Lockyer, L., Bennet, S., Agostinho, S., Harper, B. (eds.) Handbook of Research on Learning Design and Learning Objects: Issues, Applications and Technologies, pp. 330–351. IDEA group, Hershey (2008)
21. Muketha, G., Ghani, A., Selamat, M., Atan, R.: A survey of business process complexity metrics. Inf. Technol. J. **9**(7), 1336–1344 (2010)
22. Palomino-Ramírez, L., Bote-Lorenzo, M., Asensio-Pérez, J., de la Fuente-Valentín, L., Dimitriadis, Y.: The data flow problem in learning design: a case study. In: Proceedings of the 2008 8th International Conference on Networked Learning, NLC, pp. 285–292. NLC 2008 (2008)
23. Prieto, L.P., Tchounikine, P., Asensio-Pérez, J.I., Sobreira, P., Dimitriadis, Y.: Exploring teachers' perceptions on different CSCL script editing tools. Comput. Educ. **78**, 383–396 (2014)
24. Rodríguez-Triana, M.J., Martínez-Monés, A., Asensio-Pérez, J.I., Dimitriadis, Y.: Towards a script-aware monitoring process of computer-supported collaborative learning scenarios. Int. J. Technol. Enhanced Learn. **5**(2), 151–167 (2013)

25. Sánchez-González, L., García, F., Ruiz, F., Velthuis, M.P.: Measurement in business processes: a systematic review. Bus. Process Manag. J. **16**(1), 114–134 (2010)
26. Sen, C., Ameri, F., Summers, J.D.: An entropic method for sequencing discrete design decisions. J. Mech. Des. **132**(10), 1–11 (2010)
27. Sobreira, P., Tchounikine, P.: A model for flexibly editing CSCL scripts. Int. J. Comput.-Support. Collaborative Learn. **7**(4), 567–592 (2012)
28. Summers, J.D., Shah, J.J.: Mechanical engineering design complexity metrics: size, coupling, and solvability. J. Mech. Des. **132**(2), 021004-1–021004-11 (2010)
29. Suthers, D.: Technology affordances for intersubjective meaning making: a research agenda for CSCL. Int. J. Comput.-Support. Collaborative Learn. **1**(3), 315–337 (2006)
30. Wu, Y., Hernandez, F., Ortega, F., Clarke, P.J., France, R.: Measuring the effort for creating and using domain-specific models. In: Proceedings of the 10th Workshop on Domain-Specific Modeling. pp. 14:1–14:6. DSM 2010. ACM, New York, NY, USA (2010)

Supporting Collaborative Decision Making in Geo-Collaboration Scenarios

Nelson Baloian[1(✉)], Jonathan Frez[2], José A. Pino[1], and Gustavo Zurita[3]

[1] Department of Computer Science, Universidad de Chile, Santiago, Chile
{nbaloian,jpino}@dcc.uchile.cl
[2] Universidad Diego Portales, Santiago, Chile
jonathan.frez@mail.udp.cl
[3] Management Control and Information Systems Department, Faculty of Economics and Business, Universidad de Chile, Diagonal Paraguay 257, Santiago, Chile
gzurita@fen.uchile.cl

Abstract. The Geo-collaboration term is applied to collaborative activities in which data and models used by participants are strongly related to geographical locations. There are many scenarios in which Geo-collaboration is used to support a collaborative decision making process. Some of these scenarios are city planning, developing evacuations for emergencies, and developing nature protecting projects. In these situations experts with various backgrounds and knowledge contribute with their opinions and viewpoints. Ideally, the final solution should combine all these viewpoints and all specialists should agree on it. Although the literature reports about procedures for combining decision makers' opinions whose goals might be in contradiction, there are no systems which explicitly support them to reach consensus over a final joint solution. We present a tool which supports this process by allowing experts first, to propose their individual point of view, modeled in the form of beliefs according to the Dempster-Schafer evidence theory. Then, the tool lets participants visualize all proposals, discussing and combining them in a suitable consensual way.

Keywords: Geo-Collaboration · Collaborative decision making

1 Introduction

According to Kraemer and King [1], computer support for Collaborative Decision Making refers to systems which facilitate finding a solution to ill-structured problems by a team of decision makers. There are many scenarios where the decision making (DM) outcome strongly depends on geo-referenced information like city planning [2], crisis management [3], disaster management and recovery [4] natural resources management [5]. These kinds of decision making processes have often been called *Spatial Decision Making* and computer systems providing support for these activities typically include tools for input, storage and retrieval, manipulation, analysis and visualization of spatial data, including maps. Thus, Geographic Information Systems (GIS) are often considered as decision support systems involving the integration of spatially referenced

© Springer International Publishing Switzerland 2015
N. Baloian et al. (Eds.): CRIWG 2015, LNCS 9334, pp. 63–71, 2015.
DOI: 10.1007/978-3-319-22747-4_5

data in a problem solving environment [6]. The literature shows that the participation of various experts is required in many spatial decision-making scenarios [7]. The combination of Collaborative Decision Making with Spatial Decision Making has been called Geo-Collaboration [8, 9].

One of the most recurrent problems can be generally stated in the following way: *Find a suitable area to "do" something*. For example: Ghayoumian et al. [5] explain how to find specific locations for constructing artificial water recharge aquifers using floods. In this example decision makers must be experts in aquifer recharge, but they will need historical information and spatial data to design a formula which reflects the right criteria for selecting the suitable area(s). This formula is used to build a suitability map using a GIS. This map typically shows the suitability level on each point of the map satisfying the requirements. However, in ill-structured problems this criterion is complex to build because the goals are not clear and the various decision makers will tend to define different goals according to their own knowledge. The most common technique to combine the various experts' points of views in special decision making scenarios has been the Multi Criteria Decision Analysis approach [7]. Simply stated, it consists of combining the various criteria which decision makers think should be considered to evaluate the suitability of a certain option in a single objective function; there are many works centered on mathematical structure and how to combine the various attributes in order to represent the various criteria which should be included in the scenario evaluation [10]. On the contrary, the problem of supporting the various decision makers to reach consensus about which important criteria should be considered to build the suitability map in a geo-collaboration decision making scenario seems to have been neglected according to the literature. However, it should be noted support for reaching consensus has been a relevant subject for researchers working in collaborative decision making in general (not particularly in geo-collaboration). Many authors highlight the importance of reaching consensus through argumentation in successive divergent (generating options) and convergent stages (grouping, discarding, selecting best options) of the discussion [11].

Some authors consider GIS as Decision Support Systems because they are intended to support some stage of the decision making process [12]. However, others argue that according to GIS [2] offer in general appropriate techniques for data management, information extraction, routine manipulation, and visualization, but they do not have the necessary analytical capabilities to manage a decision making process. Furthermore, Malafant et al. [12] claim that at the time of publication (2010) of that paper, the existing Spatial-DSS does not provide the needed characteristics; recent literature does not show progress in this issue either. According to Nyerges [16, 17, 18] the most needed characteristics to support spatial ill-structured problems are:

- Combine data from different sources, providing degrees of certainty of each and a method to evaluate and combine data.
- Generate suitability scenarios using various hypothesis in a flexible and systematic process.
- Offer suitable tools to compare different scenarios. The comparison of two or more scenarios can provide the best solution to the problem and further information.

In this paper we propose a method and a tool intended to explicitly support discussion about scenarios and hypothesis using collaborative software based on decision support techniques.

2 Related Work

Many models have been proposed, both for individual and collaborative decision making processes encompassing several points of view, for various purposes, which have been used to design software tools supporting the process. The most important ones are presented by Antunes et al. [2]. From all these models we can distill a simplified one which has these critical stages: (1) Identifying the problem, (2) identifying and modeling the decision objective(s), (3) collecting, generating and/or combining data to generate alternative scenarios, (4) evaluating options according to stated objectives, (5) choosing an option and conducting a sensitivity analysis. If the decision makers estimate there is enough information, the process ends up with a final decision, otherwise the flow goes back to the identifying objectives stage or to the generating options stage. Like Artificial Intelligence, the boundaries for defining what falls under Decision Support Systems (DSS) seem to be diffuse. However, most authors who have tried to define them agree that one of the most important characteristics is that human judgment remains in the decision making process cycle as a key actor, generating alternatives, re-defining and re-modeling objectives since this is a task involving creativity, which cannot be mechanized. Computers, in turn, can help humans in gathering data, generating various decision options, evaluating their outcome according to the decisions goals, visualizing these results and sharing them, providing suitable tools to support discussion and exchange opinions.

Frequently, DSS deal with ill-structured problems; this means that the goals might not be totally clear and/or there is insufficient information to solve the problems in a certain optimal way. Moreover, in ill-structured problems there are many stakeholders and many decision makers, so the solution tends to be subjective and unique. Also DSS systems use various models and analysis techniques and are intended to be used by non-computer experts. Hence, a DSS must be interactive, flexible and adaptable in order to support different solution approaches. Furthermore, DSSs oriented to spatial problems must be able to model the environment and evaluate the impact of changes under various hypotheses. Also, spatial information is inherently fuzzy and uncertain [2], this implies that fuzzy analysis techniques are needed.

From the available literature about GIS used to support DM, we note there are many modelling tools available, which can generate a certain scenario for a geo-graphical area applying certain evaluation functions and showing the output, e.g., for vegetation winter survival [3], wind farms locations [4] or forest production estima-tion [5]. However, most existing GIS are not explicitly designed to support a DM cycle. Moreover, the process of generating various alternative scenarios according to various criteria and comparing them is in most cases, a difficult and time consuming task. In order to implement a DM process we need to abstract the modelling part from the DM cycle and allow the decision maker to generate multiple scenarios under various hypotheses and compare the outcomes in a simple and systematic way.

A decision making process supported by GIS typically starts with two inputs: data and expert knowledge. Models are built using experts' knowledge and alternative scenarios are constructed using different data inputs. These scenarios can be compared because they are based on the same model; however the model is based on different expert knowledge. This knowledge can change, e.g., by including or removing a person in the experts team. If the knowledge changes, it is hard to represent this change in the model; it is even harder to compare the corresponding results.

3 Scenario Building

A specific scenario consisting of a group of experts analyzing high-risk areas during earthquakes in a certain city will be used to better explain the requirements for a system supporting the previous works. The experts have varied expertise knowledge, and consequently, they can classify the danger a certain zone may pose on its inhabitants according to various criteria, e.g., an engineer will evaluate a zone according to the risks due to construction quality, while another expert will wonder on the possibility of having traffic jams during an earthquake. Someone with a healthcare background can evaluate the danger in hospitals and clinics and so on.

In the earthquake scenario, the evacuation and/or rescue problem can be classified as an ill-problem, because there is no precise information about the number of people to be evacuated or the time this operation will take. An earthquake can occur at any time and the population in the areas also change on a time basis.

We have chosen the Belief Theory of Dempster-Schafer [13] as a theoretical support because it has been successfully used to support decision making when available data is incomplete and/or uncertain. The theory states that multiple hypotheses can be proposed assigning a certain mass to a geographical area as a percentage of credibility that the hypotheses are true (belief), e.g., that there will be a certain number of persons in that area during an emergency by multiple experts. Then these hypotheses are processed generating belief and plausibility values for the whole area. These values correspond to the certainty that a hypothesis holds (belief) and the highest chance for this (plausibility). Thus time and belief based scenarios can provide suitable input to decision making when there is uncertain incomplete information, and complex modeling is needed.

We can build a set of Dempster-Shafer hypotheses which can tell us where people can be located. After a strong earthquake, several city services may fail, e.g., telecommunications, transportation, water supply, electricity. During the early stages of disaster recovery, the resources must be focused on saving lives. However, the main problem at this point is locating the places with the largest number of people in danger. Without telecommunication services this is a strong challenge, full of confusing information provided by multiple sources. In order to identify the "hotspots" (most probable locations where large amount of people in danger may be located), a risk map must be previously developed. Moreover, an earthquake can occur at any moment and the risk map is time dependent.

Multiple experts should contribute with their knowledge in order to develop useful risk maps; also multiples sources of information are usually needed. An evacuation plan for daytime, e.g., needs data from schools, hospitals and commercial centers. We propose a risk map developing methodology and tool supporting multiple experts' interactions, multiples sources validation and several scenarios manipulation. The resulting suitability map should be the result of the discussion about the plausibility of each scenario including the experts' hypotheses, known information about the area, and relevant factors that must be considered. However the final result depends on the combination methods [14].

4 Methodology

The methodology defines two roles and five stages. The normal user is the expert, who is someone with specific knowledge about data influencing the risk factor of a certain area, e.g., she/he knows about schools infrastructure, healthcare facilities, transportation networks or roads infrastructure, etc. Among the experts, one of them should play the role of coordinator who should be someone with a general knowledge of the area to be analyzed for risks; she/he is responsible for data validation, merging the viewpoints, and risk map quality. The five generic stages are: Data Gathering, Data Validation, Divergence, Argumentation and Convergence. The proposed tool supports the last three stages but the description of the first two is necessary to understand the worth of this tool.

Data Gathering: Each expert provides geo-referenced data of the area, related to her/his own expertise. It is important that no information is provided which is not backed by an expert. The coordinator can also provide information.

Data Validation: The coordinator must organize the geo-referenced data into groups of expertise or topics. Afterwards, the coordinator assigns one or more experts to each group. Each expert must analyze the data and validate, correct or reject it.

Divergence: At this stage, each expert, including the coordinator, generates scenarios which can be private or public. Scenarios can be compared, combined or discarded. The result of this stage will be a set of multiple scenarios. Each scenario can be based on the knowledge of one or more experts as a result of the combinations [14].

Argumentation: During this stage, experts argue about the plausibility of the scenarios supporting the initial hypotheses using the validated data. They can also compare and merge them performing various operations like adding, subtracting correlating and/or calculating average values for the belief and plausibility values the various maps show.

Convergence: At this stage experts should agree on a single or a reduced set of risk maps. For this purpose, the coordinator can define convergence criteria, e.g., 70 % of correlation between two scenarios allows summing or averaging them into one. After considering all possible scenarios, the resulting set can be considered as an independent group of decision support map. However, the entire group must select the most relevant ones based on their argumentation. The final result can be considered as a minimal shared independent set of decision support maps.

We do not consider that these stages should be exactly followed in this order, especially for the last three ones, which are the ones explicitly supported by the tool. We consider that experts will go back and forth generating scenarios, presenting them to their colleagues and discussing them trying to reach consensus.

5 Tool Implementation

Based on the methodology described above we propose a tool which allows the construction, discussion and combination of suitability maps. The tool supports Divergence, Argumentation and Convergence with three different views. During the Divergence stage each expert creates one or more risk scenarios. A scenario is defined by the problem characteristics and the information an expert has in order to support her/his hypotheses, e.g., a school can be considered an object that can be used for applying a hypothesis like this: "The risk in schools during an earthquake is 50 % in the morning and 75 % in cinemas in the evening and weekends". The tool extends the theory assuming that the risk mass decreases with the distance to the source location (cinemas and schools) according to a model specified by the expert. Another extension to the theory implemented by the tool is the relation between elements (facilities) and the hypothesis, which is modeled by so called rules: e.g., if the facility is located near a lake the risk mass should not be propagated to the water surface.

The expert selects the spatial propagation model, the hypotheses to be supported and the model interactions when defining a new risk scenario in the divergence stage. The tool then generates a risk map showing the risk areas according to the defined rules and hypotheses. The corresponding tool user interface is shown in Fig. 1. Each generated map will be associated to a private space belonging to the expert. The platform provides a public space to share interesting scenarios to other experts to sup-port collaborative work. A shared scenario is visible to all experts and discussion begins. The tool provides a view where each public map can be annotated, commented and voted to promote discussion about the suitability of the proposed risk map (Fig. 2). Therefore, the discussion is supported by an appropriate context [15].

Once a map is made public it can be included by other experts in their private space making a copy of it for further processing. Moreover, the platform provides tools to compare and combine private and public scenarios (Fig. 3). These tools are called operators. The implemented operators are:

- SUM: Calculates the sum of belief values for each common cell between two scenarios into the same cell in a new scenario.
- SUB: Calculates the difference of belief values for each common cell between two scenarios into the same cell in a new scenario.
- AVG: Calculates the average of belief values for each common cell between two scenarios into the same cell in a new scenario.
- CORR: Calculates the correlation of all belief values between two scenarios and returns the value and the SUB of the scenarios.

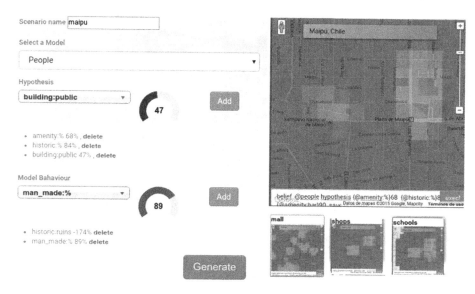

Fig. 1. The view supporting the "divergence" stage of the decision making process

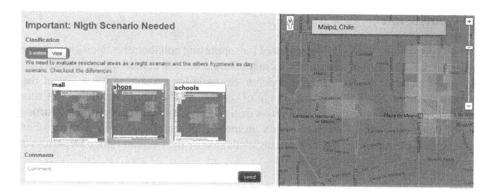

Fig. 2. The view supporting the "argumentation" stage of the decision making process

At the convergence stage the combination of scenarios can be done by the coordinator using the previous interface. After combining the possible scenarios, the resulting set will be an independent group of decision support maps. The experts can again use the argumentation view of the tool selecting one or more as an output of the full process. In order to support this step the platform provides an argument visualization combining the scenario visualization and voting system.

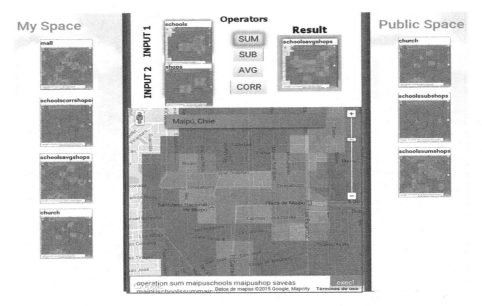

Fig. 3. The view supporting the "convergence" stage of the decision making process

6 Conclusions

We have presented a methodology and tool for supporting collaborative decision making processes for scenarios where suitability maps should be built combining the knowledge of various experts. We have used a concrete example for explaining the usage of the tool but it can be applied to a large range of scenarios. The main contribution of this work is to explicitly introduce collaborative decision making procedures to the construction of suitability maps, which has been an unexploited niche as expressed by other authors [12]. Currently the system is being evaluated by the Chilean Police Department in order to generate criminal risk maps.

References

1. Kraemer, K.L., King, J.L.: Computer-based systems for cooperative work and group decision making. ACM Comput. Surv. **20**(2), 115–146 (1988)
2. Antunes, P., Sapateiro, C., Zurita, G., Baloian, N.: Integrating spatial data and decision models in an e-planning tool. In: Kolfschoten, G., Herrmann, T., Lukosch, S. (eds.) CRIWG 2010. LNCS, vol. 6257, pp. 97–112. Springer, Heidelberg (2010)
3. Cai, G.: Extending distributed GIS to support geo-collaborative crisis management. Geogr. Inf. Sci. **11**(1), 4–14 (2005)
4. Huggins, L.J.: Comprehensive disaster management and development: the role of geoinformatics and geo-collaboration in linking mitigation and disaster recovery in the eastern caribbean. ProQuest (2007)

5. Ghayoumian, J., Ghermezcheshme, B., Feizmia, S., Noroozi, A.A.: Integrating GIS and DSS for identification of suitable areas for artificial recharge, case study Meimeh Basin, Isfahan, Iran. Environ. Geol. **47**, 493–500 (2005)
6. Cowen, D.: GIS versus CAD versus DBMS: what are the differences ? Photogram. Eng. Remote Sens. **54**, 1551–1555 (1988)
7. Malczewski, J., Rinner, C.: Multicriteria Decision Analysis in Geographic Information Science. Advances in Geographic Information Sciences. Springer, New York (2015)
8. MacEachren, A.M., Brewer, I.: Developing a conceptual framework for visually-enabled geocollaboration. Int. J. Geogr. Inf. Sci. **18**(1), 1–34 (2004)
9. Bailey, K., Grossardt, T.: Toward structured public involvement: justice, geography and collaborative geospatial/geovisual decision support systems. Ann. Assoc. Am. Geogr. **100**(1), 57–86 (2010)
10. Greene, R., Devillers, R., Luther, J., Eddy, B.: GIS-based multiple-criteria decision analysis. Geogr. Compass **5**(6), 412–432 (2011)
11. Karacapilidis, N., Papadias, D.: Computer supported argumentation and collaborative decision making: the HERMES system. Inf. Syst. **26**(4), 259–277 (2001)
12. Malafant, K., Fordham, D., Uso, J., Brebbia, C., Power, H., et al.: GIS, DSS and integrated scenario modelling frameworks for exploring alternative futures. In: Advances in Ecological Sciences. Ecosystems and Sustainable Development, vol. 1 (1998)
13. Sentz, K., Ferson, S.: Combination of Evidence in Dempster-Shafer Theory, vol. 4015. Sandia National Laboratories, Albuquerque (2002)
14. Frez, J., Baloian, N., Pino, J.A., Zurita, G.: Cooperative work for spatial decision making: an emergencies management case. In: Baloian, N., Burstein, F., Ogata, H., Santoro, F., Zurita, G. (eds.) CRIWG 2014. LNCS, vol. 8658, pp. 113–120. Springer, Heidelberg (2014)
15. Borges, M.R., Brézillon, P., Pino, J.A., Pomerol, J.-C.: Groupware system design and the context concept. In: Shen, W.-m., Lin, Z., Barthès, J.-P.A., Li, T.-Q. (eds.) CSCWD 2004. LNCS, vol. 3168, pp. 45–54. Springer, Heidelberg (2005)
16. Nyerges, T.L., Janowski, P.: Regional and Urban GIS: A Decision Support Approach. Guilford Press, New York (2012)
17. Antunes, P., Zurita, G., Baloian, N., Sapateiro, C.: Integrating decision-making support in geocollaboration tools. Group Decis. Negot. **23**(2), 211–233 (2014)
18. Zurita, G., Baloian, N.: Mobile: Collaborative situated knowledge creation for urban planning. Sensors **12**(5), 6218–6243 (2012)

Analysis of Question and Answering Behavior in Question Routing Services

Zhe Liu[1] and Bernard J. Jansen[2(✉)]

[1] College of Information Sciences and Technology, The Pennsylvania State University, University Park, State College, PA 16802, USA
zul112@ist.psu.edu
[2] Social Computing Group Qatar Computing Research Institute, HBKU, Doha, Qatar
jjansen@acm.org

Abstract. With the development of Web 2.0 technologies, social question and answering has become an important venue for individuals to seek for information that are important to their everyday lives. While prior literatures studying social question answering have suggested the possibility of routing questions to potential answerers for assistance, still little is known about how effective these question routing services are, and how individuals behave within such collaborative question answering environments. With the aim to advance the present knowledge about collaborative question answering that happens on social networking sites, in this study we collected questions and answers posted on Wenwo, a Chinese question routing service based on microblogging sites, over a ten-month period. We conduct various analyses to study individual's question and answering behavior from multifaceted perspectives, including the contributors effort in providing helps to others, the questioner's and the answerer's topical interests, and their connectedness with others through the question answering processes. Our results revealed the effectiveness of Wenwo in routing social Q&A questions to potential answerers and, in the meanwhile indicated the possible bottlenecks exist in the design of the current question routing services.

Keywords: Social question and answering · Social search · Collaborative information seeking

1 Introduction

Social networking sites (SNS), including as Facebook, Twitter, and Google+, have been widely adopted for online communication [1, 2], Besides using them for relationship formation and maintenance [3], many people also rely on SNS for information seeking [4, 5], a behavior referred to as social questioning and answering (social Q&A). Although not intentionally designed for questioning and answering, social Q&A has became a new form for online information seeking due to better search experiences over conventional information retrieval methods, such as allowing individuals to ask natural language questions to their online connections, as well as providing more personalized answers. Due to such advantages, social Q&A has attracted many researchers' attention

© Springer International Publishing Switzerland 2015
N. Baloian et al. (Eds.): CRIWG 2015, LNCS 9334, pp. 72–85, 2015.
DOI: 10.1007/978-3-319-22747-4_6

and has motivated the creation of models and tools to facilitate the information seeking process [6].

Among the proposed information seeking methods are several question routing algorithms that mostly involve expert finding techniques to solve the problem of nonguaranteed responses in a social context [7, 8]. It is assumed that question routing services, in general, can help improve the problem of low response rate in social Q&A [9], as it provides stimulus to users' participation [10]. However, still little is know about how effective these question routing services are, and how individuals behave within such collaborative Q&A environments.

To address this issue, in this study we perform detailed measurements of Wenwo, a Chinese question routing services based on microblogging sites, by conducting multi-faceted analyses on over 300,000 questions and answers posted on it during a ten-month period. We report preliminary results to identify, first, the effectiveness of question routing services in stimulating users' participation in social Q&A; second, the behavioral patterns of individuals on Weiwo, including their roles, their topical interests, and their connectedness with others through the question answering processes. Our preliminary findings indicate that Wenwo performs well in routing social Q&A questions to potential answerers. However, it relies heavily on a small number of active users and demonstrates strong separation of the roles between askers and answerers. In addition, we notice that individuals exhibit very low connectedness within the community formed by the question routing service.

2 Related Work

2.1 Analysis of Popular Community Q&A Sites

There has been a wide range of interests in understanding individual's information seeking behavior on popular collaborative portals, such as Yahoo!Answers, Stack Overflows, Quora, etc. One line of these studies has focused on utilizing quantitative methods to analyze the real-world Q&A data. For instance, Adamic et al. [11] in their study characterized the knowledge sharing behavior that occurred on Yahoo!Answers by analyzing the question categories and cluster them according to cross-categorical user interactions. Liu et al. [12] investigated the temporal patterns of knowledge contribution on Yahoo!Answers. In addition, they also successfully identified factors that affect individual's tendency to choose the questions to answer. Wang et al. [13] conducted detailed measurement on Quora using three connection networks, a graph connecting topics to users, a social graph connecting users, and a graph connecting related questions. Furtado et al. [14] categorized contributors into ten different types through a clustering analysis based on how much and how well users contribute different types of content over time.

In addition to the above-mentioned quantitative works, there are also studies using qualitative and mixed methods to understand individual's question and answering behavior from a deeper level. Treude et al. [15] examined the data collected from Stack Overflow and coded the questions asked on it into 11 different categories using a qualitative approach. Nam et al. [16] analyzed over five years Q&A data collected from KiN and noticed that higher levels of participation correlate with better performance. They also interviewed twenty six KiN users for their motivations of answering others' questions and found that altruism, learning, and competency are the top motivations for active participants on KiN. Mamykina et al. [17] adopted a mixed method that combines statistical data analysis and user interviews to uncover the reasons behind Stack Overflow's success. Based on their results, the authors also provide insightful suggestions for future design of Q&A systems, such as making competition productive, building on exiting credibility within the community, and adopting a continuous evolutionary approach to design, etc.

2.2 Analysis of Social Q&A Sites

Although the terms "community Q&A" and "social Q&A" have been mixed up and used in literatures, according to Morris et al. [4], Social Q&A is defined as the process of finding information online, especially on SNS, with the assistance of social resources. Many of the prior studies in social Q&A investigate factors that motivate people to seek information via social platforms. They found that individual's trust in friends over strangers, as well as non-urgent information needs were the major reasons that people turn to social networks to seek for information [4, 18, 19]. Besides, studies analyzing social Q&A questions also noticed more subjective questions over objective questions were asked on SNS [18].

Besides the studies of questions asked in social Q&A, there are other works examining the answers received. Paul et al. [9] noted that the majority of questions posted on Twitter received no response. They also observed that distinct question types lead to different response rates. For instance, they found that some rhetorical questions received a relatively large number of replies as compared to personal and health-related questions. In addition, the response rate was strongly related to some of the characteristics of the question askers, such as the size of their networks. Nichols and Kang [8] further confirmed this finding in their online experiment of sending questions to strangers for help. In their results, less than half of the questions received responses from strangers. Liu and Jansen [6] studied the social Q&A responses posted on Sina Weibo, the largest Chinese microblogging site. They found that the question's topic could effectively affect its response rate. For instance, they noticed that questions on the topics of Entertainment, Society, Computer, etc. received fewer responses as compared to questions from the other categories.

2.3 Question Routing in Collaborative Q&A

The concept of question routing refers to routing newly posted questions to potential answerers. According to previous studies [10, 20], the appropriateness of potential answerers was mainly measured based on their expertise as demonstrated by the archives of their previously answered questions. Numerous algorithms have been proposed to solve the problem of routing questions to appropriate answerers within the context of community Q&A. Li et al. [20] incorporated question category into their question routing model to sift out irrelevant questions in profile of an answerer for expertise estimation. Zhou et al. [21] considered the problem of question routing as a classification task, and developed a number of features that capture different aspects of questions, users, and their relations. Guo et al. [22] recommended questions to potential answerers by discovering latent topics in the content of questions as well as latent interests of users.

Given the relative low response rate in social Q&A, several studies have suggested the possibility of routing questions to potential answers to increase their response probability. Through online experiments, Nichols and Kang [8] explored the feasibility of users responding to questions sent by strangers. They found that fewer than half of the people answer questions posted by strangers. Pan et al. [23] offered a more in-depth analysis on potential answerers by leveraging users' non-Q&A social activities. Through their analysis of an inter-organizational CQA site, they found that some of the non-Q&A features can effectively predict the likelihood of one answering others' questions. Luo et al. [24] built a Smart Social Q&A system based on IBM Connected that recommends both active and inactive users for a given question based on their abilities, willingness, and readiness.

3   Research Questions

Although routing questions to potential answerers has been proposed as an effective way in solving the low response problem in social Q&A [20–24], very few studies have actually assessed the performance of the question routing method within practical context. To overcome this gap, we conducted this work evaluating a real-world question routing service called Wenwo from two perspectives:

RQ1. *How effective is the question routing service in social Q&A?*

RQ2. *How individuals behave within the question routing community?*

For our first research question, we evaluate the effectiveness of the question routing service that Wenwo offers to its users by performing some aggregated analyses on individual's question and answering behaviors. We address the second research question by analyzing individual's topical interests and their connectedness with others within the Q&A process.

4   Background on Wenwo

Wenwo[1] is a question routing application based on Sina Weibo, which is China's largest microblogging site, attracting over 600 million registered accounts by September 2014 [25], accounting for 93.60 % of the total Internet users in China. Each month, over 2 billion statuses are posted on Sina Weibo. At the time of the study, Weibo essentially adopted the same operating concept and provided very similar functions to its users as Twitter.

---

[1] http://wenwo.weibo.com/.

As a question routing service, Wenwo operates in a different manner compared to traditional community Q&A sites, such as Yahoo! Answers and Baidu Knows, in which people passively wait for the potential helpers to see their questions and to respond. In contrast, in Wenwo, individuals can either post questions directly to the site, or they can post their questions on Weibo by mentioning @微问 (@Wenwo). After receiving the questions, Wenwo will next identify a number of potential respondents based on their expertise and experience as demonstrated on their Weibo profiles, using machine-learning techniques. By routing questions to those "qualified" respondents, Wenwo effectively increases the probability of obtaining high quality response. A graphical demonstration of the question routing procedure of Wenwo is shown in Fig. 1.

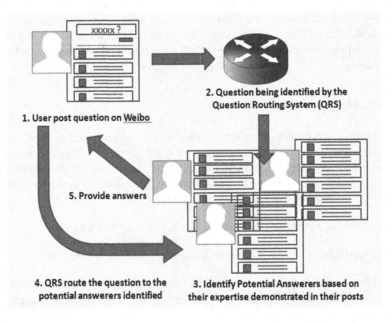

Fig. 1. Illustration of the question routing procedure of Wenwo.

Figure 2 is a screenshot of Wenwo with major sections highlighted. A question entry is created for a user if he/she posted a question either directly on Wenwo, or on Weibo by mentioning Wenwo. To better organize questions according to user's interests, Wenwo grouped all questions posted on it according to a topical hierarchy containing 13 top level categories, including: "Arts", "Business", "Computer", "Digital Electronics", "Education", "Entertainment", "Game", "Healthcare", "Life", "Resource Sharing", "Society", "Sports", and "Vexation". Under each top category, there are a number of sub-categories. All answers to the current question are listed below in a chronological thread, which makes discussions among participants easy. Another difference between Wenwo and other community Q&A sites is that, in addition to presenting the answers received, in most cases, Wenwo also informs the users to whom the question has been routed. This allowed us to know who responded a question and who did not.

Fig. 2. Screenshot of Wenwo with the major sections highlight

5   Data Collection

Since Wenwo limits the number of questions that one can view to only popular questions or questions routed to him/her, we decomposed our data collection process into two steps: identify the questions and automatically crawl the identified questions along with their answers using a web-based crawler.

To identify the questions asked or extracted by Wenwo, we adopted a tricky method by searching Sina Weibo with the keyword "I just posted a question on [Wenwo]" (我刚刚在【微问】提了一个问题). We selected this keyword because once someone successfully posts a question to or on Wenwo, as a marketing strategy, the service will generate an automatic post to the asker's Sina Weibo timeline, with the templated phrase "I just posted a question on [Wenwo]". With this keyword and Sina Weibo API, we collected 340,658 questions posted during a ten-month period from January 24, 2013 to October 18, 2013, along with the URLs linking to their Wenwo pages. Then with a Perl-written web-based crawler, we collected the question category, posting time, as well as all answers and non-responders for each identified questions. In this way, we in total collected 1,754,280 replies and 585,359 unanswered records.

6   The Performance of the Question Routing Service

To evaluate the effectiveness of the question routing service, we first conducted some aggregated analysis on the Q&A performance of Wenwo. Based on an initial examination of the dataset, we noticed that 339,878 out of all 340,658 questions in our collection received at least one answer, yielding a response rate of 99.77 %. On average, each question received 5.14 answers (standard deviation, 2.56 answers per question). Comparing with the relatively low number of answers received in natural social Q&A settings, our dataset revealed the potential of question routing in a real social Q&A service.

In order to examine the patterns of knowledge exchange in social Q&A, we further analyzed the roles that individuals played in Wenwo. In total, 671,501 Sina Weibo users participated in the social Q&A process. Among them, 22,203 (3.31 %) individuals both asked and answered questions while 221,060 (32.92 %) asked at least one question but provided no answer. In contrast, 472,644 (70.39 %) users posted no question but replied at least once on Wenwo. The 340,658 questions were asked by 243,263 unique individuals and were answered by 494,847 ones.

In Fig. 3, we plotted the distributions of the number of questions asked and the number of answers provided by each Wenwo user collected in our dataset. Surprisingly, we noticed that there were more contributors (users who posted more answers than questions) than consumers (users who posted more questions than answers) on Wenwo. Considering the large number of contributors, the high response rate on Wenwo is not surprising. Besides, while comparing our results on contributors versus consumers with the findings presented in Shah et al.'s [26] and Gyongyi et al.'s [27] observations based on Yahoo!Answers, again, we noticed the power of question routing in social Q&A context. We plotted the cumulative probability distribution of the total number of questions answered on a log-log scale and noticed that the number of questions answered on Wenwo followed a power law distribution, as the points fell closely on the straight line in the log-log plot. This indicated an uneven participation in Wenwo, where a small number of individuals contributed to a large proportion of questions and a large proportion of users only answered a few number of questions.

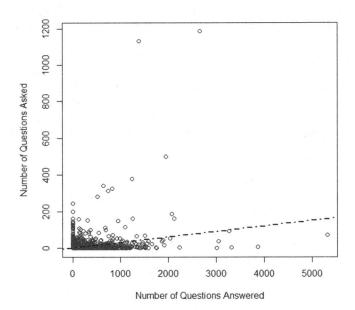

Fig. 3. Distributions of the number of questions posted and the number of answers provided

7 Question and Answering Behavior Within the Question Routing Community

In addition to our analysis on the overall performance of the question routing service, we also explored individuals' question and answering behavior within the Wenwo community from two aspects: their topical interests, and their connectedness with others via the Q&A processes.

7.1 Topical Interests

To understand individuals' topical interests when choosing questions to ask and answer, we plotted the number of questions belonging to each topical category in a bar diagram in Fig. 4(a). We observed that the topical category of "Life" contained the highest number of questions (32.05 %), followed by the category of "Entertainment" (27.72 %). These two categories accounted for more than half of the questions asked on Wenwo with the remaining 40 % of questions distributed among the other 11 categories. While examine the average number of responses received across categories, we observed in Fig. 4(b) that questions under the topics of "Entertainment", "Vexation", "Life", "Electronics", and "Arts" obtained the highest number of answers on average. We thought this might be due to the subjective nature of questions under these two topical categories, as well as the low expertise required to answer them. Examples of questions with higher number of responses from the above mentioned categories are: "Can anybody recommend any horror movie for me please?", "Has anybody used the Sony nex3n yet? Thoughts?", "Do girls really care about height that much? Like i'm 175 cm so it's minor, just curious?", etc. Conversely, questions under the topical categories of Sports, Education, and Computer received lower number of answers, indicating their relatively objective nature. Some typical factual-seeking questions under those categories include: "When should I register for the GRE test?", and "So how can i get to the reach of root of locked iphone?"

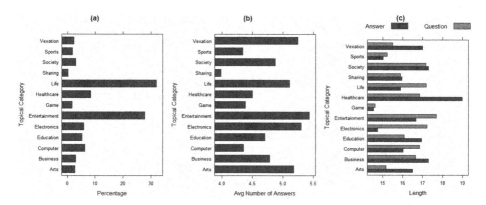

Fig. 4. (a) Topical distribution of questions asked on Wenwo; (b) Number of answers received by topic; and (c) Word length of both questions and answers across topics.

We next explored the ways individuals ask and answer questions on Wenwo. We assume that one could infer the type of information needs under each topic by examining the average question and answer length within that category. As can be seen from Fig. 4(c), which looks at length characters and terms, we noticed that questions under the topical categories "Entertainment", "Life", "Electronics", and "Computer" were asked in a fairly specific manner, whereas were answered with many short replies. For example, the question, "My IPAD suddenly go dead and after reboot all my downloads disappeared, and now I can't even download anymore! I get a warning message saying 'Make sure SD card is writeable', isn't IPAD SD card internal, what's going on?" attracted many general answers, such as, "Reset to factory settings", "Due to the loose connection of your SD card, get a replacement at Apple if within warranty", and "Better contact Apple support", etc.

In contrast, questions under the topical categories "Vexation", "Healthcare", "Education", and "Business" were phrased in a relatively general manner; for example, "Why do my gums bleed when I brush my teeth?" received long replies such as, "First rule out the possibility of blood system disease and weak liver and spleen. Then if your bleeding is caused by an accumulation of plaque around gums, ultrasonic cleaning may provide some effective relief", or "I would suggest to take a blood routine examination to check the common indices of coagulation. Most of times it is a symptom of gingivitis, pay attention to your oral health and the correct way of brushing your teeth, don't eat spicy food."

7.2 Social Connectedness

Next, to evaluate the social connectedness of the question routing community, we applied the bow tie structure analysis [28] to our dataset. The bow tie structure captures complex network structures. The key idea of the method is that a network can be viewed as a bow tie that is connected with four different components: Core, In, Out, and Tendrils/Tube, as shown in Fig. 5. The bow tie structure analysis has been used in previous studies analyzing the network structure of Yahoo!Answers [29, 30].

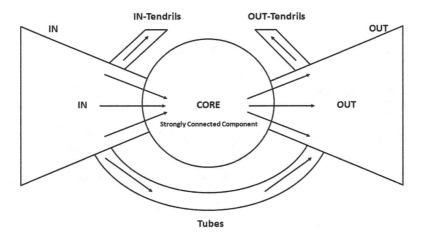

Fig. 5. The NPMI values between topic pairs (reference)

In order to fit our Wenwo data into the bow tie model, we created a questioner-answerer graph by connecting users who asked questions with users who responded to these questions. Each node within the graph represents a user who asked or answered a question, while each edge corresponded to the directed reply relationship between the questioner and the answerer. The graph contained a total of 715,209 nodes and 1,538,427 edges. The CORE component is the largest, most strongly connected component (SCC) of the questioner-answerer graph, in which any two users are mutually reachable by following the direct question-answering relationship. With the core component, we can detect the largest group of individuals who tend to help each other directly or indirectly on Wenwo. The IN component contains all nodes that are not part of the CORE but can reach it via directed paths. Users who always ask questions but rarely answer will primarily belong to the IN component. Similarly, the OUT component contains nodes that are reachable from the CORE via directed paths and, in our case, represents users who answer but infrequently ask. The Tendrils and Tube component (T&T) contains users who ask or answer only questions posted or responded by the users within the IN and OUT components.

For the Q&A graph generated using collected dataset, the CORE component contains 9,552 nodes, which corresponded to 1.33 % of all the users, which is quite different from the results as reported in previous studies on Yahoo!Answers. This indicates that the question answering process on Wenwo is not as social as one expects. Only a small proportion of users are connected on Wenwo through question and answering activities, while most of the users are quite segregated. In addition, to evaluating the reciprocal relationships between the questioners and the answerers, we also counted the number of mutual edges in our created graph. We found that among all 1,538,427 edges, 9,313 (0.60 %) were mutually connected. We believe this indicated the well-separated roles played by the contributors and consumers in social Q&A environments, like Wenwo.

To test whether user connectedness correlate with topical interest, we also measured the size of the largest SCC and the number of mutual edges within all 13 topical categories. Table 1 shows the results obtained. Compared with the SCC measurement as reported in Zhang et al.'s work [29], we observed in the table that the percentage of the nodes within the CORE for each individual category is much smaller that for the whole dataset. None of the topical categories in Wenwo were well connected, as all largest SCC contained less than 1 % of the users within that topical category. We thought this might be due to the well-separated roles of contributors and consumers on Wenwo, as we discussed in earlier section.

A further look at the results in Table 1 reveals that individuals who posted and answered questions under the topical category of Health, Vexation, and Life are relatively connected, with both a high percent of users within the largest SCC and a relatively large number of mutual edges. In other words, as compared to other topics, users focusing on those three categories were more likely to answer each other's questions. This indicated the existence of connected communities within the social Q&A process under those topics. We thought this might because of the common ground existed between individuals sharing either the same living background (as many of the Life questions were location specific, so only users from the same regions can answer those questions), or physical (individuals who experienced or known someone who had the diseases), or emotional conditions (individuals who had or known someone who suffered from the vexation). In contrast, users within the topical categories such as Arts, Sports, and Sharing were relatively less connected.

Table 1. Connectedness statistics for Q&A participants within 13 topical categories.

Topical Category	# Nodes	# Edges	CORE (%)	IN (%)	OUT (%)	T&T (%)	DISC (%)	Mutual Edge (%)
Life	242,707	472,664	0.52	23.03	6.00	56.58	13.87	0.21
Entertainment	294,473	462,439	0.32	20.02	7.15	60.02	12.48	0.09
Healthcare	49,923	106,711	0.66	30.37	1.52	62.70	4.75	0.40
Arts	27,790	40,516	0.03	2.43	0.29	39.43	57.82	0.16
Sports	19,719	22,948	0.02	1.54	0.10	63.16	35.18	0.07
Society	25,820	41,869	0.30	11.63	1.14	90.26	3.33	0.27
Business	24,024	40,042	0.22	14.01	0.76	74.34	10.89	0.17
Electronics	41,708	88,703	0.34	16.90	1.18	75.57	6.01	0.19
Education	49,514	73,637	0.23	9.21	1.11	72.68	17.01	0.16
Computer	45,098	77,479	0.35	13.79	1.09	71.80	12.97	0.19
Game	13,704	18,720	0.28	5.11	0.76	77.10	16.76	0.30
Vexation	19,359	32,639	0.59	12.12	1.88	73.73	11.68	0.44
Sharing	1,364	1,254	0.01	1.32	0.07	28.74	69.86	0.16

We also noticed that among all topical categories, there were more users contained within the IN component than in the OUT component, especially for the topical categories of Health, Electronics, Computer, and Business. This is consistent with the nature of Wenwo where users actively seek help; however, compared with our previous results as shown in Fig. 3, we noticed that the majority of answers were provided by only a smaller number of active answerers.

8   Discussion and Conclusion

In this paper, we analyzed over 340 thousand questions and 1.7 million answers collected during a ten-month period from Wenwo, which is a question routing application based on China's largest microblogging site Sina Weibo. Through quantitative evaluations, we found that overall Wenwo performed well in routing individual's questions to appropriate answers. While analyzing the number of questions asked and answered, we noticed that there were more knowledge contributors than consumers on Wenwo due to its underlying question routing mechanism, and thus yielded a much higher response probability and rate than social Q&A in natural settings. Although Wenwo seems to be effective in improving the question response rate in social Q&A, we also noticed certain concerns of such question routing services in our further analysis. First, we noticed that there is a strong separation of the roles between askers and answerers on Wenwo. Also, the total number of questions answered for each Wenwo user followed a power law distribution, indicating that within the large group of contributors on Wenwo, only a small number of them provide answers to a large proportion of questions. This means that although currently Wenwo works well with the small number of active contributors, it may later suffers from the possibility of reduced performance when active users become inactive.

In addition to measuring the overall effectiveness of the Wenwo, we also explored individual's question and answering behavior within the community formed by the question routing service. From the topical perspective, we observed the majority of questions posted in social Q&A are life and entertainment-related. More answerers chose to respond to questions required low expertise, such as questions from the topical categories of "Vexation" and "Entertainment". Also, for questions under different topical categories, individuals choose to answer them with different levels of specifities. Moreover, through a bow tie structure analysis, we found that users within the Q&A community formed by the question routing service seemed less connected than users in traditional Q&A settings. We view this lack of reciprocity as against the interactive nature of social Q&A. So we think there needs to be a better design for future question routing services in social Q&A by addressing the connectedness between individuals participated in the Q&A processes.

We believe that as a preliminary study, this work could be beneficial as it advances previous knowledge of social Q&A in two major aspects. First, to our knowledge, this is one of the first studies with large-scale analysis of knowledge sharing behavior in social Q&A within the question routing context. Our results clear quantify the necessity of question routing services for social Q&A tasks. Second, our analysis also recognizes bottlenecks that exist in the current expertise-based question routing services, and can provide valuable suggestions for future design and development of more personalized question routing mechanisms.

Noticing the importance of the small number of active users in Wenwo, for future work, we will focus on those active contributors in order to understand in more depth and details about who they are, and what drives them to share their knowledge with strangers in social Q&A. With those information, we could later build a model to identify active contributors within collaborative Q&A environments.

References

1. Zhao, D., Rosson, M.B.: How and why people twitter: the role that micro-blogging plays in informal communication at work. In: Proceedings of the ACM 2009 International Conference on Supporting Group Work 2009, pp. 243–252. ACM, Sanibel Island, FL, USA (2009)
2. Jansen, B.J., et al.: Twitter power: Tweets as electronic word of mouth. J. Am. Soc. Inform. Sci. Technol. **60**(11), 2169–2188 (2009)
3. Zhang, M., Jansen, B.J., Chowdhury, A.: Business engagement on twitter: a path analysis. Electron. Mark. **21**(3), 161–175 (2011)

4. Morris, M.R., Teevan, J., Panovich, K.: What do people ask their social networks, and why?: a survey study of status message Q&A behavior. In: Proceedings of the 2010 SIGCHI Conference on Human Factors in Computing Systems. ACM, Atlanta, GA, USA (2010)

5. Jansen, B.J., Sobel, K., Cook, G.: Being networked and being engaged: the impact of social networking on ecommerce information behavior. In: Proceedings of the 2011 iConference. ACM, Seattle, WA, USA (2011)

6. Liu, Z., Jansen, B.J.: Factors influencing the response rate in social question and answering behavior. In: Proceedings of the 2013 Conference on Computer Supported Cooperative Work 2013, pp. 1263–1274. ACM, San Antonio, TX, USA (2013)

7. Hecht, B., et al.: Search Buddies: bringing search engines into the conversation. In: Proceedings of the 6th International AAAI Conference on Weblogs and Social Media 2012, pp. 138–145, Dublin, Ireland (2012)

8. Nichols, J., Kang, J.-H.: Asking questions of targeted strangers on social networks. In: Proceedings of the ACM 2012 Conference on Computer Supported Cooperative Work 2012, pp. 999–1002. ACM, Seattle, WA, USA (2012)

9. Paul, S.A., Hong, L., Chi, E.H.: Is twitter a good place for asking questions? a characterization study. In: Proceedings of the 5th International AAAI Conference on Weblogs and Social Media 2011, Barcelona, Spain (2011)

10. Pal, A., Chang, S., Konstan, J.A.: Evolution of experts in question answering communities. In: Proceedings of the 6th International AAAI Conference on Weblogs and Social Media 2012, Dublin, Ireland (2012)

11. Adamic, L.A., et al.: Knowledge sharing and yahoo answers: everyone knows something. In: Proceedings of the 17th International Conference on World Wide Web 2008, pp. 665–674. ACM, Beijing, China (2008)

12. Liu, Q., Agichtein, E.: Modeling Answerer Behavior in Collaborative Question Answering Systems. In: Clough, P., Foley, C., Gurrin, C., Jones, G.J.F., Kraaij, W., Lee, H., Mudoch, V. (eds.) ECIR 2011. LNCS, vol. 6611, pp. 67–79. Springer, Heidelberg (2011)

13. Wang, G., et al.: Wisdom in the social crowd: an analysis of quora. In: Proceedings of the 22nd International Conference on World Wide Web, International World Wide Web Conferences Steering Committee, Rio de Janeiro, Brazil (2013)

14. Furtado, A., et al.: Contributor profiles, their dynamics, and their importance in five Q&A sites. In: Proceedings of the 2013 Conference on Computer Supported Cooperative Work. ACM, San Antonio, TX, USA (2013)

15. Treude, C., Barzilay, O., Storey, M.-A.: How do programmers ask and answer questions on the web?: Nier track, In: Proceedings of the 33rd International Conference on Software Engineering 2011, pp. 804–807. IEEE, Honolulu, HW, USA (2011)

16. Nam, K.K., Ackerman, M.S., Adamic, L.A.: Questions in, knowledge in?: a study of naver's question answering community. In: Proceedings of the SIGCHI Conference on Human Factors in Computing Systems 2009, pp. 779–788. ACM, Boston, MA, USA. (2009)

17. Mamykina, L., et al.: Design lessons from the fastest Q&A site in the west. In: Proceedings of the SIGCHI Conference on Human Factors in Computing Systems 2011, pp. 2857–2866. ACM (2011)

18. Morris, M.R., Teevan, J., Panovich, K.: A comparison of information seeking using search engines and social networks. In: Proceedings of the 4th International AAAI Conference on Weblogs and Social Media 2010, pp. 23–26, Washington, DC, USA (2010)

19. Liu, Z., Jansen, B.J.: Almighty Twitter, what are people asking for? Proc. Am. Soc. Inf. Sci. Technol. **49**(1), 1–10 (2012)

20. Li, B., King, I., Lyu, M.R.: Question routing in community question answering: putting category in its place. In: Proceedings of the 20th ACM International Conference on Information and Knowledge Management 2011, pp. 2041–2044. ACM, Glasgow, Scotland, UK (2011)

21. Zhou, T.C., Lyu, M.R., King, I.: A classification-based approach to question routing in community question answering. In: Proceedings of the 21st International Conference Companion on World Wide Web 2012, pp. 783–790. ACM (2012)

22. Guo, J., et al.: Tapping on the potential of Q&A community by recommending answer providers. In: Proceedings of the 17th ACM Conference on Information and Knowledge Management 2008, pp. 921–930. ACM, Napa, CA, USA (2008)

23. Pan, Y., et al.: To answer or not: what non-qa social activities can tell. In: Proceedings of the 2013 Conference on Computer Supported Cooperative Work 2013, pp. 1253–1263. ACM, San Antonio, TX, USA (2013)

24. Luo, L., et al.: Who have got answers?: growing the pool of answerers in a smart enterprise social QA system. In: Proceedings of the 19th International Conference on Intelligent User Interfaces 2014, pp. 7–16. ACM, Israel, Haifa (2014)

25. Bai, J.: 2014 Weibo user development report (2015). http://data.weibo.com/report/reportDetail?id=215

26. Shah, C., Oh, J.S., Oh, S.: Exploring characteristics and effects of user participation in online social Q&A sites. First Monday, 13(9) (2008)

27. Gyongyi, Z., et al.: Questioning yahoo! answers. In: Proceedings of the 16th International Conference on World Wide Web Banff, Alberta, Canada (2007)

28. Broder, A., et al.: Graph structure in the web. Comput. Netw. 33(1), 309–320 (2000)

29. Zhang, J., Ackerman, M.S., Adamic, L.: Expertise networks in online communities: structure and algorithms. In: Proceedings of the 16th International Conference on World Wide Web. ACM, Banff, Alberta, Canada (2007)

30. Chen, L., Nayak, R.: Social network analysis of an online dating network. In: Proceedings of the 5th International Conference on Communities and Technologies, pp. 41–49. ACM (2011)

An Integrative Tool Chain for Collaborative Virtual Museums in Immersive Virtual Environments

Daniel Sacher[1], Benjamin Weyers[2]([⊠]), Torsten W. Kuhlen[3],
and Wolfram Luther[1]

[1] University of Duisburg-Essen, INKO, Duisburg, Germany
{sacher,luther}@inf.uni-due.de
[2] RWTH Aachen University, Virtual Reality Group, Aachen, Germany
weyers@vr.rwth-aachen.de
[3] Forschungszentrum Jülich, Jülich Supercomputing Center, Jülich, Germany
t.kuhlen@fzj.de

Abstract. Various conceptual approaches for the creation and presentation of virtual museums can be found. However, less work exists that concentrates on collaboration in virtual museums. The support of collaboration in virtual museums provides various benefits for the visit as well as the preparation and creation of virtual exhibits. This paper addresses one major problem of collaboration in virtual museums: the awareness of visitors. We use a Cave Automated Virtual Environment (CAVE) for the visualization of generated virtual museums to offer simple awareness through co-location. Furthermore, the use of smartphones during the visit enables the visitors to create comments or to access exhibit related metadata. Thus, the main contribution of this ongoing work is the presentation of a workflow that enables an integrated deployment of generic virtual museums into a CAVE, which will be demonstrated by deploying the virtual Leopold Fleischhacker Museum.

1 Introduction

Various conceptual approaches for the creation and presentation of virtual museums are presented on annual conferences dedicated to (virtual) museums and digital heritage, as well as in publications of the virtual museum transitional network[1]. Visiting a virtual museum prior to a classical museum has many advantages [1]. Nevertheless, it is hard to find existing solutions—besides multi-user gaming environments such as Second Life—which explicitly enable visitors of virtual museums to interact with each other or to collaborate directly. Therefore, this work in progress presents an approach for the implementation of collaboration in virtual museums using immersive virtual environments and various types of display systems, including a 5-sided CAVE-like projection system. This work further discusses and evaluates other existing hardware solutions for immersive

---

[1] https://www.v-must.net.

© Springer International Publishing Switzerland 2015
N. Baloian et al. (Eds.): CRIWG 2015, LNCS 9334, pp. 86–94, 2015.
DOI: 10.1007/978-3-319-22747-4_7

virtual environments, such as low-cost implementations, which are affordable for nearly every type of user and facilitates the use at home. The presented approach further includes the use of a metadata standard called ViMCOX for the specification of virtual museums [2]. The use of an appropriate modeling language and standards is a precondition for the flexible generation of virtual museums including meta information for the artwork on display and describing the architectural structure of the museum itself. The introduction of this metadata-based description of a virtual museum into a seamless tool chain enables the implementation of virtual museums for their use in virtual environments. This workflow also provides a feedback loop of user generated content gathered in collaborative visits of virtual museums. The generated data from collaboration can range from visitor's annotations or comments regarding specific exhibits up to complete exhibit models and room (re-)designs created in a virtual environment. Nevertheless, the latter is not focus of this work at hand but presents a relevant next step. Virtual environments offer the capability to enrich 3D museum models by collaboration support through the use of different display systems and accompanied interaction techniques. The latter facilitate the use of a museum instance by more than one visitor simultaneously, a precondition for face-to-face collaboration.

In conclusion, the main contribution of this work is the presentation of a tool chain offering the deployment of virtual museums specified in the ViMCOX metadata standard into virtual environments, which enable collaborative work. Collaboration in this regard is implemented as users being co-located in the virtual museum, which enables information exchange and awareness of users actions via face-to-face communication. As mentioned above, the tool chains aims at the deployment of virtual museums to virtual reality hardware that enable the defined face-to-face communication such as a CAVE-like environment. Furthermore, the data collected during the collaborative work in the virtual museum is captured by a commenting system and can thereby be used in conjunction with the metadata for subsequent discussions or for reuse in other sessions. The solution will be evaluated by means of a virtual museum dedicated to the German-Jewish artist Leopold Fleischhacker brought into a 5-sided CAVE-like virtual environment.

The paper is structured as follows. Section 2 presents related work focusing on collaboration in virtual museums and the use of virtual environments. Section 3 introduces the tool chain and presents the software solution, where Paragraph 3.2 focuses on possible collaboration methodologies enabled through immersive virtual environments. Section 4 describes the application of this tool chain and collaboration methodology by presenting the use case of the Fleischhacker museum in the aixCAVE at RWTH Aachen University. Section 5 concludes this paper and identifies certain aspects of future work.

2   Related Work

In recent papers, the modeling and 3D visualization capabilities of the curator software suite Virtual Museum Exhibition Designer using an Enhanced ARCO Standard (ViMEDEAS) has been presented for the digitization of heritage sites or

virtual museums with access to outdoor areas ([2–5]). As visualization platforms—
for local or online presentation—VRML, X3D and X3Dom has been utilized [4].
The modeling of the exhibition areas is carried out using the Virtual Museum and
Cultural Object Exchange Format (ViMCOX) as metadata format. ViMCOX is
based on international metadata standards and uses LIDO (Lightweight Information Describing Objects) as an interchange and harvesting format for cultural
objects. ViMCOX was developed to support the hierarchical description of virtual museums and provides stylistic devices for sophisticated and vivid exhibition
design, which cannot be achieved using classic museums standards.

The use of virtual environments in the context of virtual museums has been
investigated beforehand. Roussos et al. [6] presented an approach for the use
of virtual environments in the context of collaborative learning in a distributed
setting. This approach focuses on the use of narrative concepts and story telling
for the implementation of learning systems. Roussos further published a work
on the application of immersive interactive virtual reality concepts in informal
education [7], which further lead to a work describing a use case for cultural
education [8]. Further works on the use of virtual environments for education
and learning has been published by Kriner et al. [9] as well as Taxén et al.
[10], which both concentrate on the investigation of virtual environments for the
use in learning and teaching contexts. Although these works describe important
research, none of them present a coherent tool chain, which implements a closed
loop from content creation, metadata description, up to the deployment in a
CAVE-like environment for collaborative use.

As basis for our case study serves The Virtual Leopold Fleischhacker
Museum, a joint-project initiated by Prof. Dr. Michael Brocke, director of the
Salomon Ludwig Steinheim-Institut in Essen and the University of Duisburg-
Essen [11]. The museum depicts the life and work of the German-Jewish sculptor
and artist Leopold Fleischhacker. On display are 200 photographs with metadata and descriptions as well as 30 reconstructed tombstones. The exhibition
space is organized into 10 thematic areas that span across 13 rooms and one
large outdoor area in style of an Ashkenazic cemetery.

3   Tool Chain for Applying Virtual Museums in Immersive Virtual Environments

3.1   Tool Chain

An abstract architectural overview of ViMEDEAS is presented in Fig. 1 which
is based on the work presented in [4]. Multimedia content, cultural object metadata (DC/LIDO), 3D models like (interactive) exhibits, 3D buildings or interior,
2D pictures, or floor plans as 2D point set can be used in ViMCOX. In addition,
content creators can re-use open data repositories (OAI-PMH) to include real artworks and metadata from cultural heritage institutions [5]. Algorithms can facilitate 2D floor planning and automatic determination of exhibit distribution or
room layout. Authoring tools help to modify the content base as well as ViMCOX
metadata instances [3]. The dissemination and visualization layers are middleware

for assembling and publishing virtual museum instances, locally or on the web, as well as interpreting and rendering ViMCOX metadata instances on different visualization platforms. ViMEDEAS currently supports VRML, X3D and X3Dom via Replicave. Replicave supports native export to X3D and X3Dom and supports backwards compatibility to VRML via XSL Transformations (XSLT).

The VRML models generated by Replicave are loaded by Inside, an extension of the ViSTA toolkit [12] (cf. Fig. 1). ViSTA is a software framework, which enables the implementation and execution of virtual environments and applications. It is based on OpenGL for rendering and implements various interaction methods common in virtual environments, such as flysticks or infrared tracked targets, e.g., for head tracking. Furthermore, ViSTA supports multi-display systems and stereoscopic rendering, such as needed for CAVEs and other display hardware for virtual environments. Both, the stereoscopic rendering as well as the supported interaction hardware and navigation metaphors for virtual environments are used in the collaborative museum to gain presences as well as offer tools and mechanisms for free exploration of the exhibition. The latter will be discussed in more detail in Sect. 4.

Based on the presented tools, the tool chain as shown in Fig. 1 is composed as follows: Using the authoring tools, a curator or content creator specifies a virtual museum design expressed as ViMCOX metadata file. Based on this metadata, Replicave generates a content bundle and a VRML file, which will be passed to Inside for interactive rendering in a CAVE. In this environment, the visitors virtually walk through the virtual museum. Visitors are able to access supplementary materials or comment/annotate exhibits by photographing Quick Response Codes (QR) placed in direct proximity to each exhibit item. The next section will discuss this aspect in more detail.

Since our toolchain supports X3Dom as rending platform, it is also possible to use low cost VR systems such as Google CardBoard or the Oculus Rift as well as other tangible or multi-touch interfaces, gamepad input and other VR input devices such as the Leap Motion via InstantIO and WebSockets [13]. The use of head-mounted displays as hardware solutions requires the integration of avatars into the virtual museum to offer spatial, contextual and content-related awareness for the users. As avatars offer a great potential to the collaborative use of virtual museums, we identified an extensive study as a future work for an extension of the current implementation of Replicave, for example by creating a Collada exporter to support multi-user scenarios via Second Life [14]. Nevertheless, this work focuses on the use of CAVE-like environments for collaborative work and visits of virtual museums.

3.2 Collaboration Methodologies for Virtual Museums in Immersive Virtual Environments

This section introduces the necessary interaction methodologies to implement well known aspects of collaboration, which are essential for collaborative virtual museums. As the whole concept is based on co-location of the users during the visit of the virtual museum, a CAVE-like environment is expect.

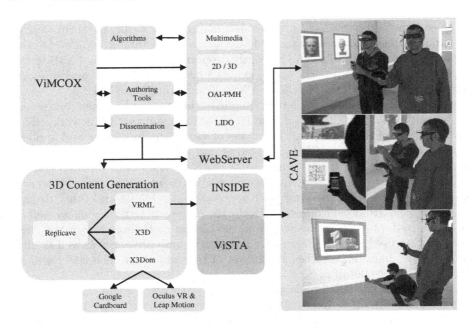

Fig. 1. Integration tool chain: On the top left part the various technologies are shown, which are used for the authoring of the virtual museum. On the lower left, the transformation technologies and tools are depicted, which deploy the content model into the virtual environment, such as a CAVE shown on the right. Here, user navigate in the museum and access metadata through scanning the exhibit's QR codes.

Awareness and Information Exchange. Both, awareness and information exchange are handled in this environment directly by the visitors' co-location in the CAVE-like environment. They are able to directly communicate with each other without the need for any computer-supported communication facilities. Pointing a co-located user's attention to specific content, a user only points to this information with a gesture. The users can further discuss all questions and problems aurally without the need of technical support. This differentiates the presented approach to classic groupware or telepresence approaches. Nevertheless, if it is needed to integrate remote users to a session, an avatar can be used to visualize the partners in the virtual museum, which is a subject of future work (see above).

Content Generation and Retrieval. As discussed in the next section, the visitors can use their own smart phones to retrieve additional information for the artwork presented by, e.g., scanning the provided QR codes in the virtual environment. This metadata is available on a shared web page accessible via the smart phone's web browser. Using the web site's form, visitors can annotated selected artwork or define further tasks for other visitors. This information can be attached to a pre-defined session to offer provenance information, such as who added the comments and when. Thus, the visitors are able to work collaboratively on specific tasks in the CAVE-like environment by directly communicating with each other and using the latter mentioned metadata and data input facilities provided by the web browser. This process can thereby be used for content generation and retrieval including the generation of provenance information. Furthermore, the web-based data access enables all imaginable post-processing and subsequent usage scenarios for this data. This includes re-use of the information in other situations, such as a school lesson in which the visit is discussed and analysed or in a follow-up meeting to pick up certain previous discussions or questions.

Navigation. Besides accessing information, one of the visitors has to lead and to navigate through the museum, which should be done in consensus with other collaborators. This could be relevant, e.g., for supporting visitors' discussions, reviewing of curator's design decisions, or in a collaborative learning scenario, as it will be presented, below. Especially relevant for the latter is the discussion emerging from the question 'where to navigate to, next?' These discussions have the potential to lead to refocusing the solution strategy, to solve a given task, or to develop a solution strategy previously.

Comparison to Groupware and Social Networks. Since our current approach is based on the concept of co-location (users work physically side-by-side), various communication concepts (asynchronous or synchronous) and awareness mechanisms (user status or content changes, etc.) as known from groupware as well as social networks are not relevant in the presented system at this preliminary stage. Nevertheless, it is crucial to combine the presented approach with the above mentioned collaborative solutions and concepts, which is enabled by the used web-based technologies and is planned as future work.

4 A Testbed for a Learning Scenario - The Fleischhacker Museum in the aixCAVE

The initial room design and layout was designed for an on-site kiosk-systems and touch-screen input. Thus, the curator Dr. Barbara Kaufhold was able to design the rooms without observing artwork and room dimensions. Therefore, we used standalone room instances that are linked via a teleporter metaphor (cf. Fig. 2, left) and enlarged the exhibits and room dimensions for proper touch-screen input. This approach is not suitable for a CAVE environment and limits the embodiment and movement freedom. Additionally, a few visitors could not keep track of their orientation and current position within the museum, which has been identified in a survey [15]. Therefore, we transformed the virtual museum rooms into a large floor plan with passages connecting other exhibition areas (cf. Fig. 3). This was achieved using connectivity graphs and our generative approach methodology [4] by varying the gaps between the paintings and inserting

Fig. 2. Metaphoric connector for changing rooms in the virtual museum. On the left a connector is shown for a web-based implementation enabling the user to teleport into another room. On the right, the solution used for virtual environments is shown, where the user navigate virtually through the door.

passages. At this exploratory stage, the outdoor area has been excluded and the room dimensions have been scaled down to prevent overlapping of rooms and to present authentic artwork dimensions. In addition, we now use generated 3D frames for each painting to achieve a more lifelike presentation of the artworks (cf. Fig. 2, right).

As mentioned above, we use QR codes to access audio recordings and other materials, which are placed in direct proximity to the exhibits, that link to our HTML-based metadata renderer and 3D object browser. Furthermore, the digital object browser allows visitors to browse the 2D/3D exhibition items and their corresponding metadata as well as rotating, zooming and panning the 3D reconstructions or watching pre-defined animations. In addition, we plan to support annotations and user feedback[2].

Our approach includes a suitable learning scenario, where students have the task to gather specific information on the life and work of Leopold Fleischhacker and his art work throughout the visit of the virtual museum in a CAVE-like environment. We tested this scenario in the aixCAVE–a five-sided CAVE located in Aachen, Germany. The scenario contains the previously mentioned interaction operations, such as to retrieve metadata, adding comments and provenance to it to finally consolidate the walkthrough in the CAVE in a, e.g., class room setting. The CAVE's dimension are 5.25×5.25 meter and it is operated with 24 cinema projectors with a resolution of 1920×1200 pixels each. The rendering is performed by a 24 node cluster, which enables the installation to render stereo images at the desired resolution and appropriate frame rates, which are at a minimum of 60fps. The running museum in the aixCAVE is shown in Fig. 1 on the right.

---

[2] http://examples.x3dom.org/v-must/index.html.

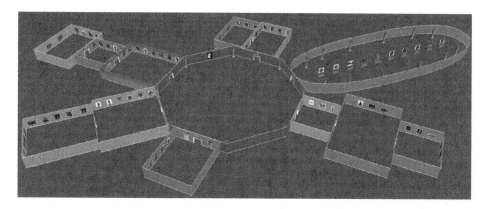

Fig. 3. Room layout as bird eye's view of the Leopold Fleischhacker virtual museum as it has been deployed to the aixCAVE at RWTH Aachen University. All rooms are arranged around a central room, which enables the access to the different exhibition's topics.

5   Conclusion and Future Work

This paper introduced a tool chain for the modeling of virtual museums, which includes the description of single exhibits up to complete exhibitions, metadata and room concepts. Furthermore, the tool chain provides the extraction of 3D models in various formats and includes a software that supports the rendering and the integration of virtual museums in a CAVE-like environment. Using QR codes and metadata provided through a web server, we were able to show the feasibility of the approach for an exemplary learning scenario. Future work comprises an extensive evaluation of the presented approach. The goal of this study will be to quantify how far our approach supports the visit of virtual museums or learning scenarios as well as identifying the impact of immersion in comparison to classic interaction on computer screens or other projections. We further aim at extending the approach to the use of head mounted displays, especially because decent solutions are affordable. Finally, our solution will be used in an interactive installation enriching a real museum exhibition on-site. Therefore, we are going to develop a cooperative interaction concept for navigation and interaction with the museum in a non-stereo projection environment. This will be accompanied with a further evaluation to gather data on the specific use case as well as on newly developed interaction concepts.

References

1. D'Alba, A., Jones, G.: Analyzing the effects of a 3D online virtual museum in visitors discourse, attitudes, preferences, and knowledge acquisition. In: Cases on 3D Technology Application and Integration in Education, pp. 26–47 (2013)

2. Biella, D., Luther, W., Baloian, N.: Beyond the ARCO standard. In: 16th International Conference on Virtual Systems and Multimedia (VSMM), pp. 184–191 (2010)
3. Biella, D., Luther, W., Sacher, D.: Schema migration into a web-based framework for generating virtual museums and laboratories. In: 18th International Conference on Virtual Systems and Multimedia (VSMM), pp. 307–314. IEEE (2012)
4. Sacher, D., Biella, D., Luther, W.: A generative approach to virtual museums. In: Krempels, K.-H., Stocker, A. (eds.) 9th International Conference on Web Information Systems and Technologies (WEBIST 2013), pp. 274–279. SciTePress (2013)
5. Sacher, D., Biella, D., Luther, W.: Towards a versatile metadata exchange format for digital museum collections. In: Proceedings of the 2013 Digital Heritage International Congress (Digital Heritage), pp. 129–136 (2013)
6. Roussos, M., Johnson, A., Leigh, J., Barnes, C.R., Vasilakis, C.A., Moher, T.G.: The nice project: narrative, immersive, constructionist/collaborative environments for learning in virtual reality. In: Proceedings of Ed-Media/Ed-Telecom, vol. 97, pp. 917–922 (1997)
7. Roussou, M.: Immersive interactive virtual reality and informal education. In: Proceedings of User Interfaces for All: Interactive Learning Environments for Children (2000)
8. Roussou, M.: The interplay between form, story, and history: the use of narrative in cultural and educational virtual reality. In: Balet, O., Subsol, G., Torguet, P. (eds.) ICVS 2001. LNCS, vol. 2197, p. 181. Springer, Heidelberg (2001)
9. Kirner, T.G., Kirner, C., Kawamoto, A.L., Cantão, J., Pinto, A., Wazlawick, R.S.: Development of a collaborative virtual environment for educational applications. In: Proceedings of the Sixth International Conference on 3D Web Technology, pp. 61–68. ACM (2001)
10. Taxén, G., Naeve, A.: A system for exploring open issues in vr-based education. Comput. Graph. **26**(4), 593–598 (2002)
11. Sacher, D., Brocke, M., Heitmann, M., Kaufhold, B., Luther, W., Biella, D.: The virtual leopold fleischhacker museum. In: Proceedings of Museums and the Web (2013)
12. Assenmacher, I., Kuhlen, T.: The vista virtual reality toolkit. In: Proceedings of the IEEE VR 2008 Workshop Software Engineering and Architectures for Realtime Interactive Systems (SEARIS), pp. 23–28 (2008)
13. Olbrich, M., Franke, T., Rojtberg, P.: Remote visual tracking for the (mobile) web. In: Proceedings of the 19th International ACM Conference on 3D Web Technologies. Web3D 2014. ACM, New York, NY, USA, pp. 27–33 (2014)
14. Urban, R.J.: A second life for your museum: 3d multi-user virtual environments and museums (2007)
15. Sacher, D., Weyers, B., Biella, D., Luther, W.: Towards an evaluation of a metadata standard for generative virtual museums. In: Hervás, R., Lee, S., Nugent, C., Bravo, J. (eds.) UCAmI 2014. LNCS, vol. 8867, pp. 357–364. Springer, Heidelberg (2014)

A Behaviour Awareness Mechanism to Support Collaborative Learning

Esunly Medina[1], Roc Meseguer[1(✉)], Sergio F. Ochoa[2], and Humberto Medina[3]

[1] Department of Computer Architecture, Universitat Politècnica de Catalunya, Barcelona, Spain
{esunlyma,meseguer}@ac.upc.edu
[2] Computer Science Department, Universidad de Chile, Santiago, Chile
sochoa@dcc.uchile.cl
[3] Department of Aerospace, Electrical and Electronic Engineering,
Coventry University, Coventry, UK
humberto.medina@coventry.ac.uk

Abstract. Awareness has been identified as a key element that affects the quality of collaboration. Several studies indicate that awareness mechanisms to support collaborative learning activities should include factors and stimuli from the students' context and social interactions. This contributes to enhance the collaboration process and the learning experience of the students. This paper proposes a behaviour awareness mechanism to support collaborative learning in undergraduate learning scenarios. This mechanism has been designed to provide personal and social awareness to students about both, their own and their peers learning behaviour. Moreover, this mechanism encourages reflection and promotes social interactions among students in order to improve the effectiveness of collaborative learning. The article also describes and evaluates a prototype of the proposed mechanism and its implementation in a collaborative mobile learning application, using a case study. The preliminary results show that this proposal helps promote collaborative learning in undergraduate learning contexts.

Keywords: Collaboration awareness · Reflective learning · Collaborative learning · Visual feedback

1 Introduction

Recent learning paradigms suggest that, in order to be successful, learning should be highly situated, collaborative, informal and mobile. Therefore, meaningful learning activities can take place not only in a confined space-time context, but also across multiple scenarios and involving several types of students.

The diversity and complexity of contexts where collaborative learning may occur makes challenging the measurement and assessment of the collaboration process [1, 2]. Usually, the instructor and students have low visibility of such a process while it is being conducted, and therefore its assessment is done once it is concluded, which is too late to try intervene (e.g., by providing feedback to students and instructors). This situation shows a need to count on automatic mechanisms that monitor team members' activities

© Springer International Publishing Switzerland 2015
N. Baloian et al. (Eds.): CRIWG 2015, LNCS 9334, pp. 95–110, 2015.
DOI: 10.1007/978-3-319-22747-4_8

and provide feedback accordingly. These mechanisms could be embedded in collaborative learning applications to help students evaluate their own and their teammates' performance, and react on time in case of need. Thus, such collaborative learning applications could help improve the students learning experiences.

The findings of previous research studies highlight that: (i) the effectiveness of a student team is determined by a combination of cognitive, social and motivational processes, and (ii) collaboration should not only be assessed by the quality of its outcomes or achievements [2–4]. Although social interaction has been identified as a key element that influences the quality of collaborative learning [5], there are still various social interaction areas that are unexplored in the context of Computer-Supported Collaborative Learning (CSCL) [2].

Furthermore, awareness has been considered as an extremely valuable feature of collaborative systems [6] that affects motivation [7] and group coordination [4], and therefore the quality of any collaboration process. Consequently, many interesting works in CSCL have been prompted by the need of providing appropriate awareness support to promote active learning and coordinate students' activities [3, 4]. In that line, feedback has been regarded as an extremely important awareness mechanism, which influences positively the learning process by providing learners with information that allows them to improve their performance and learning behaviour [8].

Considering the importance of social interactions in the quality of collaboration and performance of students' teams, this paper proposes a visual feedback mechanism to support CSCL applications. This mechanism was named *BAM (Behaviour Awareness Mechanism),* and it provides awareness of the students' social behaviour, as well as individual and cognitive elements that affect collaborative learning. A prototype of the *BAM* was designed to be embedded in a mobile collaborative learning application, aimed at providing feedback that encourage reflection and promote social interactions among students.

This awareness mechanism helps provide personal and social awareness on the learning collaborative behaviour and patterns of the students, delivering feedback in a direct, dynamic and holistic fashion. To the best of our knowledge, such a type of awareness provision method has not been previously explored in CSCL. We also believe that this mechanism can positively impact the quality of collaboration in several other application areas; therefore, it can be embedded in several types of collaborative applications.

This article also report a use case, and the results obtained from an evaluation process. The results suggest that the proposed *BAM* is a valuable design element that could be included as part of the awareness support of CSCL applications, as a way to encourage reflection and foster social interactions between students.

Next section presents a review of related work. Section 3 describes the design of the prototype developed to provide visual feedback to students. Section 4 reports results of an evaluation performed to assess the usefulness of our prototype. In addition, Sect. 5 presents a use case that shows how the proposal can be applied in a real-world learning scenario. Finally, we conclude with a summary of the main contributions of our research and the future work.

2   Related Work

Many studies have addressed the feasibility of providing visual feedback functions in software systems supporting collaborative learning activities. For example, the work presented in [7] proposes the introduction of two different tools in wiki systems to increase awareness of each editor's contribution and of task conflict. The first tool is a paragraph-based edit history and a word-based content authorship, for providing awareness on contributions. The second tool provides feedback of task conflicts by assigning different background colours to words or sentences, based on the computation of the severity of the conflict.

In [4] a Web-based group coordination tool for an online course is described and evaluated. The tool includes functions to visualize the assessments of the members of a team about their group processes and performance. It also allows comparing theses values with those from other teams.

Another work that explores the role of awareness in CSCL environments is introduced in [9]. The authors enhance an existing groupware application with services for supporting peer feedback and reflection. The Radar tool, for peer feedback, facilitates the collection and display of information about the social and cognitive performance of a student, from a personal and team perspective. Moreover, Radar was evaluated to assess its usefulness in providing individual and group awareness about the students' collaborative behaviour.

The previous proposals differ from the *BAM* mainly in two different aspects: (i) they focus on a particular type of awareness, such as individual contributions, conflict or peer feedback, whereas our proposal includes a wider range of sources for feedback, providing both subjective and objective information, (ii) their methods of feedback provision are restricted to particular contexts; i.e., the previously mentioned solutions provide awareness only within the context of a specific collaborative activity, and they are linked to a particular collaborative application. By contrast, our proposal is intended to be used across different CSCL systems and contexts, and thus, it provides dynamic as well as longitudinal feedback to the users.

3   Design of the Behaviour Awareness Mechanism

As explained before, we developed a prototype of the *Behaviour Awareness Mechanism (BAM)* to provide feedback about the students' collaborative learning behaviour. Our design is based on two basic facts: (i) any awareness mechanism must provide an understanding of the activities of others as a context for the activities of the individual [6], and (ii) the feedback provision in CSCL must ensure that the students are able to relate their current state of learning and performance with specific targets or standards [10]. Next we describe the design considerations and the components of the proposed awareness mechanism.

3.1   Design Considerations

As stated in [2], many educational teams are "ad hoc". That is, most collaborative learning teams only exist during specific tasks or courses, because they were only established for that particular purpose. For that reason, the provision of awareness to support collaborative learning is frequently focused on a specific activity or project; therefore, the supporting application provides only the feedback that is relevant within that particular context. Nevertheless, individual experiences in previous collaborative tasks are usually transferred to collaboration events in the future, and they influence new group interactions and outcomes. To a large degree, we based the design of the feedback mechanism on such an assumption. Hence, we took into account collaborative and individual experiences of the students, as they are clear indicators of their future behaviour. Our aim is to make students aware of their previous and current social behaviour, and based on that, make recommendations (e.g., actions that they could take) that help improve their collaboration attitude and learning practices.

There is a large amount of literature supporting the fact that there is an intrinsic relationship between the individual, social, motivational and cognitive aspects involved in collaborative learning [1–4], and that such a relationship also determines the effectiveness of a team. Consequently, our proposal takes a holistic approach and provides awareness about each one of these aspects.

On the other hand, many research works focus on specific collaboration tools, and provide indirect feedback about underlying aspects of the collaborative behaviour extracted from how the users have interacted among them using these tools. The objective is to make the user reflect on their previous actions, and promote collaboration through higher engagement with a particular collaboration tool [7]. By contrast, we decided to use direct feedback, specifying concrete collaboration aspects that should be improved, not limiting it to a specific activity or to the use of a particular supporting application.

Regarding strategies for providing awareness information, the literature presents several alternatives; some of them are based on automatic data capture and others require a conscious user feedback [11]. Our proposal followed a mixed approach to generate the awareness information, and therefore it considers both implicit and explicit feedback of the users. Consequently, our design requires for the mobile application that embeds the *BAM* to include some metrics collected automatically in an unobtrusive way (e.g., from application logs, smartphone-based sensing, etc.) and also information gathered from the user feedback (e.g., self-assessments, surveys, etc.). This help us provide awareness about a wider range of aspects, integrating multiple data sources and including both qualitative and quantitative measures of the learning experiences.

We have also identified in the literature three different kinds of awareness that are essential for supporting effective collaborative learning, and therefore they should be considered in our proposal: *behavioural*, *cognitive* and *social* awareness [12]. We have also considered the *motivational* awareness as a forth awareness type to be included because it usually has high relevance in these collaboration processes. Thus, our proposal intends to contribute to the development of CSCL systems, providing a comprehensive awareness that considers the following features:

- *Integral Awareness.* The visual representations consider behavioural, cognitive, social and motivational information of the users.
- *Aggregated Information.* The awareness provides representations of the historic collaborative and learning behaviour of the users, regardless of the collaborative process or activity being supported. Thus, it is possible to identify behaviour patterns of the users.
- *Mixed Feedback.* The proposed awareness includes a combination of implicit and explicit feedback.
- *Dynamic Information.* It provides real-time awareness information that indicates the current behaviour (and also its evolution) of the students.
- *Multiple Data Sources.* This awareness can represent information from several data sources, such as surveys, self-reports, software logs and information collected automatically through the sensors of the mobile device.
- *Explicit Feedback.* BAM provides synthesized and direct awareness information that indicates what needs to be improved in the collaboration or learning process.

3.2   Components of the Awareness Mechanism

The proposed awareness mechanism has the following components: the *Personal Awareness Component (PAC)* and the *Social Awareness Component (SAC)*. Next we describe these components.

Personal Awareness Component (PAC).   This element provides awareness about the collaborative patterns of a specific student, and it represents several features of the student's behaviour. It is important to notice that these features reflect two important aspects of CSCL: *positive interdependence* and *individual accountability* [13]. As a result, the *PAC* component provides feedback on aspects related to the way in which the students interact within different teams, as well as personal features of these students that affect their collaboration and learning. Hence, the *PAC* is a simple visual representation of both, (i) collaboration processes and outcomes, and (ii) motivational and social aspects. In addition, this component of the awareness mechanism allows the students to compare their own behaviour with the behaviour of their peers.

The collaborative behaviour features that should be represented in the *PAC* were determined based on previous research work about quality assessment of computer-supported collaboration processes [14–17]. We found seven basic dimensions related to the effectiveness of collaboration, and classified them according to the awareness types provided by *BAM*. Nevertheless, we condensed such dimensions into five types, because we considered that some of them were strongly related to each other. Consequently, the resulting five dimensions correspond to the features of the students' collaborative behaviour represented in the *PAC* component: ***communication, coordination, motivation, performance*** and ***satisfaction***. Table 1, summarizes the relationship between the types of awareness considered in the proposal, the collaboration dimensions found in the literature, the collaborative behaviour features and the metrics that can be used to assign a value to these collaborative features.

Table 1. Awareness types and collaborative behaviour features

Awareness types	Collaboration dimension	Collaborative behaviour feature	Metrics
Behavioural: Informs about learners' activities	Communication	Communication	Based on knowledge and information exchange, and collaboration flow
	Joint information processing		
	Coordination	Coordination	Presence of roles, planning activities, time management, and reciprocal interactions
	Interpersonal relationship		
Cognitive: Determines how well the student's output meets the expected values	Performance	Performance	Scoring of both individual and group outcomes (achievements)
Social: Determines the functioning of the group, as perceived by the collaborators	Satisfaction	Satisfaction	Measurement of the students satisfaction about both, the collaboration process and outcomes
Motivational: Represents the awareness of the student motivation	Motivation	Motivation	Measurement of motivational outcomes

In order to represent the five features of the students' collaborative behaviour, we divided the *PAC* visualizations into two subcomponents. The first one, the *PAC-CBI* (Fig. 1a), displays an overview of the collaborative learning behaviour by combining the collaborative features through a global rating scheme, defined by the *Collaborative Behaviour Index (CBI)*. This index is calculated as the average of the features represented (or *CBI* elements), and therefore it provides a representation of the overall collaborative behaviour of a student. Once the *PAC-CBI* is displayed, the

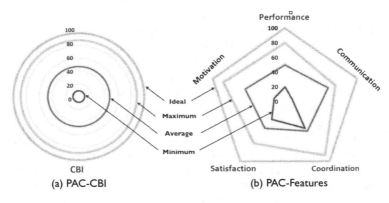

Fig. 1. Design of the visual representations of the *CBI* and the collaboration features

user can have more information through the visualization of the second subcomponent, the *PAC-Features* (Fig. 1b), which shows specific details about each collaborative feature included in the previous subcomponent.

As we can observe in Fig. 1a, the *PAC-CBI* subcomponent is represented with a coloured circle, whose size correspond to the *CBI* value within a normalized scale from 0 to 100. The four concentric circles in the figure represent the theoretical ideal, the normalized minimum, average and maximum values of the *CBI* for the overall group of students considered in the representation. This allows us to provide awareness of the behaviour of a student in comparison to the behaviour of his peers.

Figure 1b shows the *PAC-Features* subcomponent, represented using a radar diagram. Thus, each feature of the students' collaborative behaviour is depicted as a vertex of a coloured pentagon. The pentagon size corresponds to the normalized value of the features. Similar to the *PAC-CBI*, we depict four concentric pentagons; one regular and the other three of variable size and shape. The regular pentagon represents the theoretical ideal value expected for all the behaviour features. The pentagons of variable size represent the normalized minimum, average and maximum values of the features for the overall group of students. This enable a student to compare, for each feature, his own performance to the one of his peers.

Notice that both the *PAC-CBI* and the *PAC-Features* visualizations represent the behaviour of the specific student to whom the feedback is being displayed as colour-filled shapes (a circle and a pentagon, respectively).

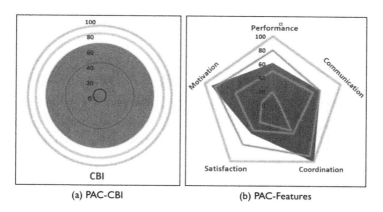

Fig. 2. Example representations displayed for the *Personal Awareness Component*

Considering the previous design, Fig. 2 shows an example of the visual representation of a student behaviour as displayed in the *Personal Awareness Component*. As we can observe, it is composed by the *CBI* index (Fig. 2a), as a measure of the overall collaborative behaviour, and also a detail of the five previously explained collaborative dimensions (Fig. 2b).

Social Awareness Component (SAC). This component provides social awareness and proposes possible suitable collaborators (i.e., other students) to the user. In order to identify potential collaborators, we use the Multi-Dimensional Scaling (MDS) method to represent students as points in a 2D space [18]. By performing MDS, the values of the five collaboration features (5D space) of the *CBI* can be mapped into a point in a 2D space, in such a way that distances between points are preserved. Thus, we can represent, in the *SAC,* two students that have similar behaviour as two points located at a short distance from each other. However, it could happen that students having similar *CBI*, could also have very dissimilar values of the several collaboration features that compose this index. In that case, the MDS also allows us to represent such students as two distant points in the *SAC*; therefore, these students will not be suggested as potential collaborators.

Moreover, we defined two different criteria to propose collaborators, depicted as the *"highly recommended collaborators"* and the *"other recommended collaborators"* areas of the *SAC*, respectively. The former includes at least one potential collaborator that is located at the closest MDS distance from the represented student, and the latter area includes the previous one and it has a range that covers at least a 20 % of the closest potential collaborators. This percentage was decided on the basis of the Pareto's principle or 80-20 rule [19], which states that "80 % of all effects result from 20 % of all causes". Accordingly, we considered that 20 % of all possible collaborators can produce the most significant impact in the collaboration process. Figure 3 shows the design proposed for the visualization of the *SAC* component.

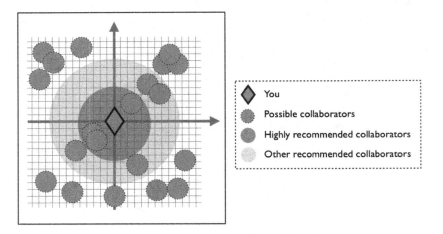

Fig. 3. Design of the visual representations displayed by the *Social Awareness Component*

This method for suggesting collaborators is based on the correlation between values of the *CBI* components for several students. Hence, we only propose collaborators with similar behaviour. That is, only students who have similar values in the same collaboration features will be encouraged to collaborate. Two alternative methods for providing this feedback are the following: (i) suggesting as possible collaborators only those students who have complementary behaviour or skills, and (ii) proposing collaborators with both similar and complementary behaviour.

Figure 4 shows examples of *SAC* representations, using these alternative methods. Figure 4a represents the feedback provided to a student, where only those possible collaborators with complementary behaviour are proposed. Thus, those students who have high values of certain behaviour features will be suggested as potential collaborators of other students who have small values in such features and vice versa. By contrast, Fig. 4b corresponds to the visual representation displayed to a student, where other students with similar or complementary behaviour are suggested as collaborators. As we can observe in both figures, we represent possible collaborators using two different colours, depending on whether we recommend them, because they have a behaviour similar or complementary to the student that is receiving the feedback.

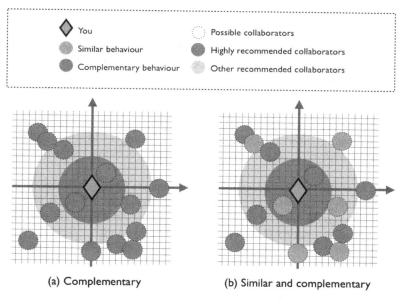

Fig. 4. Design of the visual representations of the *Social Awareness Component*

All the methods proposed to recommend collaborators have the purpose of promoting collaboration among students, helping them to improve their own behaviour and their learning experience. However, determining which method is the most appropriate to fulfil such a purpose is beyond of the scope of this work.

4   Evaluation of the BAM Prototype

In order to evaluate the usefulness of the proposed awareness mechanism, we embedded it in the *Moodle* learning platform used by the *Universitat Politècnica de Catalunya (UPC)*, in Spain, to support undergraduate courses. Therefore, this platform allowed us to provide feedback visualizations to students, including both the *PAC* and *SAC* components. The *Moodle* platform was also used to collect the answers of the students concerning the evaluation tasks and questionnaires. Next sections present the evaluation methodology and the obtained results.

4.1 Evaluation Methodology

The evaluation process involved real students and the collaborative learning environment that these students use every day to support their learning activities. Twenty four students were recruited; all of them were third year students enrolled in the course *"Design of Applications and Services (DSA)"* delivered at the *Castelldefels School of Telecommunications and Aerospace Engineering*, of the *UPC*. We also used a real data set from students of the DSA course to create the visualizations presented to the participants of the study.

The dataset included information from the students' activities and opinions while working within the formal learning environment as well as outside the classroom in an informal and unplanned way. The data sources used to gather the information included surveys and log files. The surveys investigated the students' feelings, opinions and behaviour during the course (both inside and outside the classroom). On the other hand, the log files, collected from the learning supporting platform, had information about the students' activities and performance while working in the course project.

The visualizations used in the study consisted of three different figures, corresponding to the *PAC-CBI*, *PAC-Features* and the *SAC* components of our awareness mechanism.

In order to evaluate the fitness of the awareness proposal for the intended application, we asked participants to complete three tasks; one for each visualization type. Consequently, for each representation the students had to perform a classification task, indicating whether those figures represented "poor", "average" or "good" student performance, or if some students represented in the *SAC* were "highly recommended", "recommended" or "not recommended" as collaborators. For simplicity, we named the classification tasks according to the rating levels that they represent as *"good"*, *"medium"* or *"bad"*.

In addition to the classification tasks, we asked participants to answer several questions to assess the usability of the three components of the *BAM*. These questions were taken from the *Usability Perception Scale (UPscale)* [20] and the *Post-Study System Usability Questionnaire (PSSUQ)* [21]. Both tools were adapted to suit the purposes of our study and formatted in a 5-point Likert scale. The resulting usability questionnaires included questions designed to evaluate attributes of the visualizations, such as ease of interpretation, learnability, usefulness, relevance and intention of use.

4.2 Evaluation Results

The prototype evaluation considered the analysis of the perceived usefulness of the feedback model, and also its suitability to be used as part of the awareness support of collaborative learning applications. The next sections present and discuss the obtained results.

On the one hand, the results from the classification tasks were useful to provide insights on how suitable the proposed awareness mechanism is to classify different learning behavioural patterns and suggest possible collaborators. Figure 5 shows the results of the classification tasks for the three elements of the *BAM*, which compose the visual representations of our proposal. As we can observe, there is a high rate of correct answers (94.91 % in average) for all the figures, which supports the suitability of our feedback proposal.

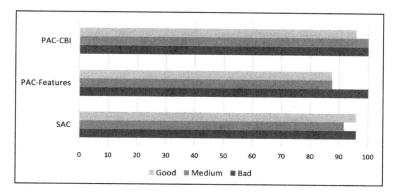

Fig. 5. Results of the classification tasks

On the other hand, results from the usability questionnaires helped us evaluate the students' perceived satisfaction concerning the information quality and its representation. We also evaluated the usefulness and comprehensibility of the feedback. Figure 6 shows the results obtained from the *UPscale* that suggest very positive participants' perceptions about the usability (70.42 % in average) and engagement (65.69 % in average) of the three kinds of visualizations.

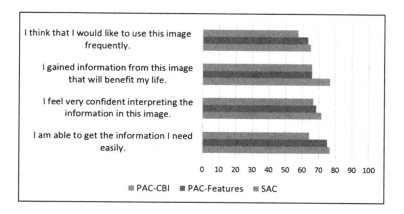

Fig. 6. Results of the *UPscale* questionnaire

Similarly, the results from the *PSSUQ* questionnaire, depicted in Fig. 7, indicate a high rate of participants' satisfaction (76.31 % in average) for such visualizations. Considering both usability questionnaires, it is important to notice that the results revealed the highest satisfaction with the representation provided by the *SAC* component, followed by the *PAC-Features* and the *PAC-CBI* respectively. This means that the *SAC* awareness component was the representation with the highest score in this evaluation.

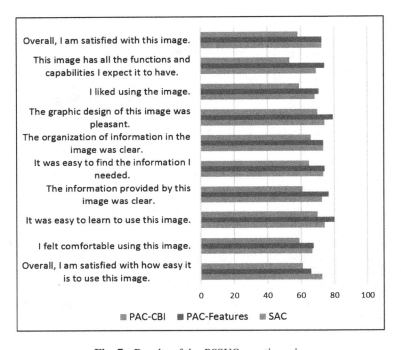

Fig. 7. Results of the *PSSUQ* questionnaire

5   Use Case

The awareness mechanism proposed in this paper can be integrated into collaborative learning applications in order to provide visual awareness about the collaborative learning behaviour of the users. As a proof-of-concept of such an integration, in this section we present a use case that describes the implementation of a mobile collaborative application that combines information from different types of data sources, and displays a dynamic and explicit feedback to users using the *Behaviour Awareness Mechanism*.

5.1   Data Sources

In order to generate the information required to provide awareness, we used data traces collected from students' behaviour during an academic semester. The traces corresponds to the participants in the previously mentioned *DSA* course, and they contain information about the students' actions while working in teams in a software development project. More specifically, we gathered data from the following sources:

- *Moodle* platform. In order to collect information about the students' performance, communication and coordination, we used the *Moodle* regular services. Examples of data traces collected through this mechanism are the number of tasks completed in time, number of forum messages posted by the students, number of group tasks submitted in time, and the individual and group grades.
- *Trello* web-based project management application. We used software logs from this tool to generate information related to the coordination among the team members, such as activity planning, collaboration flow, group interaction and group hierarchy. Examples of traces from this source are the number of tasks assigned, updated or finished on time by each member.
- *Online surveys* to collect communication, satisfaction and motivation information. We recorded the students' answers to a number of surveys, including questions about the collaboration with peers and the learning experience.
- *GitHub* web-based version control system. Logs from this software helped us obtain data about certain aspects related to the team coordination and performance. Examples of the collected information are the coding frequency and the number of pull request and open issues of the team members.

In order to calculate the five collaborative behaviour features considered in this study, we used different combinations of data traces from different sources. Hence, each feature is calculated using specific traces, normalizing (from 0 to 100) the measurements that each trace provides, assigning weights as multiplying factors depending on the number of traces, and aggregating the resulting values. This process can be summarized through the following equation:

$$Feature_x = \sum_{n=1}^{\text{\# of data traces}} \alpha_n \left(Trace_n \right) \tag{1}$$

where $Feature_x$ represents the collaborative feature to be calculated, n is the number of data traces used, α_n corresponds to the multiplying factors, and $Trace_n$ is the measurement from the particular data trace normalized from 0 to 100.

From the previous equation and for the considered feature, we obtain a value within the range $0 - 100$. As an example, let us consider that we use three data traces to calculate the "Performance" collaborative feature of a specific student. Such traces include individual and group grades of *Moodle* assignments and also the coding frequency as calculated by *GitHub*. In this case, the resulting equation for performance would be the following:

$$
\begin{aligned}
Performance \\
&= 0.4 \, (\textit{Individual grades on Moodle}) \\
&+ 0.4 \, (\textit{Group grades on Moodle}) \\
&+ 0.2 \, (\textit{GitHub coding frequency})
\end{aligned}
\tag{2}
$$

We must take into account that the measurements from each data trace can lay within any possible range of values; therefore we must normalize the values of such metrics. For example, the *"GitHub coding frequency"* indicates the number of items added by a particular student to the software project repository. We can normalize the *GitHub coding frequency,* assigning the values of 0 and 100 respectively to the theoretical maximum and minimum number of expected additions for a specific time period. Thus, 0 and 100 correspond to a coding frequencies of 1 and 5 additions per week respectively. Also, notice that in this case we assigned different weights to the multiplying factors, giving more importance to some measurements than to others. However, determining the weight that should be given to each metric is not part of this research work.

5.2   Sample Visualizations

Using the information gathered from the previous sources, the application classifies the data according to the five collaborative features and combines it appropriately in order to compute a value for each feature (within a normalized scale from 0 to 100). In addition, the *CBI* index is calculated as the average of the features.

Finally, based in the features and *CBI* values of a specific student and his peers, the application performs various MDS operations to represent, with a short distance, the students that have similar behaviour. Figure 8 depicts an example of the visual representations of the students' collaborative behaviour, provided by the *Behaviour Awareness Mechanism*, as shown in the students' smartphones.

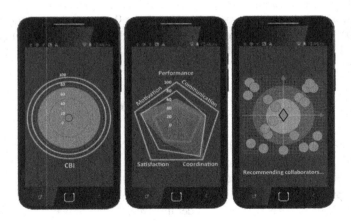

Fig. 8.   Interface of the *Behaviour Awareness Mechanism*

6   Conclusions and Future Work

This paper proposes a *Behaviour Awareness Mechanism (BAM)* as a method to provide visual feedback to support collaborative learning. It was initially proposed to support undergraduate courses, but it could also be suitable to be used in other learning scenarios.

In order to determine the usability and usefulness of this proposal, we conducted a proof-of-concept in an undergraduate course at the *Universitat Politècnica de Catalunya (UPC)*, Spain. This evaluation included a use case considering a group of students working collaboratively during a software development project and using a mobile collaborative application that implements the proposed awareness mechanism.

Although preliminary, the evaluation results indicate that the proposed awareness mechanism is useful to provide aggregate feedback about the students' behaviour and performance in educational contexts. The results also indicate that this mechanism represents properly the different collaborative learning behavioural patterns of the students and also the suggestions of potential suitable collaborators for them. Although these findings are still preliminary, they could help researchers and developers of CSCL applications to provide dynamic, direct and holistic awareness on the learning patterns and collaborative behaviour of the users.

Next steps in this research work involve a more in depth evaluation of *BAM*. This will allow to improve the design of these visualizations and investigate how the provision of feedback about the collaborative patterns may affect behaviour and collaboration dynamics of the students.

Acknowledgements. This work has also been partially supported by Fondecyt (Chile), grants: 1150252; by the Spanish Ministry of Science and Innovation (MCI) and FEDER funds of the EU under the contracts TIN2013-47245-C2-1-R, by the Community Networks Testbed for the Future Internet (CONFINE), Large-scale Integrating Project: FP7-288535, and also by the Generalitat de Catalunya as a Consolidated Research Group 2014-SGR-881.

References

1. Gress, C.L., Fior, M., Hadwin, A.F., Winne, P.H.: Measurement and assessment in computer-supported collaborative learning. Comput. Hum. Behav. **26**(5), 806–814 (2010)
2. Strijbos, J.W.: Assessment of (computer-supported) collaborative learning. Learn. Technol. IEEE Trans. **4**(1), 59–73 (2011)
3. Fransen, J., Kirschner, P.A., Erkens, G.: Mediating team effectiveness in the context of collaborative learning: The importance of team and task awareness. Comput. Hum. Behav. **27**(3), 1103–1113 (2011)
4. Kwon, K., Hong, R.Y., Laffey, J.M.: The educational impact of metacognitive group coordination in computer-supported collaborative learning. Comput. Hum. Behav. **29**(4), 1271–1281 (2013)
5. Kreijns, K., Kirschner, P.A., Jochems, W.: Identifying the pitfalls for social interaction in computer-supported collaborative learning environments: a review of the research. Comput. Hum. Behav. **19**(3), 335–353 (2003)
6. Antunes, P., Herskovic, V., Ochoa, S.F., Pino, J.A.: Reviewing the quality of awareness support in collaborative applications. J. Syst. Softw. **89**, 146–169 (2014)
7. Wu, K., Vassileva, J., Sun, X., Fang, J.: Motivating wiki-based collaborative learning by increasing awareness of task conflict: a design science approach. In: Baloian, N., Burstein, F., Ogata, H., Santoro, F., Zurita, G. (eds.) CRIWG 2014. LNCS, vol. 8658, pp. 365–380. Springer, Heidelberg (2014)

8. Schneider, J., Börner, D., van Rosmalen, P., Specht, M.: Augmenting the senses: a review on sensor-based learning support. Sensors **15**(2), 4097–4133 (2015)
9. Phielix, C., Prins, F.J., Kirschner, P.A., Erkens, G., Jaspers, J.: Group awareness of social and cognitive performance in a CSCL environment: effects of a peer feedback and reflection tool. Comput. Hum. Behav. **27**(3), 1087–1102 (2011)
10. Nicol, D.J., Macfarlane-Dick, D.: Formative assessment and self-regulated learning: a model and seven principles of good feedback practice. Stud. High. Educ. **31**(2), 199–218 (2006)
11. Buder, J.: Group awareness tools for learning: Current and future directions. Comput. Hum. Behav. **27**(3), 1114–1117 (2011)
12. Bodemer, D., Dehler, J.: Group awareness in CSCL environments. Comput. Hum. Behav. **27**(3), 1043–1045 (2011)
13. Wang, Q.: Design and evaluation of a collaborative learning environment. Comput. Educ. **53**(4), 1138–1146 (2009)
14. Meier, A., Spada, H., Rummel, N.: A rating scheme for assessing the quality of computer-supported collaboration processes. Int. J. Comput. Support. Collaborative Learn. **2**(1), 63–86 (2007)
15. Chounta, I.-A., Hecking, T., Hoppe, H.U., Avouris, N.: Two make a network: using graphs to assess the quality of collaboration of dyads. In: Baloian, N., Burstein, F., Ogata, H., Santoro, F., Zurita, G. (eds.) CRIWG 2014. LNCS, vol. 8658, pp. 53–66. Springer, Heidelberg (2014)
16. Kahrimanis, G., Meier, A., Chounta, I.-A., Voyiatzaki, E., Spada, H., Rummel, N., Avouris, N.: Assessing collaboration quality in synchronous CSCL problem-solving activities: adaptation and empirical evaluation of a rating scheme. In: Cress, U., Dimitrova, V., Specht, M. (eds.) EC-TEL 2009. LNCS, vol. 5794, pp. 267–272. Springer, Heidelberg (2009)
17. Lin, C., Standing, C., Liu, Y.C.: A model to develop effective virtual teams. Decis. Support Syst. **45**(4), 1031–1045 (2008)
18. Buja, A., Swayne, D.F., Littman, M.L., Dean, N., Hofmann, H., Chen, L.: Data visualization with multidimensional scaling. J. Comput. Graph. Stat. **17**(2), 444–472 (2008)
19. Hardy, M.: Pareto's law. Math. Intelligencer **32**(3), 38–43 (2010)
20. Karlin, B., Ford, R.: The usability perception scale (UPscale): a measure for evaluating feedback displays. In: Marcus, A., (ed.) Design, User Experience, and Usability. Design Philosophy, Methods, and Tools. LNCS, vol. 8012, pp. 312–321. Springer, Heidelberg (2013)
21. Lewis, J.R.: Psychometric evaluation of the PSSUQ using data from five years of usability studies. Int. J. Hum. Comput. Interact. **14**(3–4), 463–488 (2002)

Exploiting the Use of Wikis to Support Collaborative Writing: A Case Study of an Undergraduate Computer Science Class

Oluwabunmi Adewoyin[✉], Kewen Wu, and Julita Vassileva

University of Saskatchewan, Saskatoon, Canada
bunmi.adewoyin@usask.ca, semiwenwen@gmail.com,
jiv@cs.usask.ca

Abstract. Use of wikis in education reflects a shift in the education paradigm from lecture and individual homework-based to a paradigm emphasizing student engagement and the construction of knowledge through collaboration and peer-help. Existing research work on the use of wiki in collaborative writing had given mixed results. The goals of this research are to investigate whether wiki supports learning of writing and argumentation skills, and whether the students are motivated to use it and see it as a useful learning tool. Our participants comprise ten senior undergraduate students of a Computer Science class, who engaged in collaborative writing using wiki for four weeks. Their contributions were graded by a designated TA. The grades assigned to both their final articles and individual contributions, and the wiki logs were analyzed to determine the quality and volume of their weekly contributions, while feedback was taken from them using questionnaire to sample their perception of the use of wiki in writing. Our results showed that the use of wiki is helpful in improving their writing skill. However, participants are not happy with the further use of wiki in their course work. Also, we found that they require extrinsic motivation, in form of feedback (grades) from the TA and acceptance of their contribution by their peers, to increase their participation in wiki writing.

Keywords: Collaborative writing · Motivation · Collaborative learning · Wiki

1 Introduction

Wikis are web pages that allow users to add, modify or delete contents, in collaboration with other users [26]. Wikipedia is the most famous application of wiki technology, ranking 5th, with 1.2 billion unique visitors, among all the websites [25]. Use of web 2.0 technologies like wikis in education reflects a shift in the education paradigm from lecture and individual homework-based to a paradigm emphasizing student engagement and the construction of knowledge through collaboration and peer-help, which according to the socio-constructivists are powerful sources of knowledge transfer [16]. Existing research works had focussed mainly on how wiki can enhance students' collaboration in collaborative learning and writing. Some of these studies had mixed results [11, 13]. While some researchers found that wikis posses features that would be of great benefit

© Springer International Publishing Switzerland 2015
N. Baloian et al. (Eds.): CRIWG 2015, LNCS 9334, pp. 111–123, 2015.
DOI: 10.1007/978-3-319-22747-4_9

to collaborative learning when an apt attention is given to sound pedagogy in its implementation [5], others found that wikis do not necessarily encourage collaboration among students [13]. Hence, the benefits of wiki in supporting collaborative learning still require further exploration with regards to whether it supports learning and collaboration. In this research, we used a modified wiki to support collaborative essay writing in a senior undergraduate Computer Science class, in order to discover whether it supports learning of writing and argumentation skills, and whether the students are motivated to use it and see it as a useful learning tool.

2   Related Work

In higher education, wikis are being used in collaborative learning and writing because of their ease of use and the availability of options for editing by different contributors with different levels of privileges [4, 5, 11, 13]. For example, [13] studied the use of wiki to support collaborative writing in an undergraduate class. In their study, participants were organized into four writing groups, each with a group leader, and they were engaged in a writing project which was broken down into four stages with deadlines. The researchers used the wiki logs to collect data about the volume of contributions of each participant, the degree of collaboration and interaction among group members, and the division of labor among them. Their findings showed that work was not evenly distributed among the group members and the group leaders made most of the wiki entries. Overall, they found a limited collaboration among the participants using the wiki, while they did bulk of their discussion and sharing of ideas via email. [21] also engaged 216 students in voluntary wiki writing over a period of two years, at the end of which their exam performance was used to judge the benefits of wiki writing. Their findings showed that students who were actively involved in the wiki writing performed better than the less active students in their final exams. One short coming of this study is that little or no emphasis was placed on participation in the wiki writing and there was no incentive to motivate participants to contribute [21]. [11] assessed students' collaborative learning behaviour using wiki. Their findings showed a high overall level of participation. However, they also found that the use of wiki does not necessarily enhance collaboration.

On the other hand, [4] discovered that wiki was a great tool to enhance collaboration among students, though with certain reported difficulties. However, their findings were based solely on self-reported data from the participants using questionnaires and not on log data or performance evaluation [4]. Self-reported data can give useful insights into the learner's acceptance of wiki technology and their perception of its usefulness to support learning. However, it is subjective and prone to bias [20].

We discovered that most of the research on wikis in education, particularly for collaborative writing in classrooms, rely on either self-reported data from participants (their perception of knowledge gained) or on wiki logs to determine whether wiki actually supports collaborative learning by various measures. Also, the few that combined both the wiki logs and students' feedback, however, did not investigate the quality of students' contribution and the helpfulness of using wiki on their writing skill over time [19, 22, 23].

Also, none of the existing works looked at factors that could motivate participation for wiki users in collaborative writing. Some researchers have proposed general strategies for motivating contributions to the online environments [3, 12, 18]. [3] described some principles that can aid collaborative learning, most importantly in online environments. Two of these principles are *positive interdependence*, which is to ensure that coursework and assessment are designed in a way to make the success of the individuals in the group depend on the success of the group; and *individual and group responsibilities*, which is used to give individual participant a sense of responsibility by grading their individual contributions [3].

[18] classified motivating factors into psychological and economic. Psychologically, some users are self-motivated to contribute, while few are obliged to keep contributing as a result of self-preservation considering the fact that they have invested their time and that their contributions are important to the online community [10, 14, 12] stated anticipated reciprocity, increased recognition and sense of efficacy as the three motivations to contribute in online communities. [9] suggested three social rewarding mechanisms (implemented in MediaWiki) using: (1) quality and number of references, (2) rating of articles and (3) number of views on articles. The values along these three metrics can be combined in a two-step calculation process (*revision basis* and *author basis*) to find the active participants in the wikis. "*Revision basis*" refers to scoring every revision to an article based on the three social rewarding mechanisms, while "*author basis*" refers to assigning the sum of all scores accrued from every revision an author has made to the author [9]. Another approach proposes instantly rewarding editors with barnstars, points or warning signs that correlate with the quality of their contributions [7]. However, measuring the quality of contribution (participation) in wiki has always been an open research problem.

Many variables have been used to measure the quality of participation in wiki systems. A popular measure is the use of edit count, which is the number of characters or words that the editors contributed to the wiki. However, this metric gives the same credibility to both high quality and substandard contributions [24]. [6] suggested the use of edit sessions, which are the labor hours that each wiki editor puts into making contributions to the wiki articles. Although a slight correlation was found between edit session and edit count metrics, edit session as described by [6] might result in neglecting time spent behind the scenes doing other critical wiki activities. Also, the between session threshold of one hour might incorporate non-wiki activities, thereby overestimating the labor hours. Another measure is the use of editors' contributions that survive revisions by the other editors or administrators [1]. This refers to the number of characters, from the editors' contribution, which are not deleted from the wiki article or changed by the other editors. We see this approach as the most efficient, productive but inexpensive way to measure quality of participation since it considers only the useful contribution made by the editors.

Since the results from current studies have been inconclusive on the helpfulness of wiki in collaborative writing, due to their mixed results; in this study, we aim to clarify the effects of using wiki for collaborative writing in an undergraduate class and define the motivation strategies that can encourage both group and individual contributions in wiki collaborative writing. To do these, we will answer the following research questions:

Does collaborative writing using wiki help students to improve their writing skill?
What is the students' perception of the use of wikis for collaborative writing?
What strategies can be used to improve students' participation in collaborative writing
using wiki?

To measure the editors' contribution, we used the metric by [1], which is the editors'
contribution that survived revision by the other editors.

3   Research Tool

We developed a research tool, a wiki system, called *WikiMentor*, which is a customized
MediaWiki system with a content authorship module. Therefore, a login is mandatory
in *WikiMentor*. By comparing the content differences between every former and latter
revision of an article, *WikiMentor* is able to figure out the authorship of each character
and send email notification to the authors when their contents have been modified by
others (see Fig. 1).

Fig. 1. Sample email notification

These emails only inform the editors that their contents have been changed, no further
details are provided. Also, we modified the interface of the system by adding a dialog
box (see Fig. 2) in each wiki article page. The dialog box is triggered when the user
revisits a page after she has edited some texts and there have been subsequent edits by
others of her text. Two sub-functions are embedded in the dialog box, namely *content
changes* and acceptance/*evaluation of changes*. '*Content changes*' lists all modifications
of an article made between the newest version and the latest version contributed by the
user in reverse chronological order. It further helps users to locate the modifications by
highlighting the added (or deleted) content in the original place of the text.

In this way, the users become aware of every change made to the article after the last
time they logged into the system and made edits. For each change of content contributed
by the user, there is the function "Accept change", which allows the user to accept or
reject the change. The acceptance is considered equivalent to a positive rating (+1),
referred to as r in the formula below, and rejection – to negative rating (−1), referred to

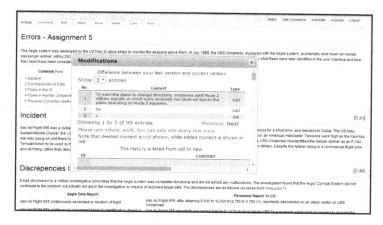

Fig. 2. Dialogue box showing content changes & acceptance/evaluation of changes

as s in the formula below. We compute the user's reputation from the acceptance or rejection, collected from the different users whose contributions were edited by the user using the formula below [15].

$$T = (r + 1) / (r + s + 2)$$

Where T refers to reputation, r refers to the number of accepted changes, while s refers to the number of rejected changes. For example, an editor would have a reputation of 0.67 at a point when r =+1 and s = 0. In addition to the generic features of a wiki system, we included the following features to the WikiMentor:

Email notification when changes are made to editor's contribution;
Highlighting changes made to every editor's contribution;
Opportunity to accept or deny changes made to their contribution;
Computation of each editor's reputation based on the acceptance or denial of their contribution or changes.

While the reputation value was not visible to the editors, it was used in the analysis to check the editors' responses with the system data.

4   Research Method

We recruited 10 undergraduate students of a senior undergraduate computer science class on ethics, who engaged in four collaborative writing sessions required for their coursework using WikiMentor. Therefore, the wiki editors in our case were the students. The coursework required the students to write collaboratively essays on different topics assigned by the instructor each week. The students created the wiki page dedicated for the weekly assignment. There was no designated author responsible for each wiki page. The students were encouraged to contribute to the wiki assigned each week using pseudonyms. Students could add new contents, edit and delete the existing contents of the wiki. In order to ensure that students make distinct and meaningful contribution, their contributions to each wiki article were graded by a designated teaching assistant (TA), who is a senior graduate student and has taught the class as Sessional instructor. We only had one marker in order to prevent increase in the cost of the experiment since the TAs (markers) would be paid and also to avoid complexity that might arise from giving conflicting feedback to the students from different markers. The grading was done by assigning one grade for the final article and then deviations of this mark (both positive and negative within 15 %) were assigned to individual students based on how substantial was their individual contribution, judged by the TA. In this way we aimed to create positive interdependence among the students and as well enforce both group and individual responsibilities, since they all know that not only does the entire group contribution matter, but their individual contributions also count towards their final grades. In order to mitigate the subjectivity of the marks given by the TA, the grading of their final article was based on three criteria with some weights assigned to each criteria, (1) issues raised, weight 0.3; (2) completeness and logic of the argumentation, weight 0.4; and (3) writing style and grammar, weight 0.3. Students had seven days to make contributions to each wiki article, after which the article was locked and grading started.

For every edit made to their contribution, each student got notified by email and the resulting changes were highlighted within the individual interface of the wiki system. Therefore, the user could either accept or reject the changes and this translated into a rating value of the change, that could be either positive ($+1$/accept) or negative (-1/deny), and was used in computing the reputation of the student who did the change as described in the previous section. We did not reveal the calculated reputation values to prevent the students from cheating or gaming the system. However, they were aware that their edits to others' contributions would either be accepted or rejected.

For each participant, we collected data on the number of characters contributed and the number of characters of their contributions that survived revisions by the other participants, the revisions that they made, the time they spent making their contributions and revisions, the numbers of their revisions that were accepted or rejected by the authors. Also, we kept history of their contributions and revisions, which could be viewed from the "history" tab once they logged in to the wiki system. At the end of the term, participants were given an exit questionnaire to evaluate their experience.

5   Results and Discussion

5.1   Does Collaborative Writing Using Wiki Help Students to Improve Their Writing Skill?

The participants engaged in collaborative writing using wiki for 4 weeks. There was no designated group leader or author. Therefore, anybody could start each wiki article while others joined in adding more texts. At the end of each weekly article, we sent them the grades assigned to both their final article and their individual contributions, by the TA. These grades were used to ensure group and individual responsibilities [3]. Grades assigned to the final articles over the four weeks are shown in Fig. 3. We found that there was a positive improvement in their grades from 75 % in the first week to 90 % in the fourth week.

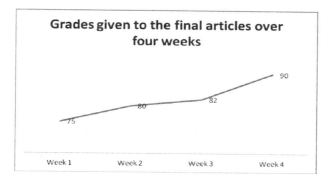

Fig. 3. Grades given to the final articles for the four weeks

We also found a growing trend in their average individual grades over the four weeks from 78.60 % in the first week to 91.89 % in the fourth week (Table 1).

Table 1. Grades assigned to individual contributions

Users	Wiki1	Wiki2	Wiki3	Wiki4
A	75.00	90.00	87.00	95.00
B	80.00	80.00	82.00	95.00
C	77.00	80.00	82.00	85.00
D	85.00	85.00	94.00	93.00
E	75.00	75.00	77.00	87.00
F	77.00	80.00	90.00	90.00
G	75.00	90.00	100.00	100.00
H	85.00	90.00	77.00	97.00
I	77.00	–	75.00	–
J	80.00	75.00	77.00	85.00
Average	**78.60**	**82.78**	**84.10**	**91.89**

We collected data on the number of their contributed characters that survived revision by the other participants. The individual weekly contribution quality (WCQ) for each student was calculated using the formula (results in Table 2).

Table 2. Weekly contribution quality for each student

User	Week 1	Week 2	Week 3	Week 4
A	0.9895	0.9058	0.9975	1
B	No contribution	0.5527	0.6967	0.9422
C	1	0.993	0.908	1
D	0.8201	0.9981	0.9336	0.9993
E	1	0.7008	0.9545	0.9282
F	1	1	0.9778	0.911
G	0.9523	0.7222	0.9973	0.9501
H	0.9994	0.9911	1	1
I	1	No contribution	0.9846	No contribution
J	0.9991	0.7897	0.9925	0.332
Average	**0.9734**	**0.8504**	**0.9443**	**0.8959**

$WCQ_i = $ (*#characters owned by i in the final version*)/(*#characters contributed by i over the week in total*).

The results show a growing trend in the quality of the weekly contributions of some of the participants, except in week 1 when they mostly had very high weekly contribution quality. One reason that can be attributed to these high values is that majority of the students gave their contributions towards the deadline, when it was practically impossible for the other students to edit their contributions. The result also shows a decline from a high class average in week 1 to a lower class average in week 2. This can be attributed to the last minute contributions made by the students, which had a huge impact on the overall class average. There was a growing trend in the subsequent weeks, except in the week 4, when the values dipped lower (and there was an outlier of 0.332), still a good trend on the overall.

5.2 What is the Students' Perception of the Use of Wikis for Collaborative Writing?

Participants were given exit questionnaire. The exit questionnaire contained questions aimed at sampling their opinions about the competence of other contributors, the helpfulness of the wiki system in improving their writing, their satisfaction with the wiki system and the motivational strategies, which we included in the wiki system, that helped their writing and learning. We received 10 responses, though few of them abstained from answering certain questions.

We asked questions about their general impression of the other contributors to the wiki articles. The options given and the summary of their responses are presented in Table 3.

Table 3. Participants' perception of other contributors

Options	Number of respondents (out of 10)
Competent	6
Provided detailed contribution	6
Helpful	6
Not helpful	1
Not competent	1
Lacked substance	1

Participants found other contributors to be competent, detailed and helpful on the average, which is also confirmed in their comments. e.g.

"I found sometimes people were too thorough, and by the time I went to record my thoughts, everything I wanted to say had already been said."

We asked to know if they were actually comfortable with using wiki system and 80 % said they were very comfortable. Although they used pseudonyms while contributing to the wiki articles and they expressed that they were comfortable with using wiki, we discovered from their comments that few of them have reservation for editing other contributors' contents, while some did not have problem with this. Some of their comments are quoted below:

"It was uncomfortable deleting other people's work, but I was comfortable expressing my own ideas"
"… I have no reservations about editing."

Also, 60 % of the participants objected to the further use of wiki in their coursework. Some of the reasons that they gave are quoted below.

"…the wiki was a forced exercise in frustration, boredom, and annoyance"
" With the wiki, what I wanted to say was often already said by someone else"

This shows that, although there was a noticeable improvement in their writing, participants did not like to use Wiki in their collaborative writing, because they see it as a forceful and boring exercise.

We found out that participants found other contributors to be competent, helpful and detailed in their contributions. Although, 80 % of participants feel they were comfortable with using the wiki system, we found out that some of them still hold some reservation for editing other contributors' contents. Many factors could have contributed to this that we hope to found out in our future work. Despite their positive attitude towards other contributors and their expressed competence in the use of wiki, participants were generally not happy with the further use of wiki in their collaborative writing.

5.3   What Strategies can be Used to Improve Students' Participation in Collaborative Writing Using Wiki?

We asked participants about the features of the wiki system that motivated them to keep participating in the collaborative writing process. Participants could select as many features as were applicable to them on the list. See Table 4 for the summary of the options and the selection made by the participants.

Table 4. Participants' preference for motivation strategies

Options	Number of respond-ents (out of 10)
The open contribution format of collaboration	6
Free writing style in wiki	6
The email notification when changes were made to their contents,	3
The highlighting of the changes made to their contents,	4
Their perceived status to their peers	7
Use of pseudonyms	2
Marks given by the TA	6

As shown in Table 4, only four of the options were chosen by more than five participants at a time. These are "The open contribution format of collaboration" (6), "Free writing style in wiki" (6), "The perceived status to their peers" (7) and "Marks given by the TA" (6).

These results showed that wiki editors actually required motivation, even if used for educational purpose. Their perceived status was borne out of their reputation score, which was not visible to the participants, but computed from the acceptance or rejection of their contribution to the wiki articles. This showed that participants care about the acceptance and rejection of their contributions by other participants, and the awareness of such feature could motivate them to ensure that they always make reasonable contribution. Also, participants got to see both their group and individual marks from every weekly article, before they moved on to the next wiki article. The results here showed that they are motivated by the feedback from the marks and the marker's comments that they received weekly from their contributions. Overall, students are generally motivated by approval or feedback from their peers and an authority figure, in this case, the teaching assistant (TA). Two selected options, free writing style and open contribution, are characteristic of any wiki system, which corroborates the findings by [5] that the ease of use of wiki makes it a valuable tool in collaborative learning. The other two popular options (perceived status to their peers and marks given by the TA) correspond to enhanced performance feedback that can be usefully and easily incorporated in educational wiki systems. It was disappointing to find that the other new features introduced in our wiki, aiming to increase awareness of peer-feedback (the email notification when changes were made to their contents, the highlighting of the changes made to their contents, emphasizing fact that other editors are accepting or rejecting their contents, and the use of pseudonyms to encourage students to be more critical) were not chosen as motivating students to participate in the system. Yet the students could only be aware of their reputation by being aware of the accepted changes that they made to their classmates' contributions. So it is possible that in answering this question, they focused on the higher motives for participation, assuming that the others (not selected items) are just technical means to achieve them. Further research will seek to clarify this issue.

6 Conclusion

A lot of research that had been conducted on wiki and collaborative learning were mostly targeted at whether wiki actually encourages collaboration or not. However, in this research, we studied the effects of the use of wiki as a source of peer feedback on improving writing skill and helping participants in collaborative learning. We also looked at the motivation strategies that can trigger meaningful contributions to wiki. The participants felt that wiki was not really helpful and it was rather a boring activity; however, the quality of their writing improved, both measured by the proportion of contributed text that remained in the final article and the grades assigned by the marker (TA) based on the quality of the collaboratively written article and the individual contributions to it. The findings from this study show that the wiki writing exercises are helpful in improving students writing skill and that self-report from users is not enough when measuring cognitive and affective states. Our results also suggest that students require extrinsic motivation in form of feedback from their peers and an authority figure (e.g. instructor, TA) to enhance their quality of contribution to wiki.

There are few limitations to this study. This study was designed with ten participants, which is a small sample size. Hence, the results from the study cannot be generalized. However, it serves as a basis for future studies with large sample size. Also the participants only worked as one group, comprising of ten participants working together on a wiki article at the same. However, research had shown that for wiki to be effective as a collaborative writing tool group interaction and discussion are necessary conditions [8]. Research had also shown that small groups enhance group interaction and cohesion [17]. Therefore in our future work, we will deploy the wiki tool in a larger class, where students will be grouped into small group sizes (3 to 4 in each group) for collaborative writing. In addition, we only had one marker. To improve the reliability of the grades assigned, we could use two expert markers and calculate the discrepancy in their scores. However, this will significantly increase the costs in an already costly experiment in a real class environment and may produce conflicting feedback to the students.

Despite the limitations, this study is pivotal for teachers, who will like to deploy wiki for collaborative writing in their classrooms. The findings here show that students require extrinsic motivation to participate in wiki writing. Therefore, teachers should consider the use of appropriate motivational features while deploying wikis, and that they should not only rely on the feedback from the students, but also feedback from an authoritative person (TA or marker), to measure the impacts of the use of wiki in collaborative writing.

References

1. Adler, B.T., De Alfaro, L., Pye, I., Raman, V.: Measuring author contributions to the wikipedia. In: Proceedings of WikiSymp, 10 p. ACM (2008)
2. Antin, J., Cheshire, C., Nov, O.: Technology-mediated contributions: editing behaviors among new wikipedians. In: Proceedings of the 2012 Conference on Computer Supported Cooperative Work, CSCW 2012, pp. 373–382 (2012)
3. Barkley, E.F., Cross, K.P., Major, C.H.: Collaborative Learning Techniques: A Handbook for College Faculty. Jossey-Bass Publishers, San Francisco (2005)
4. Deters, F., Cuthrell, K., Stapleton, J.: Why wikis? students' perception of using wikis in online coursework. MERLOT J. Online Learn. Teach. 6(1), 122–134 (2010)
5. Engstrom, M.E., Jewett, D.: Collaborative learning the wiki way. TechTrends 49(6), 12–15 (2005)
6. Geiger, R.S., Halfaker, A.: Using edit sessions to measure participation in wikipedia. In: Proceedings of the 2013 Conference on Computer Supported Cooperative Work, pp. 861–870 (2013)
7. Geiger, R.S., Ribes, D.: The work of sustaining order in wikipedia: the banning of a scandal. In: Proceedings of the 2010 Conference on Computer Supported Cooperative Work, CSCW 2010 (2010)
8. Hadjerrouit, S.: A collaborative writing approach to wikis: design, implementation and evaluation. Issues Informing Sci. Technol. 8, 431–449 (2011)
9. Hoisl, B., Aigner, W., Miksch, S.: Social rewarding in wiki systems – motivating the community. In: Schuler, D. (ed.) HCII 2007 and OCSC 2007. LNCS, vol. 4564, pp. 362–371. Springer, Heidelberg (2007)
10. Joyce, E., Kraut, R.E.: Predicting continued participation in newsgroups. J. Comput. Mediated Commun. 11, 723–747 (2006)
11. Judd, T., Kennedy, G., Cropper, S.: Using wikis for collaborative learning: assessing collaboration through contribution. Australas. J. Educ. Technol. 26(10), 341–354 (2010)
12. Kollock, P.: The economies of online cooperation: gifts and public goods in the cyberspace. In: Smith, M., Kollock, P. (eds.) Communities in Cyberspace, pp. 220–239. Routledge, London (1999)
13. Leung, K., Chu, S.K.W.: Using wikis for collaborative learning: a case study of an undergraduate students' group in Hong Kong. In: ICKM 2009: The 6th International Conference on Knowledge Management (2009)
14. Ling, K., Beenen, G., Ludford, P.J., Wang, X., Chang, K., Li, X., Cosley, D., Frankowski, D., Terveen, L., Rashid, A., Resnick, P., Kraut, R.: Using social psychology to motivate contributions to online communities. J. Comput. Mediated Commun. 10(4) (2005)
15. Noorian, Z., Marsh, S., Fleming, M.: Multi-layer cognitive filtering by behavioral modelling. In: Proceedings of 10th International Conference on Autonomous Agents and Multiagent Systems (AAMAS 2011), pp. 871–878 (2011)
16. Piaget, J.: The Judgement and Reasoning in Children. Routledge and Kegan, London (1928)

17. Bothos, E., Apostolou, D., Mentzas, G.: IDEM: a prediction market for idea management. In: Weinhardt, C., Luckner, S., Stößer, J. (eds.) WEB 2008. LNBIP, vol. 22, pp. 1–13. Springer, Heidelberg (2009)

18. Rafaeli, S., Ariel, Y.: Online motivational factors: incentives for participation and contribution in wikipedia. In: Barak, A. (ed.) Psychological Aspects of Cyberspace: Theory, Research. Applications. Cambridge University Press, Cambridge (2008). ISBN 0-521-87301-0

19. Ravid, G., Kalman, Y.M., Rafaeli, S.: Wikibooks in higher education: empowerment through online distributed collaboration. Comput. Hum. Behav. **24**(5), 1913–1928 (2008)

20. Sorensen, J.: Measuring Emotions in a Consumer Decision-Making Context – Approaching or Avoiding. Working Paper Series. Department of Business Studies, Aalborg University, Aalborg (2008)

21. Stafford, T., Elgueta, H., Cameron, H.: Students' engagement with a collaborative wiki tool predicts enhanced written exam performance. J. Assoc. Learn. Technol., 22 (2014). doi: http://dx.doi.org/10.3402/rlt.v22.22797

22. Tetard, F., Patokorpi, E., Packalen, K.: Using wikis to support constructivist learning: a case study in university education settings. Paper presented at the System Sciences, 42nd Hawaii International Conference on System Sciences, HICSS 2009 (2009)

23. Tsai, W.T., Wu, L., Elston, J., Yinong, C.: Collaborative learning using wiki web sites for computer science undergraduate education: a case study. IEEE Trans. Educ. **54**(1), 114–124 (2011)

24. Wikipedia (2014). Wiki. URL: http://en.wikipedia.org/wiki/Wiki. Accessed 27 June 2014

25. Wikipedia (2014). Wikipedia: Editcountitis URL: http://en.wikipedia.org/wiki/Wikipedia: Editcountitis. Accessed 17 April 2014

26. Wikipedia (2015). Wiki. URL: http://en.wikipedia.org/wiki/Wiki Accessed 1 April 2015

Where to Begin? Using Network Analytics for the Recommendation of Scientific Papers

Laura Steinert[(✉)], Irene-Angelica Chounta, and H. Ulrich Hoppe

University of Duisburg-Essen, Lotharstr. 63, Duisburg, Germany
{steinert,chounta,hoppe}@collide.info

Abstract. This paper proposes a network analytic approach for scientific paper recommendations to researchers and academic learners. The proposed approach makes use of the similarity between citing and cited papers to eliminate irrelevant citations. This is achieved by combining both content-related and network-based similarities. The process of selecting recommendations is inspired by the ways researchers adopt in literature search, i.e. traversing certain paths in a citation network by omitting others. In this paper, we present the application of the newly devised algorithm to provide paper recommendations. To evaluate the results, we conducted a study in which human raters evaluated the paper recommendations and the ratings were compared to the results of other network analytic algorithms (such as Main Path Analysis and Modularity Clustering) and a well known recommendation algorithm (Collaborative Filtering). The evaluation shows that the newly devised algorithm yields good results comparable to those generated by Collaborative Filtering and exceeds those of the other network analytic algorithms.

1 Introduction

One task any researcher has to face quite often, regardless the research field, is literature research. Whether a scientist is new to a field or exploring a new idea, the time consuming task of skimming seemingly hundreds of papers lies ahead in order to find the few precious papers that are of interest. "Nowadays, [...] there are too many articles to read [...], and as a result, intelligent recommender systems [...] play a crucial role in recommending articles." [5, p.1830]. By providing a user with literature recommendations he or she is also indirectly presented scientific communities that may fit his or her interests. In this way, we aim to support a new researcher to place himself within a community and identify potential useful collaborations and connections.

A strategy applied by many researchers when they look for relevant papers is to pursue a chain of citations. However, not all citations are followed because not all citations are equally important to the topic of interest. This could be expressed by weighing the citations differently. Notwithstanding, in previous research citations were usually considered to be equal in citation analysis [5]. Garfield [7] lists 15 reasons to cite a document, additionally saying that these

© Springer International Publishing Switzerland 2015
N. Baloian et al. (Eds.): CRIWG 2015, LNCS 9334, pp. 124–139, 2015.
DOI: 10.1007/978-3-319-22747-4_10

are only some of the possible reasons. Accordingly, a "purely quantitative citation analysis" is heavily criticized [18, p.103]. Hence, whenever a citation network – i.e. a graph where nodes are papers and edges represent citations among
them – should be used to generate reading recommendations, only citations that
contribute to the main topic should be taken into account. Therefore, a method
is needed to weight citations in a citation network in order to reflect the relevance
of citations. This is also pointed out by Liu and Lu [11].

This paper proposes a method to generate reading recommendations based on
citation networks that additionally takes the relevance of citations into account.
This relevance is calculated by combining content-related similarity measures
with similarities derived from the structure of the citation network. It is assumed
that a cited paper that is similar in content and citation patterns to the paper
citing it, is a relevant citation. The innovative key idea is to consider the paths
of citations humans follow to generate reading recommendations. This idea was
originally inspired by Main Path Analysis [2,9]. Hence, the new approach is
grounded in network analytic methods. By adapting the human approach to
find relevant literature, the new method is more intuitive to understand than
existing methods. Moreover, we believe that by using the structure of the citation
network to generate recommendations, the quality of recommendations can be
improved compared to algorithms that consider all papers as recommendations.

The next section of the paper provides an overview of related work. Afterwards, a novel algorithm to recommend papers is presented alongside two known
algorithms that are also adapted for this task. In Sect. 4, we present a study
where the results of the aforementioned algorithms were evaluated. The results
are discussed in Sect. 5. The paper ends with a conclusion and a prospect of
future work.

2   Related Work

The need to find literature on a given topic is closely intertwined with scientific research. As such, many tools came up over the preceding decades to aid
researchers in that quest. Nowadays, many platforms exist that allow researchers
to traverse citation networks easily – e.g. CiteSeerX[1]. Although citation networks
enable a user to find literature on a given topic, not all cited papers are relevant.
This is because not all papers linked via a citation are related in topic as has
been mentioned previously.

Pohl et al. [14] recommend papers based on a co-download measure of papers
to indicate topic similarity / relatedness. Others rely on textual similarity alone
to recommend papers. For example Lee et al. [10] use all papers published by a
querying user and compare the abstracts and titles of these to a corpus of papers.
They use a vector space model and cosine similarity to calculate the similarities
between papers. The papers most similar to the querying user's papers are then
recommended.

---

[1] http://citeseerx.ist.psu.edu, as seen on March 9th 2015.

Other recommender systems for scientific papers make use both of the textual information as well as the citation network. Sugiyama and Kan [17] use a user's papers as a profile against which the similarities of possible recommendations are calculated. They construct a feature vector for each paper of the user by calculating term-frequencies. Additionally, the feature vector encodes the similarity of the paper to its citing and cited papers. Hence, they partly make use of the information given by the citation network. Recommendation candidate papers – for which similar feature vectors are constructed – are then compared to the feature vectors of the user and the most similar papers are recommended.

Torres et al. [19] generate reading recommendations for scientific papers by combining collaborative filtering (CF) and content-based filtering (CBF). Both methods can be run in parallel or sequentially. As input a user has to select one paper that is used to generate his profile of interest. For the content-based filtering the approach uses *term frequency-inverse document frequency* (tf-idf) on the text of papers, which are subjected to stopword removal and stemming beforehand. The CF approach is taken from McNee et al. [12], where k-nearest neighbour is used. A matrix where rows are papers and columns are citations is generated. An entry in the matrix denotes whether a paper has cited another paper. By computing the cosine similarity between the rows of the matrix – i.e. the citation patterns of papers – the CF algorithm recommends papers with a high similarity to the paper selected by the user. Overall they test a variety of combinations of the two modes. If run in parallel, the results of both algorithms are merged to generate recommendations with papers highly recommended by both algorithms ranking higher in the overall results. If run sequentially the output of one algorithm is the input of the other. In [19] variants are presented where any one of the two is the first algorithm.

Closely related to recommending papers to read is the task of recommending papers to cite, which is for e.g. done by Strohman et al. [16]. In their approach both the citation network as well as textual similarities are combined. As an input the user has to enter a text about the topic he is writing about. To retrieve a set of candidate papers, they compute the text similarity of the input text to over one million papers in a database and return the 100 most similar papers as the set R. However, they note that in the database used – Rexa – only approximately 10 percent of the entries contain full text information. In a second step they add all papers to R that any paper in R cites. Adding additional papers to that set, e.g. by adding the papers cited by the newly entered entries, does not improve the results. They report that R usually contains 1000 to 3000 documents and contains 90 percent of the papers researchers actually cite given the input text. They then rank the papers in R according to a mix of six features – publication year, text similarity, co-citation coupling, same author, Katz graph distance and citation count – and recommend those ranked highest.

A network analytic algorithm not intended for recommending papers but that might very well be suited for this task is the so called *Main Path Analysis* (MP). This algorithm discovers the path along which information is dispersed among scientific publications. As such the found main path can yield information about the most influential papers and therefore can serve as a reading suggestion for scientists new to this field. Originally proposed by Hummon and Doreian [9], the first step of the algorithm was considerably improved by Batagelj [2]. For a given directed acyclic graph a single source vertex and a single sink vertex are added and connected to the previously present sources or sinks. A source is defined as a vertex with an indegree of zero, whereas a sink has an outdegree of zero.

The MP algorithm then is a two stepped procedure that first calculates a flow for the graph. A flow is a function that maps every edge to a natural number and all vertices (except the source and the sink) fulfill Kirchoff's current law, i.e. the sum of the flows of all incoming edges equals the sum of the flows of all outgoing edges. In the second step the (local) main path is derived from the calculated SPC weights. The algorithm starts in the source vertex and always selects the outgoing edge with the highest SPC weight. If two or more edges exist that have the highest weight, the main path splits and continues along all of these edges. Upon reaching the sink the main path ends.

3   Method of the Study

A scientist searching for literature usually traverses a citation network starting from a single paper and following a subset of all possible citations. As mentioned before, this is because not all citations are relevant. However, although some of the approaches mentioned in Sect. 2 use the structure of the citation network to determine the similarity between papers, none make use of the network to actually generate the set of candidates. Most approaches look at *all* papers, calculate their similarity and recommend the most similar. But why should an algorithm not mimic the human approach? One might argue that a researcher would gladly look at all papers in the citation network if only he or she had the time. Moreover, a researcher often does not have access to the whole citation network but only sees the literature at the end of each paper. However, maybe there is more to the human strategy of finding relevant literature. Therefore, we propose an algorithm that mimics the way humans search for literature (cf. Sect. 3.1). Furthermore, we adapt other algorithms that were not initially designed for giving reading recommendations but that exploit the structure of the underlying graph (cf. Sects. 3.2 and 3.3). All three algorithms are network analytic approaches to the problem.

Figure 1 illustrates the overall process to recommend literature. First of all, the citation network has to be extracted. Afterwards, content-related and graph-based similarities are calculated and combined. Finally, the literature recommendations can be generated. These steps are described in the following subsections.

Extracting the Citation Network. In order to receive reading recommendations a user has to name one paper that covers the topic he or she wants to explore further. The citation network used in this paper was gathered by extracting it from CiteSeerX[2] by starting from the paper the user provided as a seed.

---

[2] http://citeseerx.ist.psu.edu, as seen on 9th March 2015.

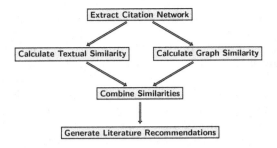

Fig. 1. The overall process to recommend literature

From there, the citations and inverse citations – i.e. the *cited by* relations – were crawled up to a given depth. Papers were added as vertices only if the abstract was provided on CiteSeerX and if it was written in English. Additionally, the title was extracted. Citations were added as edges to the extracted graph. The edges always point from the citing to the cited papers, i.e. backwards in time.

Calculating the Similarity. In our approach textual similarities are combined with similarities based on the structure of the citation network to generate the *topic-structure similarity* (tss), since Strohman et al. [16] report that using such a combination outperforms recommendations based on only one of the similarity measures. This was also done by He et al. [8]. As a measure based on the structure of the citation network the strength of the co-citation coupling is used.

The co-citation coupling was defined by Small [15] and is a subject similarity indicator. It measures how often two articles are cited together in relation to their overall individual citations. The strongest co-citation couples seem to be papers that are also directly liked by citation, yet this does not apply to all strongly coupled papers. It is believed to be a better subject similarity indicator than bibliographic coupling.

The strength $CoCitS$ of the coupling is calculated using Eq. (1) suggested by Garfield [6]. In this equation, $coCit(u,v)$ stands for the number of co-citations of u and v, whereas $cit(u)$ gives the overall number of citations of text u. Since every co-citation is counted twice in $cit(u) + cit(v)$, the number of co-citations has to be subtracted in the denominator from the overall number of citations.

$$CoCitS(u,v) = \frac{coCit(u,v)}{cit(u) + cit(v) - coCit(u,v)} \tag{1}$$

The topic-structure similarity was only calculated for papers citing each other, i.e. that are directly connected in the citation network. This similarity was encoded as an edge weight. In order to find the linguistic algorithms best suited for calculating the content-related similarity, a small evaluation was conducted using different text similarity algorithms in combination with various key phrase extraction and preprocessing algorithms, e.g. lemmatizing. A set of papers from three different scientific domains was taken and the similarity between every pair calculated. Afterwards, modularity clustering [4] was applied. The results were then scored depending on how well the generated clusters resembled the three expected clusters. The combination of *Co-occurrence Graph key phrase extraction* and *Greedy-String-Tiling* (GST) yielded very good results with a very good runtime behaviour. Hence, it was selected to calculate the content-related similarity used in this paper.

The algorithm called *Co-occurrence Graph key phrase extraction* is a variant of the *TextRank* algorithm by Mihalcea and Tarau [13]. It is an unsupervised method to extract key phrases from natural language texts. Unsupervised means that the system does not need to be trained on a corpus. The algorithm first constructs a graph from a given natural language text. The vertices are sequences of words from the texts. An edge is established between two vertices if the corresponding word sequences co-occur within a section of the text that is maximally N words long. N is also referred to as the *window size*. However, words occurring in the same window have to belong to the same sentence. Additionally, the words making up the vertices can be further filtered by word class. In this variant only nouns are permitted. The minimal length of key phrases is two and the maximum size is set to four. The window size is set to two. After the graph has been created, a score for every vertex is calculated, encoding how well it can be used as a key phrase for the text. In this work the implementation provided by *DKPro Keyphrases*[3] is used.

The Greedy-String-Tiling algorithm as described by Wise [20] is an algorithm to calculate content-related similarity by detecting equal substrings in two texts. A pair of matching substrings is called a *tile*. For this only substrings of a minimal length of three are considered. Moreover, tiles never overlap.

The algorithm seeks to maximize the tiling of the two texts, i.e. it tries to maximize the number of tokens belonging to tiles. However, since this problem is probably NP-hard, if multiple tilings are possible GST is set to prefer larger tiles. This increases the chances of finding significantly similar passages versus mere chance similarities as produced by smaller tiles. The similarity is then the percentage of the first text that is covered by tiles. The implementation used was provided by the DKPro Similarity[4] library.

In order to calculate the content-related similarity of two papers in our approach the title and abstract information was subjected to key phrase extraction using *Co-occurrence Graph key phrase extraction*. Here all extracted key phrases regardless of their weight were considered. The content-related similarity between the key phrases of both papers was then calculated using GST. This process is illustrated in Fig. 2. Both the content-related similarity as well as the co-citation coupling strength were then summed up, resulting in a topic-structure similarity $tss(u, v) \in [0; 2]$ for two vertices u and v. This is also shown by Eq. (2).

$$tss(u, v) = CoCitS(u, v) + GST(u, v) \qquad (2)$$

---

[3] http://code.google.com/p/dkpro-keyphrases/, as seen on March 9th 2015.
[4] https://code.google.com/p/dkpro-similarity-asl/, as seen on March 13th 2015.

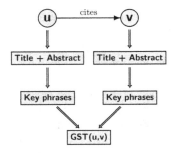

Fig. 2. The calculation of the content-related similarity of two papers u and v

Once the citation network has been extracted and the edge weights have been calculated, a reading recommendation can be calculated by using one of the following three algorithms.

3.1 Finding Highly Connected Components

A citation network is a directed acyclic graph. Hence, strongly connected components cannot exist. Therefore, a weakly connected component will be referred to as *component* only.

By construction the citation network is a single component. However, edges with a low weight – i.e. low topic-structure similarity – are of little interest. By repeatedly deleting the edges with the lowest weights the graph will be segmented into different components until eventually only isolated vertices exist. However, assuming that papers covering the same topic are highly connected among one another with high edge weights they should be found in the same component up until very late in the process. In order to generate reading recommendations one could therefore look at this largest component and give its set of vertices as recommendations. The problematic part is up to which edge weight edges shall be deleted.

Let θ be the threshold such that all edges with an edge weight below it are deleted. If one only considers the largest component, i.e. the component with the most vertices, for any θ, the sum of edge weights and the average edge weight describe functions nearly monotonic in nature. With an increasing θ, the sum of edge weights in the largest component decreases since all edge weights are greater or equal to zero and for $\theta = 0$ the highest number of edges – all edges – are in the largest component. However, as more and more edges with lower weights are deleted, the largest component will have an increasing average edge weight. This is depicted in Fig. 3 for a real world citation network. Here, the topic-structure similarity edge weights were normalized beforehand. The seed of this citation network is a paper by Fortunato[5]. The depth of the retrieved citation network

---

[5] Fortunato, S.: Community detection in graphs. Physics Reports 786(3), 75–174 (2010).

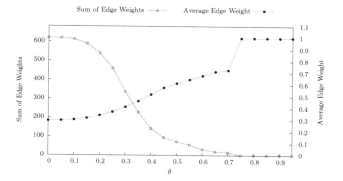

Fig. 3. The sum and the average edge weight for the largest component of a real citation network - generated by taking a paper by Fortunato as seed

---

Algorithm 1. LC Seed

Require: weighted Citation Network *graph*
  N = ∅
  for $\theta \leftarrow 0$ **to** 1 **do**
    Delete edges with weight $< \theta$
    C = largest components
    for $c \in C$ **do**
      if $seed \in V(c)$ **then**
        if $|V(c)| > minSize$ **then**
          N = V(c)
        end if
      end if
    end for
  end for
  return N

---

was three, i.e. if edge direction is ignored, any vertex in the graph is connected to the seed vertex by a path of maximally length three. It contains 1451 vertices.

In order to find the θ that determines the largest component that is returned as a reading recommendation, two variants are possible. The first assumes that since the seed paper concerns the topic of interest, the highest θ for which the largest component still contains the seed paper should be taken. However, this is the case where all vertices are isolated, i.e. the seed vertex forms a component of its own. Thus, a constraint should be added that only largest components that contain more than $minSize$ vertices are considered. For all evaluations described in this paper $minSize$ was set to one. This method is described in Algorithm 1 and will be called *LC Seed*.

The second variant seeks to find the optimal θ thus that all topic-structurally not very similar papers have been disconnected from the largest component but that all highly similar papers are still connected. Inspired by the diagram depicted in Fig. 3 we introduce an intersection heuristic. The θ for which the

---

Algorithm 2. LC Intersection

Require: weighted Citation Network *graph*
  min = $|V(graph)|$
  N = $\emptyset$
  maxSum = SumOfWeights(graph)
  for $\theta \leftarrow 0$ **to** 1 **do**
    Delete edges with weight $< \theta$
    C = largest components
    c' = $\emptyset$
    for $c \in C$ **do**
      c' = c
      if *seed* $\in V(c)$ **then**
        break {If there are multiple largest components, prefer that with the seed vertex}
      end if
    end for
    $\Delta = |avgWeight(c') \cdot maxSum - sumOfWeights(c')|$
    if $\Delta < min$ **then**
      $min = \Delta$
      $N = V(c')$
    end if
  end for
  return N

---

function of the average edge weight and the function of the sum of edge weights intersect is selected and the respective vertices in the largest component returned as reading recommendations. This could be approximated by increasing the θ discretely and finding the θ for which the two functions differ the least. However, before the two functions can be compared, their ranges need to be equalized. First of all, since the topic-structure similarity lies in $[0; 2]$ it can be normalized by dividing all weights by the highest occurring topic-structure similarity. Then the average edge weight lies within $[0; 1]$. By multiplying it with the maximal sum of edge weights – which is the sum of edge weights of the whole citation network – the ranges of the two functions can be equalized. This approach is described by Algorithm 2 and will be called *LC Intersection*.

Both *LC Seed* and *LC Intersection* can be run using the topic-structure similarity as an edge weight. However, by multiplying the topic-structure similarity with the SPC weights generated by the first step of the Main Path Analysis and using that as edge weights the notion of the evolution of a scientific field can also be taken into consideration. These variants will be called *LC Seed SPC*topSim* and *LC Intersection SPC*topSim*.

3.2 Weighted Main Path

This normal calculation of the main path is only based on the citation network but not on the content-based similarity of the papers. By combining the SPC weights with the topic-structure similarity via a multiplication – as was done in [3] – and finding the main path on these altered edge weights this problem can be overcome. Hence, this weighted Main Path contains only papers that are important concerning the SPC weights where adjacent papers are additionally topically and structurally similar. Thus, this weighted main path might contain good reading recommendations. But one problem remains: The weighted main path might not contain the seed paper and might thus be concerned with a different topic than the one for which recommendations are sought. This might be overcome by adding a restriction that the main path must contain the seed paper. This algorithm will be called *weighted Main Path* or *WMP*.

3.3 Modularity Clustering

Papers concerning the same topic should have a high topic-structure similarity. Moreover, it is likely that they are well connected among one another since papers on the same topic might cite each other. Hence, clustering that takes edge weights into account can be applied. Suitable for this is *Modularity Clustering*, applied to the undirected citation network [4]. The implementation provided by the *igraph* library of the programming language R was used[6]. For this algorithm the number of expected clusters is not a required parameter. The cluster containing the seed vertex represents the set of papers given as reading recommendations. This approach will be called *MC*.

4   Analysis and Results

In order to evaluate the recommendations produced by the different algorithms, an online survey was conducted. The different algorithms generated reading recommendations based on a single citation network. These recommendations were then rated by users.

4.1 Survey Setup

As a seed for the citation network a survey paper by Fortunato on graph clustering was taken. First of all, survey papers are a good starting point for scientists to embark on a new field. Secondly, they usually cite many papers and thus the resulting citation networks generated from them as starting points will contain many papers. The citation network generated from this paper used a depth of three and contained 1451 vertices.

Table 1 shows the number of reading recommendations (excluding the seed paper if it was given as a recommendation) given by the different algorithms. Those marked with a † were evaluated in the online survey. All others were omitted, either because they gave too many reading recommendations – e.g. MC – or too few – e.g. LC Seed SPC*topSim.

---

[6] http://www.inside-r.org/packages/cran/igraph/docs/fastgreedy.community, as seen on March 24th 2015.

Table 1. Number of reading recommendations per algorithm

Algorithm	No. of Recommendations
LC Seed†	20
LC Intersection	389
LC Seed SPC*topSim	1
LC Intersection SPC*topSim†	11
MP†	14
WMP†	5
MC	217

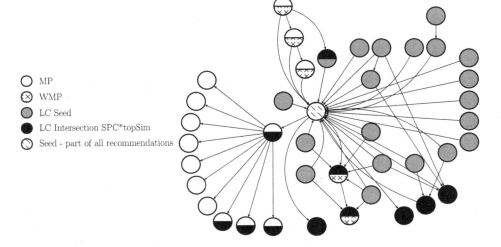

○ MP
⊗ WMP
◑ LC Seed
● LC Intersection SPC*topSim
◌ Seed - part of all recommendations

Fig. 4. The 40 papers recommended by the four algorithms evaluated in the survey and the seed node with their citations among each other

Figure 4 shows how the seed paper and the 40 papers recommended by the algorithms MP, WMP, LC Seed and LC Intersection SPC*topSim are connected in the citation network. The papers recommended by the MP algorithm clearly form a path in the citation network – as was expected – that only diversifies in the second last node on the path. The recommendations generated by the WMP show a single path that partially overlaps with that generated by the MP algorithm. The papers recommended using LC Seed are overall not very well connected among another, but mostly only connect via the seed paper. The recommendations generated by LC Intersection SPC*topSim on the other hand overlap with all recommendations from all other three algorithms. They are not as clearly connected as those recommended by the MP or WMP, but more connected than those generated with LC Seed. Papers from different recommendations are sometimes connected, especially the papers recommended by LC Seed and LC Intersection SPC*topSim.

4.2 Evaluation

In the conducted online survey the quality of the 40 papers recommended by the four different algorithms was evaluated. At the beginning of the survey the user was provided with the author information, title and abstract, as well as reference of the seed paper by Fortunato[7]. This information, as well as all other used in the survey, was reproduced from CiteSeerX or comparable web services and was hence publicly available.

The task was that the user was to assume that he or she wanted to find further literature on the topic covered by the seed paper. He or she was then asked to provide additional information with respect to his level of expertise in computer science, graph clustering and social network analysis on a 4-point Likert scale from one to four ("No expertise at all", "I have heard of it", "I am familiar with the field" and "I am a scientific researcher in this field"). This enabled us to ensure a high level of expertise of the raters.

The survey provided the same information as for the seed paper (title, author, abstract and reference) for all 40 papers to be rated. We limited the given information to the abstracts and titles instead of providing full papers because we assumed that scientific researchers familiar with a field can estimate the topic of a paper given only the abstract and title. For each of these 40 papers the user was asked to rate the quality of each as a reading recommendation compared to the topic of the seed paper on a 5-point Likert scale from one to five ("Very Bad", "Bad", "Neutral", "Good" and "Very Good"). The information on the recommended papers alternated with the questions to rate the quality. During the whole time the information on the seed paper were visible for comparison. The user was unaware that the recommendations had been generated by different algorithms. Moreover, the papers were ordered by the last name of the first authors.

In the survey 17 raters participated with a high average expertise in computer science (3.76), a medium average expertise in graph clustering (2.76) and a medium average expertise in social network analysis (2.65). The survey evaluated the recommendation quality of the different recommended papers. The second and third columns of Table 2 give the standard deviations and rounded average rating results of the four algorithms obtained by averaging the ratings the papers that were recommended by a specific algorithm got. If all participants stating their level of expertise in graph clustering to be *1* or *2* are omitted – which leaves 10 participants – the average results look like given in column four of the same table. As can be seen, the results do not differ much. The interrater reliability as given in Table 3 was measured by ICC(2,1). According to Andresen [1], an ICC value between 0.4 and 0.75 is a moderate to good reliability which is the case here. However, since the number of participants was very small, a higher interrater reliability was not expected. The survey task was also formulated openly in regards to the rating of the quality of recommendations. It highly depended on the criteria used for the rating by the different raters, e.g. whether

---

[7] Fortunato, S.: Community detection in graphs. Physics Reports 786(3), 75–174 (2010).

Table 2. Results of the first survey

Algorithm	All Raters		Clustering Med-Exp[a]	
	Avg. Rating	σ	Avg. Rating	σ
MP	2.32	0.45	2.19	0.34
WMP	3.11	1.01	3.04	1.00
LC Intersection	3.37	0.75	3.22	0.91
SPC*topSim				
LC Seed	3.88	0.55	3.73	0.54

[a]Expertise in Graph Clustering 3 or 4 on 4-point Likert scale; 10 Raters

Table 3. Interrater reliability for survey 1 using ICC(2,1)

	All Raters	Clustering Med-Exp[b]
Consistency	0.546	0.505
Absolute Agreement	0.507	0.482

[b]Expertise in Graph Clustering 3 or 4 on 4-point Likert scale; 10 Raters

they wanted to find other papers on graph clustering in general or papers on very specialized forms of graph clustering.

Finally, the four algorithms are compared to an algorithm that generates reading recommendations while considering all papers in the citation network as candidates. A variant of the *Item-Item Collaborative Filtering* algorithm proposed by McNee et al. [12] is used to recommend papers based only on the structure of the citation network. This algorithm is used as a baseline against which to compare all other algorithms. For the citation network the (undirected) adjacency matrix is calculated. In order to recommend papers every column of the matrix is compared to the column representing the seed paper and the cosine similarity is calculated for every pair. The N most similar papers are taken as the reading recommendations. This algorithm will be referred to as *CF*.

A weighted variant – weighted CF (WCF) – was also considered, that incorporates the topic-structure similarity by encoding it in the adjacency matrix. The reading recommendations are generated as in the CF approach. For the evaluation the value of N was set to ten for both variants.

Table 4. Results of the second survey

Algorithm	Avg. Rating	σ
CF	3.73	0.73
WCF	3.7	0.91

Table 5. Interrater reliability for survey 2 using ICC(2,1)

	All Raters
Consistency	0.504
Absolute Agreement	0.471

Both variants were tested in a survey structured identically to the first one. Moreover, the same dataset was used. Both variants recommended a total of 14 different papers. The second study was conducted by six participants with a high average expertise of 3.83 in computer science, medium expertise in graph clustering (2.33) and a medium expertise in Social Network Analysis (2.33). Table 4 gives the rounded average rating results and standard deviations of the two algorithms. The interrater reliability as given in Table 5 was measured by ICC(2,1) and is again moderate but slightly worse than for the first survey. However, since the second survey had only six participants, a low interrater reliability was to be expected.

5   Discussion

The papers recommended by the MP algorithm received on average a low rating of (2.32, $\sigma = 0.45$) that does not qualify the results as good. Slightly better rated were the papers recommended by WMP, which were rated neutrally. This indicates that the recommendations benefited from the used topic-structure similarity, as was expected. LC Intersection SPC*topSim received a neutral-positive rating of (3.37, $\sigma = 0.75$). Yet LC Seed received the highest ratings with (3.88, $\sigma = 0.55$) or (3.73, $\sigma = 0.54$) by the experts on a 5-point Likert scale, which is considered to be a *good* rating. Moreover, the standard deviation is low. Considering, that the ratings reflect precision, the ratings of LC Seed are even better since it is the algorithm that recommended the most papers. The recall of the generated recommendations could not be measured since ground truth on the quality of all 1451 papers in the citation network was not available.

Overall, it is indicated that the LC algorithm is better suited for recommending papers than the MP algorithm. Moreover, the usage of topic-structure similarities improves the ratings, whereas the usage of Main Path's SPC weights seems to lower them.

Since the MC algorithm recommended far too many papers, it could not be evaluated in a user study. However, 13 of the 20 papers recommended by LC Seed were also recommended by the MC algorithm. One paper recommended by LC Intersection SPC*topSim was also recommended by MC. There was no overlap with the recommendations generated by MP or WMP. The small overlap with LC Intersection SPC*topSim might be explained by the usage of the different edge weights. The same holds for the nonexistent overlap with the recommendations by MP and WMP, however these two algorithms additionally only greedily select the locally highest edge weights which might also explain the difference in recommendations.

The seven recommendations not in the intersection of MC and LC Seed received an overall average rating of (3.51, $\sigma = 0.63$) if all raters are considered or (3.26, $\sigma = 0.53$) if only modularity clustering experts are considered. Hence, good and moderately good recommendations are not in the intersection. The 13 nodes in the intersection however received a rating of (4.08, $\sigma = 0.40$) or (3.98, $\sigma = 0.35$) by the experts. This is another improvement in the rating compared to the rating of all 20 papers recommended by LC Seed which is (3.88, $\sigma = 0.55$) or (3.73, $\sigma = 0.54$). Hence, focusing the results of the MC algorithm by intersecting them with the results of the LC Seed algorithm might result in a very good reading recommendation algorithm.

The survey rating the recommendation quality of the CF and WCF algorithms shows that the LC Seed algorithm was rated more or less equally compared to the CF and WCF approaches. However, since the LC Seed recommended twice as many papers, the high rating can be valued even more highly.

So far the recommendations generated by the algorithms have only been analyzed for one input paper – a survey paper from graph theory. It would be interesting to see how the type of the seed paper – survey paper, short paper etc. – and accordingly the shape of the extracted citation network affect the quality of results.

6   Conclusion and Future Work

In this paper a novel algorithm – LC – was presented to recommend scientific papers to read. It incorporates a topic-structure similarity and makes high usage of the structure of citation networks in order to recommend papers. Furthermore, two other algorithms were adapted to recommend papers based on the structure of the citation network – Modularity Clustering and Main Path Analysis. In an online user study the algorithms were evaluated. It was found that the novel algorithm produced the best results. Incorporating the SPC weights from Main Path Analysis on the other hand seemed to worsen the quality of recommendations. All algorithms were furthermore compared to an existing CF based approach to recommend papers. It was shown that the novel algorithm produced an equally high precision but generated more recommendations. The results indicate that a combination of the novel algorithm with Modularity Clustering might further improve the results.

However, since only a small amount of users participated in the studies, these results need to be verified in future surveys. In these the participants will be asked to select the seed paper themselves in order to ensure their expertise when rating the quality of the recommendations.

References

1. Andresen, E.M.: Criteria for assessing the tools of disability outcomes research. Arch. Phys. Med. Rehabil. **81**, 15–20 (2000)
2. Batagelj, V.: Efficient algorithms for citation network analysis (2003). arXiv preprint cs/0309023
3. Charles, C.: Analysis of Communication Flow in Online Chats. Master's thesis, University of Duisburg-Essen (2013)
4. Clauset, A., Newman, M.E., Moore, C.: Finding community structure in very large networks. Phys. Rev. E **70**(6), 066111 (2004)

5. Ding, Y., Zhang, G., Chambers, T., Song, M., Wang, X., Zhai, C.: Content-based citation analysis: the next generation of citation analysis. J. Assoc. Inf. Sci. Technol. **65**(9), 1820–1833 (2014)

6. Garfield, E.: Abcs of cluster mapping. 1. most active fields in the life sciences in 1978. Curr. Contents **40**, 5–12 (1980)

7. Garfield, E., et al.: Can citation indexing be automated. In: Statistical Association Methods for Mechanized Documentation, Symposium Proceedings, pp. 189–192 (1965)

8. He, X., Zha, H., Ding, C.H., Simon, H.D.: Web document clustering using hyperlink structures. Comput. Stat. Data Anal. **41**(1), 19–45 (2002)

9. Hummon, N.P., Doreian, P.: Connectivity in a citation network: the development of dna theory. Soc. Netw. **11**(1), 39–63 (1989)

10. Lee, J., Lee, K., Kim, J.G.: Personalized academic research paper recommendation system (2013). arXiv preprint arXiv:1304.5457

11. Liu, J.S., Lu, L.Y.: An integrated approach for main path analysis: development of the hirsch index as an example. J. Am. Soc. Inf. Sci. Technol. **63**(3), 528–542 (2012)

12. McNee, S.M., Albert, I., Cosley, D., Gopalkrishnan, P., Lam, S.K., Rashid, A.M., Konstan, J.A., Riedl, J.: On the recommending of citations for research papers. In: Proceedings of the 2002 ACM Conference on Computer Supported Cooperative Work, pp. 116–125. ACM (2002)

13. Mihalcea, R., Tarau, P.: Textrank: bringing order into texts. In: Proceedings of EMNLP, vol. 4, p. 275, Barcelona, Spain (2004)

14. Pohl, S., Radlinski, F., Joachims, T.: Recommending related papers based on digital library access records (2007). CoRR abs/0704.2902

15. Small, H.: Co-citation in the scientific literature: a new measure of the relationship between two documents. J. Am. Soc. Inf. Sci. **24**(4), 265–269 (1973)

16. Strohman, T., Croft, W.B., Jensen, D.: Recommending citations for academic papers. In: Proceedings of the 30th Annual International ACM SIGIR Conference on Research and Development in Information Retrieval, pp. 705–706. ACM (2007)

17. Sugiyama, K., Kan, M.Y.: Scholarly paper recommendation via user's recent research interests. In: Proceedings of the 10th Annual Joint Conference on Digital Libraries, pp. 29–38. ACM (2010)

18. Teufel, S., Siddharthan, A., Tidhar, D.: Automatic classification of citation function. In: Proceedings of the 2006 Conference on Empirical Methods in Natural Language Processing, pp. 103–110. Association for Computational Linguistics (2006)

19. Torres, R., McNee, S.M., Abel, M., Konstan, J.A., Riedl, J.: Enhancing digital libraries with techlens+. In: Proceedings of the 4th ACM/IEEE-CS Joint Conference on Digital Libraries, pp. 228–236. ACM (2004)

20. Wise, M.J.: Yap 3: improved detection of similarities in computer program and other texts. In: ACM SIGCSE Bulletin, vol. 28, pp. 130–134. ACM (1996)

Every Answer Has a Question: Exploring Communication and Knowledge Exchange in MOOCs Through Learning Analytics

Irene-Angelica Chounta[(✉)], Tobias Hecking, and H. Ulrich Hoppe

University of Duisburg-Essen, Duisburg, Germany
{chounta,hecking,hoppe}@collide.info

Abstract. This paper aims to explore the use of common learning analytics methods, such as activity metrics and network analytics, in order to study and analyse the activity of users and the communication flow in discussion forums that serve Massive Open Online Courses (MOOCS). We particularly seek to identify trends and patterns that may potentially be used to support the communication and information exchange between MOOCs participants. To that end, we applied existing metrics and methods on the log files of a discussion forum that supported participants' communication for a Coursera MOOC. We present the methodology of the study as well as the results and findings with respect to knowledge exchange and information flow in the case of a massive online course.

Keywords: Moocs · Learning analytics · Activity metrics · Network analytics · Discussion forums

1 Introduction

Over the past few years, Massive Open Online Courses (MOOCs) have gained the attention focus in the research fields of collaborative and technology-enhanced learning. MOOCs became increasingly popular after 2012 when traditional educational learning spaces shifted into online contexts [1] with examples such as Coursera (https://www.coursera.org/.). The greatest benefit of MOOCs, besides openness and accessibility, is the social interaction of individual learners with large communities. Discussion forums are used to facilitate communication and information exchange between MOOCs participants within a social context. However, the massive participation makes extremely difficult the analysis and assessment of communication and information flow. In addition, it is not clear what kind of user interactions can be characterized as meaningful, thus promoting communication and, consequently, information exchange and knowledge building [2].

The main objective of this paper is to explore the use of automated and semi-automated metrics that derive from traditional learning analytic approaches in a MOOC context. In particular, we look for meaningful metrics that could potentially provide insight with respect to participation behavior in MOOCs and could be further used to characterize and assess the communication, information exchange and knowledge

© Springer International Publishing Switzerland 2015
N. Baloian et al. (Eds.): CRIWG 2015, LNCS 9334, pp. 140–147, 2015.
DOI: 10.1007/978-3-319-22747-4_11

building patterns in such learners groups. For the purpose of our study, we used the log files from a discussion board that supported a 2-months MOOC to extract metrics of user activity. In addition, we applied network analytics to trace the information flow between the participants of the course. Finally, we compared the different set of metrics in order to discover communication patterns existing in MOOCs.

2 Related Work

The term "learning analytics" is used to describe the activity of collecting and analyzing data of learners in order to understand and support the learning process. Although qualitative analysis of such data is necessary to gain a deep understanding of learning activities, data-driven approaches can provide valuable insight and suggest ways for further improvement [3]. This is particularly challenging nowadays with the explosion of big and the multi-dimensional data [4]. Plain metrics that represent activity volume, such as the sum of messages or the average number of words are commonly used to assess students' practice [5]. Additionally, network graphs and social network analysis techniques are quite popular in the field of technology-enhanced learning. Metrics from network theory, such as density and centrality, are used to assess the communication and coordination among users during learning activities [6, 7].

Online discussions, in terms of knowledge exchange, have attracted researchers over decades. One of the main goals is to define and identify expertise in such online forums. Measures of expertise can be based on the quantity of questions and answers users post to a forum or their position in the Q/A communication network [8]. However, there can be huge differences in the function and communication structure of different discussion forums. Little is known about the structure of knowledge exchange through forums in online courses although it is known that only a small fraction of registered participants on a large MOOC or discussion forums are really engaged over to complete course, completing all course activities [9]. There are often a few highly active users who have an influence on the whole community [10]. Regarding the vulnerability of the communication processes and the diffusion of information, Gillani et al. [2] have showed that it is often sufficient to take out a small amount of important users in order to interrupt the communication and information flow significantly.

3 Method of the Study

3.1 Background

In this paper, we study a Coursera MOOC, named "Introduction to Cooperate Finance" that took place over a two-month period, from November 2013 to end of December 2013 [11]. The dataset provided no information with respect to the performance of users and the success of students regarding the learning objective. The Finance MOOC was supported by a discussion forum that facilitated the communication between participants. The discussion forum consisted of multiple subforums that were divided thematically (e.g. general discussion, assignments, course feedback etc.) and each subforum consisted of multiple user-created threads. A user could start a new thread by simply creating a new post. Moreover, a user had the right to comment on an existing post. The MOOC participants could post or comment in the discussion forum either using a personalized user account or anonymously. However, the anonymous users (1826 logfile entries from "anonymous" users with no further identification, such as IP address etc.) were removed from the analysis due to the fact that we aim to use personalized metrics.

3.2   Metrics and Application

For the purposes of our study, we have used activity metrics that derive from the log files of the discussion forum and represent volume and ratio of activity per user. These metrics are: the number of threads that a user has submitted a post (*#threads*); the number of sub forums that a user has submitted a post (*#forums*); the number of posts of a user (*#posts*); the average number of words per message per user (*wordratio*); the average sum of votes per message per user. Each user can add a ($\pm$) to a post (*voteratio*).

In addition, the forum posts were used to extract networks and apply network analytics metrics. For the network extraction, we classified the posts in categories according to their content. For the classification, we used a tag set classifying posts into four categories, namely "questions", "answers", "social" and "other". Other tag sets are more fine-grained differentiating between different types of questions and answers [12]. Since we aim to distinguish between active information givers and active information seekers as in [13], the reduced tag set is sufficient. As social posts, we identify posts that have a social dimensions (people looking for study groups or participants from the same country etc.) while as "others" we identify the posts that do not fall in any of the three, previous categories. Taking into account the posts classified as "questions" and "answers", we build a network of posts that link to each other. In order to build this network, we applied the following rules:

- Questions within threads are usually followed by answers. Therefore, we decompose threads as linked activity between sequences of questions and answers.
- Each post that is classified as an answer is linked directly to its parent post, provided the parent post is a question.
- An answer that is posted as a comment to a previous answer is considered to provide further information and therefore is linked to the outgoing neighbors of the parent post.

Additionally, we used similarity measures to identify lexical overlap among sequential posts. In discussion, disentanglement of chats or unstructured forums structural rules for linking contributions are often accompanied by measures of similarity between sequential posts [14]. We used lexical overlap to further refine the links between posts. The post network was further projected into a user network [15] that was used to extract the following metrics, used in this study:

- Z-score: The z-score [8] measures the deviation of the communication pattern of a forum user compared to an imaginary random poster. The z-score is defined as:

$$z - score\,(user) = \frac{a - q}{\sqrt{(a + q)}}$$

- A user who posts more answers than questions has a positive z-score while the opposite is the case for frequent help-seeker. Users who seek for help and give help equally often should have a z-score close to 0.
- Authority score: In the sense of a directed network between forum users based on question-answer relations, a user with a high authority score would be a help seeker who receives help from many other help seekers.
- Hub score: Hubs in forums according to the HITS definition [8, 16]) are those users who give help to many other strong help-givers. A user with high hub score can be considered as extraordinary important for the knowledge exchange in the network since other help-givers rely on the user's advice.

Inreach and outreach: The inreach and the outreach combine posting quantity and network centrality measures. Given a single node i in a weighted and directed network, the diversity of its in and outgoing relations can be characterised by a measure of entropy. Eq. (1) calculates the diversity of outgoing relations for a node i, where $w(e_{i,j})$ is the weight/multiplicity of an edge from i to j and $od(i)$ is the out-degree i (taking into account edge weights), which is equal to the number of its help giving posts.

$$H_{out}\,(i) = -\frac{1}{od\,(i)} \sum_{j \in outneigh(i)} w\left(e_{i,j}\right) * \log\left(\frac{w\left(e_{i,j}\right)}{od(i)}\right) \tag{1}$$

The value for the neighbourhood entropy of node i reaches its maximum if all posts of i address different users and its minimum 0 on the other extreme. In order combine diversity and help giving activity the number of help giving posts of node i (= $od(i)$) can be multiplied with ($H_{out}(i) + 1$) resulting in Eq. (2) for the outreach.

$$outreach\,(i) = od\,(i) - \sum_{j \in outneigh(i)} w\left(e_{i,j}\right) * \log\left(\frac{w\left(e_{i,j}\right)}{od(i)}\right) \tag{2}$$

As a result the outreach of i is at minimum the number of its help giving posts, if all posts address the same user. The formula for the inreach (help-seeking behaviour) replaces the out-degree in the formula in-degree.

4   Analysis and Results

4.1   Analysis

For the purpose of the study, we applied the aforementioned activity and network metrics on the Coursera MOOC dataset. From the dataset we removed the outliers, i.e. users who contributed no posts or that their activity could not be linked to the activity of other users or the community. Eventually, the dataset that we studied consisted of 857 participants who created 5028 posts, while the main part of the activity was spread over

31 threads and 11 forums. The 82.87 % of the participants contributed less than 10 posts overall throughout the duration of the MOOC, while only a 1.28 % of the participants contributed 50 posts or more. The 78.79 % of the users posted in less than five different threads while only the 1.05 % of the users posted in more than half of the existing threads. Finally, the 46.39 % of the participants posted in one or two subforums but only 0.23 % of the population participated in all subforums. The distribution of users over the number of posts, threads and subforums is presented in Fig. 1.

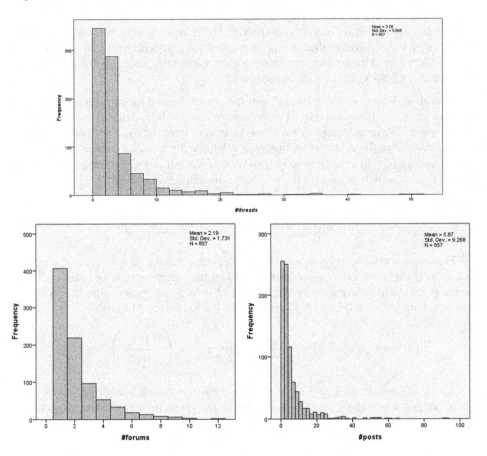

Fig. 1. Distribution of users over number of posts, threads and subforums

4.2 Results

The descriptive analysis of the dataset indicated that the distribution of users over the discussion forum was concentrated over specific threads and that the participants did not scattered over different thematic areas (subforums). In addition, it was shown that most of the participants had a small contribution, in terms of posting activity, and mostly focused on asking and answering questions. In order to explore this further, we extracted a network of users based on their posting activity and in particular, the help-giving relations between the users. On the aforementioned network we applied network analytic metrics and further studied the results in relation to the logfile activity metrics, as described earlier. To that end we used the Spearman's Rank correlation coefficient ρ since the data are not normally distributed. Regarding the activity metrics as calculated per participant, the number of threads, forums and posts that participants are active all correlate highly ($\rho > 0.8$, $p < 0.01$). Users who have a high volume of activity also spread a lot among threads and forums. The volume of activity (number of posts, threads and forums) also correlates with the number of votes received on average per user. This finding possibly indicates that the most active forum users, usually considered as "gurus" or "help-givers", and other participants use to show appreciation or preference by voting for their posts. The average number of words that participants use per post does not correlate significantly with any other metric, other than the vote ratio (on a low level, $\rho = 0.163$, $p < 0.01$). On the one hand, high posting activity does not necessarily lead to long posts. On the other hand, it is expected that well-elaborated comments, thus longer, will get more votes from other users.

In addition, we studied the distribution of the network metrics of the participants described in Sect. 3.2. The majority of the participants have low scores for the network metrics that were used in this study. The distribution of the inreach and outreach is similar, showing that the users of the forum are asking questions and providing answers equally. Moreover, most of the users portray low authority and hub scores. This means that they do not contribute significantly in the knowledge exchange and they do not have a key role in the communication and information flow. This finding comes in agreement with the results from the activity metrics analysis and confirms that the majority of the participants might be perceived as circumstantial users of the discussion forum that support the course, rather than exchanging information and communicating.

Some of the high correlations among the network measures and between the network measures and the z-score are not surprising. In reach and authority score as well as outreach and hub score both increase with the number of ingoing and respectively outgoing connections. Therefore, the correlations between these measures are extraordinary high. However, between in reach and outreach there is no and between authority score and hub score there is only little correlation ($\rho = 0.222$, $p < 0.01$). Consequently, the users in the forum can be seen either as help givers or help seekers but not both in most cases. The high negative correlation ($\rho = 0.78$, $p < 0.01$) between in reach and z-score results from the fact that help seekers with more question post than answer posts have a negative z-score but a higher in reach. More interesting are the statistically significant correlations between the network measures and the other activity metrics. Outreach correlates higher with the number of threads and forums compared to in reach. This could mean that users who are help-givers spread information in a more diverse way while help-seekers tend to ask their questions in dedicated threads and sub forums. There is also a slight correlation between outreach and votes ratio ($\rho = 0.166$, $p < 0.01$) as well as between hub score and vote ratio ($\rho = 0.127$, $p < 0.01$). Consequently, help givers are more likely to receive votes for their posts than help seekers.

5   Conclusion and Future Work

This paper presents the application of common learning analytics in MOOC discussion forums. The main objective of the study was to track and study the interactions among participants of a 2-months MOOC with respect to the communication and the knowledge exchange between them. A discussion board was used in order to facilitate the communication of users. We used the user data from the discussion board in order to build a network based on user interactions (questions – answers, posts - comments) and then we applied user activity metrics and network analytics. From the descriptive analysis of the activity metrics, it was shown that the majority of posts in a MOOC discussion forum can be classified as questions & answers (63.76 %) while the "social" posts are considerably less (14.70 %). Furthermore, it was evident that the majority of participants were not particularly active, with about 82.7 % of the users contributing less than 10 posts in a two months period and keeping focus on certain threads. However, the participants with high posting activity, also spread among threads and sub forums. These participants are identified as "help-givers" since they provide more answers than questions and get voted more from the rest of the community. The structure and the placement of the node, i.e. to whom the particular participant provides answers, is crucial and reveals the need to motivate users to contribute more.

These findings pinpoints the vulnerability of communication between participants in MOOCs as well as the inadequacy of existing tools to support knowledge exchange and promote participation on a massive scale. However, the advantage of MOOCs is partly this massiveness and the opportunity to learn and socialize with and through a large community. In order to benefit from what is considered to be one of MOOCs greatest advantages, i.e. learning within a large group and through social interaction – there is the need to motivate participants not only to contribute in discussions and information sharing but also to guide these contributions. Furthermore, the need of methods and tools to provide insights on the meaningful activities that participants should be engaged in as well as to assess the effectiveness of communication and knowledge building is also evident. In future work, we aim to explore and study what kind of user interactions are critical for the effective communication among MOOCs participants and in what ways we can promote and assess knowledge building in MOOC communities.

References

1. Kay, J., Reimann, P., Diebold, E., Kummerfeld, B.: MOOCs: so many learners, so much potential. IEEE Intell. Syst. **28**, 70–77 (2013)
2. Gillani, N., Yasseri, T., Eynon, R., Hjorth, I.: Structural limitations of learning in a crowd: communication vulnerability and information diffusion in MOOCs. Sci. Rep. 4, (2014)
3. Siemens, G., Long, P.: Penetrating the fog: analytics in learning and education. Educ. Rev. **46**, 30 (2011)
4. Mayer, M.: Innovation at Google: the physics of data. In: PARC Forum (2009)
5. Voyiatzaki, E., Avouris, N.: Support for the teacher in technology-enhanced collaborative classroom. Educ. Inf. Technol. **19**, 129–154 (2014)

6. Hoppe, H.U., Engler, J., Weinbrenner, S.: The impact of structural characteristics of concept maps on automatic quality measurement. In: International Conference of the Learning Sciences (ICLS 2012), Sydney, Australia (2012)
7. Chounta, I.-A., Hecking, T., Hoppe, H.U., Avouris, N.: Two make a network: using graphs to assess the quality of collaboration of dyads. In: Baloian, N., Burstein, F., Ogata, H., Santoro, F., Zurita, G. (eds.) CRIWG 2014. LNCS, vol. 8658, pp. 53–66. Springer, Heidelberg (2014)
8. Zhang, J., Ackerman, M.S., Adamic, L.: Expertise networks in online communities: structure and algorithms. In: Proceedings of the 16th international conference on World Wide Web. pp. 221–230. ACM (2007)
9. Clow, D.: MOOCs and the funnel of participation. In: Proceedings of the Third International Conference on Learning Analytics and Knowledge. pp. 185–189. ACM (2013)
10. Wong, J.-S., Pursel, B., Divinsky, A., Jansen, B.J.: An Analysis of MOOC Discussion Forum Interactions from the Most Active Users. In: Agarwal, N., Xu, K., Osgood, N. (eds.) SBP 2015. LNCS, vol. 9021, pp. 452–457. Springer, Heidelberg (2015)
11. Rossi, L.A., Gnawali, O.: Language Independent Analysis and Classification of Discussion Threads in Coursera MOOC Forums
12. Kim, S.N., Wang, L., Baldwin, T.: Tagging and linking web forum posts. In: Proceedings of the Fourteenth Conference on Computational Natural Language Learning, pp. 192–202. Association for Computational Linguistics (2010)
13. Stump, G.S., DeBoer, J., Whittinghill, J., Breslow, L.: Development of a framework to classify MOOC discussion forum posts: methodology and challenges. In: NIPS Workshop on Data Driven Education (2013)
14. Hoppe, H.U., Göhnert, T., Steinert, L., Charles, C.: A web-based tool for communication flow analysis of online chats. Networks 11, 39–63 (2014)
15. Harrer, A., Hever, R., Ziebarth, S.: Empowering researchers to detect interaction patterns in e-collaboration. Front. Artif. Intell. Appl. 158, 503 (2007)
16. Kleinberg, J.M.: Authoritative sources in a hyperlinked environment. J. ACM JACM. 46, 604–632 (1999)

Dynamic Credibility Threshold Assignment in Trust and Reputation Mechanisms Using PID Controller

Mohsen Mohkami[✉], Zeinab Noorian, and Julita Vassileva

Department of Computer Science, University of Saskatchewan,
Saskatoon, Saskatchewan, Canada
{m.mohkami,z.noorian,jiv}@cs.usask.ca

Abstract. An e-marketplace is an example of a multi-agent system where buyers try to find the best seller with best Quality of Service (QoS). The uncertainty of open marketplaces have resulted in the design of reputation systems that help buyers find honest feedback from their peers (advisers). Despite the advances in this field, there is no systematic approach for setting the honesty threshold as an acceptable level of honesty of advisers in the Trust and Reputation Management (TRM) systems. Having an appropriate honesty threshold is important in these systems, since having a high threshold would filter away possibly helpful advisers, or the opposite - having a low value for it may permit malicious advisers to badmouth good services. In this paper we propose a self-adaptive honesty threshold management mechanism that adopts PID feedback controller from the field of control systems. Experimental results on a real-world dataset show that having a dynamic honesty threshold increases the successful transaction rate of buyers in a marketplace, and improves the accuracy of the TRM system used in that marketplace.

Keywords: Credibility mechanism · Honesty threshold · Multi-agent systems · Trust modeling · E-commerce

1 Introduction

After almost 20 years since the emergence of the first e-marketplaces, buyers still cannot be completely sure about the honesty of the seller they want to purchase from. This uncertainty is mainly due to the openness of e-marketplaces. All kinds of people can interact in these marketplaces hiding their actual identities. We can expect that malicious sellers may impersonate benevolent ones. Online marketplaces provide consumers with the ability to leave feedback about sellers. However, buyers may be deceived by the number of positive reviews a seller has received, if the reviews are fake. In current e-marketplaces, buyers decide to make a purchase based on reviews left by anyone, and not just by those people who they trust.

© Springer International Publishing Switzerland 2015
N. Baloian et al. (Eds.): CRIWG 2015, LNCS 9334, pp. 148–163, 2015.
DOI: 10.1007/978-3-319-22747-4_12

The performance of an e-commerce systems is a function of a large number of parameters, such as information quality with respect to the accuracy of provided feedback [2], buyers satisfaction and their net benefits [3], service quality of providers, and assurance including the adopted credibility and security measures [22].

Designing reputation systems for open marketplaces seems to be an effective approach to ensure that only participants with satisfactory qualities can prosper [9,26]. Reputation systems assist buyers in their decision making process by providing them with trustworthiness assessment techniques to thoroughly evaluate the credibility of other buyers (advisers), considering various parameters and environmental circumstances.

Different trust and reputation mechanism have been proposed in the literature which model the trustworthiness of participants via different approaches such as socio-cognitive [25], game theoretical [12,28], and probabilistic models [7,24,29]. Although these and other trust models [20] have shown very promising results in accurately modeling the trust of participants, there are certainly opportunities for further optimization with respect to the accuracy of the model. More specifically, existing reputation systems perform under the assumption of the existence of a credibility threshold to retain only trustworthy advisers. The credibility threshold sets a decision boundary on the behavioral model of advisers and characterized them as honest and malicious. These systems suffer from a lack of a systematic approach for adjusting the honesty threshold to the dynamic environmental conditions[1].

Defining the threshold for acceptable level of honesty of advisers is very important. The foremost drawback of having a static honesty threshold is that an inappropriately set threshold would filter away possibly good advice, or the opposite - allow malicious buyers to badmouth good services. A low threshold will result in a plenty of possible advisers, but the quality of advice may be low. In this situation, deceitful advisers who maintain a minimum level of trustworthiness remain undetected and could actively contribute into a buyer's decision making process. On the other hand, a higher credibility threshold leads to the contribution of a smaller number of advisers and can make it impossible to find advisers. Clearly, adjusting a threshold value is a trade-off between the number of credible advisers and the risk of being misled by deceptive peers.

This paper proposes a method by feedback on the performance of the marketplace in terms of QoS metrics to dynamically determine appropriate value for honesty threshold to optimize the market performance. We built a controller that monitors the quality of e-marketplace and uses a Proportional-Integral-Derivative (PID) feedback controller technique [21] to determine new values for the honesty threshold. Buyers then dynamically re-evaluate their network of trustworthy advisers according to the new recommended value.

Our approach was validated experimentally by integrating our PID-based honesty threshold controller into a simulated e-marketplace with different

---

[1] Throughout the paper, the terms *credibility threshold* and *honesty threshold* are used interchangeably.

population tendency. Experimental results show that adaptively tuning the honesty threshold to the market performance enables honest buyers to obtain higher quality of services and more accurately detect malicious advisers in comparison with the static threshold values defined based on designer intuition that are used in previous work.

This work situates well within the context that [10] outlines as the central concern for future research in multi-agent trust modeling. According to [10], artificially adjusting the credibility threshold value might be inappropriate since one of the ways in which trust models can fail to be robust is in relying on a set of untrustworthy advisers. The methods we outline in this paper seek to address this concern.

A credibility evaluation mechanism guided by the PID-based threshold adjustment creates the opportunity of designing self-improving trust and reputation systems which learn from the state of the e-marketplace promoting the acceptance of web-based agent-oriented e-commerce by human users.

The rest of the paper is organized as follows. We discuss in Sect. 2 how our research resides with other approaches for setting credibility threshold. In Sect. 3, we present the credibility evaluation mechanism to provide context to our proposals and to the experiments which follows. We then describe our proposed approach of adaptive credibility threshold adjustment in Sect. 4. In Sect. 5, we provide experimental results on the real-world dataset demonstrating the effectiveness of our approach in comparison with other static threshold management approach. Finally, we conclude our current work and propose some directions for future research in Sect. 6.

2   Related Work

Generally speaking, in most current e-commerce websites such as eBay and Amazon all of the users act as advisers for each other. That is, the trust and reputation management systems within these websites calculate the global reputation of entities, sellers and products. As a result of these cumulative ratings for a seller or item, the users of that system decide whether to buy that item (e.g. in Amazon), or conduct business with a seller (e.g. in eBay).

A global reputation is not the best approach for these marketplaces. It is not rational to consider everyone as our advisers without thinking about who these users may be. This is not logical for two main reasons:

1. In any e-marketplace, even in a marketplace in the real world, there inevitably exist users who intentionally want to deceive others through their advice or ratings. For example, it is widely known and a lot of the ratings on several websites are fake [16,18], introduced by either malicious users who collude with restaurant or hotel owners to raise their reputation or to badmouth the competitors. They mostly entrap victims to lead them to do their desired actions, which is purchasing desirable items from their favorite sellers. These malicious users usually try to take advantage of the market system's limitations to achieve their goals. Considering these circumstances, we do not want to be misled by invalid ratings.

2. Even if we ideally think of a malicious-free society, there are other factors that we should take into account. Not all users are alike and think the same way. The members of a marketplace can give feedback and rate products and sellers based on their interests, preferences, priorities. Naturally, we prefer to use those users' ratings who have the same interests as we do, (i.e. our taste-mates).

Consequently, a way to help the users of a community is by allowing them to make decisions based on the feedback of users similar to them. Thus, they only receive advice from those users who are trustworthy enough to overcome the first issue, and have a similar way of thinking to address the second problem.

This idea is the basis of the collaborative filtering method developed in the Recommender Systems area. As the authors in [8] lay out, neighborhood-based collaborative filtering methods have three steps:

1. Calculating the similarity of all users with the active user
2. Choosing a subset of similar users as advisers
3. Computing a prediction for items based on advisers' ratings

However, generally, collaborative filtering systems do not involve the second step mentioned in the list above. They take into account all users that have had the same experience as the active user to be advisers [13, 14, 23]. As authors mention in [8], it is expensive in terms of computation to calculate the similarity of all users that can be considered as advisers. Moreover, it is not useful and effective as there may be only a few users who share the same taste with the active users. As a result, to help the system achieve better performance in terms of accurate predictions, several studies have considered limiting the number of advisers in a system [6, 8]. In order to do so, they use two techniques to determine the number of advisers for each user. The first technique is setting an absolute correlation threshold. This threshold decides which users are qualified to be assigned as an adviser for the active user. For the second technique, they limit the number of advisers to the best n number of users who have the highest values in terms of similarity.

As study [8] shows, there is a conspicuous inverse relationship between the correlation threshold and coverage in the results. In other words, if the system chooses a higher correlation threshold, fewer advisers for a user will remain. Therefore, the user can predict the rating value of fewer items due to the lack of information and advice from its advisers. On the other hand, the value of the correlation threshold has a direct impact on the accuracy of the system. The user can make sure the remaining advisers have a minimum proven predicting value and that they provide a more accurate rating than when there are unreliable advisers helping the user as well. As we can see, there is a trade-off between having high coverage and high accuracy by choosing a correlation threshold value. Study [6] attempts to limit the number of advisers in a trust and reputation management system. As Gorner mentions in [6], we have to find an appropriate "sweet spot" that brings us the most reliable results. Therefore, he tries to find the parameters for the threshold value and the maximum number of neighbors that provide more accurate trust-modeling results. Based on their experimental results, he recommends the value 0.55 for the threshold value and 30 as the best value for the maximum number of advisers.

3　Credibility Evaluation Mechanism

Our proposed credibility evaluation mechanism adopts a variation of our previous work, *Prob-Cog* model [19], and formalizes the credibility degree of advisers in different steps.

Suppose that a buyer c sends a query to advisers requesting information about sellers $P = \{p_1, p_2, .., p_j, .., p_m\}$ on the outcomes of the interactions between the advisers and sellers occurring within a time threshold t (which diminishes the risk of changeability in sellers' behaviour). Adviser a_i responds by providing a rating vector R_{ij} for each seller, for example p_j. It contains a tuple $\langle r, s \rangle$, which indicates the number of successful (r) and unsuccessful (s) interaction outcomes with seller p_j respectively. Once the evidence is received, for each R_{ij}, buyer c calculates the expected value of the probability of a positive outcome ($P_r(R_{ij})$) for seller p_j based on a beta distribution [11] as follows:

$$P_r(R_{ij}) = \frac{r+1}{r+s+2} \tag{1}$$

Clearly, $0 < P_r(R_{ij}) < 1$ and as it approaches 0 or 1, it indicates *unanimity* in the body of evidence [31]. That is, particularly large values of s or r provide better intuition about an overall tendency and quality of sellers. In contrast, $P_r(R_{ij}) \approx 0.5$ (i.e. $r \approx s$) signifies the maximal conflict in gathered evidence, resulting in increasing the uncertainty in determining the quality of sellers. Based on these intuitions, we are able to calculate the degree of reliability and certainty of ratings provided by advisers. More formally, let x represent the probability of a successful outcome for a certain seller. Based on the Definitions (1) and (3) in [31], the *reliability degree* of each R_{ij} can be defined as follows:

$$Conf(R_{ij}) = \frac{1}{2} \int_0^1 \left| \frac{x^r(1-x)^s}{\int_0^1 x^r(1-x)^s \, dx} - 1 \right| \, dx \tag{2}$$

Theoretical analysis [31] demonstrates that, for a fixed ratio of positive and negative observations, the reliability increases as the number of observations increases. On the contrary, given a fixed number of observations, as the extent of conflict increases, the reliability of the provided observations decreases accordingly. That is, reliability is at a minimum when $P_r(R_{ij}) = 0.5$. As such, the less conflict in their ratings, the more reliable the advisers would be.

However, buyer c should not strictly judge the advisers with rather low reliability in their R_{ij} as deceptive advisers since this reliability factor could signify both the dishonesty of advisers and the dynamic and fraudulent behaviour of sellers reported by the advisers. For example, some malicious sellers may supply satisfactory quality of products in some situations when there is not much at stake and act conversely in other occasions associated with a large gain.

To address this ambiguity, buyer c computes $P_r(R_{cj})$ and $Conf(R_{cj})$ based on her personal experience, R_{cj}, with a set of sellers P with whom the advisers also have experience.[2] Through the comparison of advisers' metrics with the buyer's experience, the buyer would have more trust in those advisers with a similar rating pattern and satisfactory level of honesty. More formally, buyer c measures an average level of dishonesty of a_i by:

$$D_h(a_i) = \frac{\sum_{j=1}^{|P|} | P_r(R_{cj}) - P_r(R_{ij}) |}{|P|} \qquad (3)$$

It may also happen that an honest adviser lacks experience with sellers. Thus, despite her inherent honesty, its reliability degree is low and it should not be highly trusted. To address this, we introduce an uncertainty function $U_n(a_i)$ to capture the intuition of information imbalance between c and a_i as follows:

$$U_n(a_i) = \frac{\sum_{j=1}^{|P|} | Conf(R_{cj}) - Conf(R_{ij}) |}{|P|} \qquad (4)$$

Given the level of dishonesty of adviser a_i, the honesty of the adviser could be calculated as $1 - D_h(a_i)$. Similarly, given the uncertainty of adviser a_i, the certainty of the adviser would be $1 - U_n(a_i)$. Thus, a credible adviser should achieve higher honesty and certainty simultaneously. The *credibility degree* of adviser a_i is then calculated by reducing her honesty based on her certainty degree as follows:

$$CR(a_i) = (1 - D_h(a_i)) \times (1 - U_n(a_i)) \qquad (5)$$

To retain only the most trustworthy advisers, an *honesty threshold*, β where $0 \leqslant \beta \leqslant 1$, is used to determine behavioral patterns of advisers. That is, if $CR(a_i) \geq \beta$, a_i will be counted as a *credible* adviser. In contrast, if $CR(a_i) < \beta$, a_i will be detected as *malicious* adviser and would be filtered out from the buyer c's advisers network.

4   PID-based Credibility Threshold Management

Inspired by the existing electronic commerce quality models[3] [2,3,22], we consider three factors that contribute to performance of e-marketplaces, including, (1) market liquidity (denoted by $Mliq$), (2) information asymmetry, and (3) buyers satisfaction.

Market liquidity describes a marketplace's ability to facilitate trading of the products promptly without transaction cost (i.e., having to considerably reduce

---

[2] Here, we choose a set of sellers $P \subset \{p_1, ..., p_m\}$ with whom buyer c has sufficient experience, to make sure that the buyer has sufficient knowledge to judge the advisers.

[3] Different from other approaches, we ascribe the performance of the e-commerce system only to the quality of its participants (buyers and sellers) in conducting transaction.

their price) [4]. It also denotes the ability of buyers to find products with desirable features, when needed. However, the open nature of e-commerce, the existence of variety of products with competing features, and the lack of honesty enforcement mechanism make buyers uncertain in discovering the best-suited transaction partners (i.e., trust-wise and profit-wise),thus affecting the liquidity of the market.

Information asymmetry measures whether a buyer has sufficient information to make rational purchase decision in the e-marketplace. Higher information asymmetry is particularly salient in online environments. The buyers suffer from the risk of purchasing the low quality products, which differ from the descriptions claimed by sellers. The availability of credible advisers can effectively reduce the information asymmetry [27].

Finally, *buyer satisfaction* can be measured using the ratio of transactions with successful outcome to all the transactions conducted by buyers.

Through the proposed credibility threshold management, each buyer can further adjust her social network of credible advisers by considering the overall performance of the e-marketplace. For example, a marketplace with poor performance might imply that a considerate amount of advisers and sellers might be malicious. In this case, each buyer might want to carefully check other buyers' qualification as her advisers by increasing the credibility threshold β. In other words, when the community is populated with deceitful advisers, buyers would find it difficult to access honest feedback about sellers. Hence, the buyers should require more credible advisers by increasing β. This can help them to detect and exclude more dishonest advisers from their network, and thus obtain opinions of higher quality advisers.

If $\text{SuccessNum}_{(c)}$ denotes the number of successful outcomes achieved by c in a time stamp t, $\text{transactionNum}_{(c)}$ indicates the number of transactions conducted within t, $\text{purchaseNum}_{(c)}$ denotes the number of transactions that c initially *intended* to perform within t as indicated in its purchase mission[4], we can formulate the *transaction success rate* (throughput) and the *transaction rate* of the buyer c denoted by $tp(c)$ and $tr(c)$ for the time stamp t as follows:

$$tp(c,t) = \frac{\text{SuccessNum}_{(c,t)}}{\text{transactionNum}_{(c,t)}} \qquad (6)$$

$$tr(c,t) = \frac{\text{transactionNum}_{(c,t)}}{\text{purchaseNum}_{(c,t)}} \qquad (7)$$

To accurately adjust β, the central server should have a global observation of the system performance. Therefore, buyers are asked to periodically share their $tr(c)$ and $tp(c)$ with the *e-marketplace central server* (ECS). The values of $tr(c)$ and $tp(c)$ reflect the behavior of participants in the e-marketplace. For example, having a high transaction rate $tr(c)$ but a low transaction success rate

---

[4] We assume that buyers have a pre-determined purchase missions such that they enter the market to buy certain products.

$tp(c)$ signifies the situation in which a buyer c is misled by dishonest advisers in her network; therefore, could not find high quality sellers.

Given these quality metrics, we propose the performance measures for e-commerce systems as follows:

$$Q(t) = \frac{2 * tp(t) * Mliq(t)}{tp(t) + Mliq(t)} \tag{8}$$

Where $Mliq(t) = \frac{\sum_{i=1}^{n} tr(c_i)}{n}$ and $tp(t) = \frac{\sum_{i=1}^{n} tp(c_i)}{n}$ are the average of all $tr(c)$ and $tp(c)$ shared by buyers at time stamp t, and $Q(t)$ is the *harmonic mean* of the e-commerce quality metrics described above. Since the performance of the marketplace is a function of these quality metrics, we use a harmonic mean to balance them by mitigating the impact of the one with a larger value and aggravating the impact of the other with a lower value.

To adjust β accordingly, ECS adopts the idea of feedback controller, specifically, PID controller [30]. Given a designated goal in a system, called the reference r, the feedback control system calculates the error by differentiating the actual outcome, called y, and the reference r. PID controllers provide a means to minimize the error in a system based on the received feedback [21].

In e-commerce systems, the ultimate goal is to maximize the performance of marketplaces in terms of buyers' satisfaction degree and market liquidity, achieving $Q(t) = 1$, so we initialize the goal r to $r = 1$. We designate error, $e(t)$, in the e-commerce system as the difference between the actual performance of the system $Q(t)$ and the goal r which is $e(t) = r - Q(t)$.

In the ideal e-commerce systems in which no malicious buyers exist $Q(t)$ could converge to one. However, in a realistic situation where the marketplace is populated with different participants with various behavioral dispositions, it is not reasonable to expect the perfect performance of the system; therefore, the system will have $Q(t) < 1$.

Given these values, ECS calculates a new value for β that improves $Q(t)$ to reach the idealistic goal $r = 1$. To this end, ECS incorporates PID controller to determine the extent that it has to change the value of β.

The new recommended value of β for the next time stamp $t + 1$ is formulated as follows:

$$\beta(t + 1) = \beta(t) + \beta_0(t + 1) \tag{9}$$

in which $\beta_0(t + 1)$ is formalized using the PID controller presented as,

$$\beta_0(t + 1) = k_p e(t) + k_i \int_0^t e(\tau) d\tau + k_d \frac{de(t)}{dt} \tag{10}$$

Where k_p, k_i, and k_d are the coefficients that leverage the contribution of *Proportional* **P**, which captures the error $e(t)$ calculated in the time stamp t, *Integral* **I**, which accumulates all errors from the start of the e-marketplace, and *Derivative* **D**, which calculates the deviation of current error $e(t)$ from its previous value $e(t - 1)$, respectively.

Input: t : starting time of e-marketplace;
              t_i: current time of e-marketplace;
              t_n: end of time of e-marketplace;
              $\beta(t)$: β initially set to 0.55 ;
              A : set of advisers;
              C: set of buyers;
Output: $\beta(t_n)$;
while $t_i \leq t_n$ **do**
    foreach $c \in C$ **do**
        c filters its advisers in A, based on $\beta(t_i)$;
        c shares $tr(c)$ and $tp(c)$ with ECS;
    end
    ESC computes *mean* of transaction success rate, $tp(t_i)$;
    ECS computes *mean* of transaction rate, $Mliq(t_i)$;
    ECS computes $Q(t_i)$ using Eq. 8;
    if $|Q(t_i) - Q(t_i - 1)| > \sigma$ **then**
        ECS computes $\beta_0(t_i + 1)$ using Eq. 10;
        ECS computes $\beta(t_i + 1)$ using Eq. 9;
    else
        $\beta(t_i + 1) := \beta(t_i)$;
    end
    $t_i = t_i + 1$;
end

Algorithm 1. PID-based honesty threshold adjustment algorithm

Since in the e-marketplace it is unrealistic to expect $Q(t)$ reaches the value of r (due to the activity of malicious participants), ECS would stop adjusting β if $Q(t)$ reaches a stable point.

More formally, ECS updates the value of β for the next time stamp $t + 1$, given the following conditions:

$$\beta(t + 1) = \begin{cases} \beta(t) + \beta_0(t + 1) & |Q(t) - Q(t - 1)| > \sigma \\ \beta(t) & \text{otherwise} \end{cases} \qquad (11)$$

Where σ is a trigger threshold.

The pseudo code summary of adjusting β in the proposed PID-based credibility threshold management is shown in Algorithm 1.

5   Experiments

To show that the proposed approach can function well in the real world the proposed approach is tested on a real-world dataset. The dataset gathered from the website Yelp.com has attributes that make it suitable to test the proposed approach. And this dataset is widely used in literature as in [15,16]. Yelp.com is one of crowdsourcing websites which consumers use to provide their opinions about local businesses. These opinions are gathered in the forms of 5-star likert scale ratings and comments as text. Yelp call its members (users) Yelpers, and these Yelpers have written over 61 million local reviews, according to [1]. This website has been quite successful in attracting users and obtaining their reviews and in 2011 it had more than 10 million reviews [15]. Each review written by every user in this website is shown to the public. The rating given to a business affects its overall reputation in the system since the reputation of a business is simply the average of all the ratings that business has received.

This dataset obtained on October 11, 2014 and containing data about five cities: Phoenix, Las Vegas, Madison, Waterloo and Edinburgh. Generally, Yelp has 22 categories for businesses, and 42,153 businesses have registered on the website. Almost 18,000 of the businesses registered on the website are under the Food and Restaurants categories, so these two categories include the majority of businesses on the website followed by shopping with more than 6,000 businesses. Note that each business can be categorized under more than one category. Almost 253,000 users exist in the system, providing it with approximately 1,125,500 reviews. Roughly 70 % of these reviews have been given to businesses under the Restaurants and Foods categories. More than 75 % of users have given at least one review in these two categories. In order to evaluate our proposed approach, we consider businesses under the Restaurants and Food categories that include the majority of businesses.

To adjust the dataset for our needs we consider each business as a seller and reviews as purchases that buyers(users) make.

5.1 Experimental Settings

In order to be able to measure the efficiency of the PID thresholding approach, the trust modeling has to be able to model the trust values in the system. As described in detail in previous chapters, the trust model used for this experiment works based on similar businesses that users have interacted with. Since in the dataset exist users who have given a few number of reviews for businesses and it affects the operation of the TRM system, we need to remove these users and keep users who have had interactions with similar businesses. Therefore the TRM system can model the trustworthiness values of users. As a result, in this experiment we only considered users in the system who have left at least 50 reviews. This limitation left us with acceptable numbers of users, businesses and reviews used for experiments in literature. This experiment is conducted with 1348 users, 15537 businesses and 128586 reviews. The date of reviews considered for the experiment is from 2011-01-01 to 2014-07-16.

The TRM system models the trust values that each user has in other users between the year 2011 and 2012. After modeling their trust values they are assigned as advisers for the user, if they are credible enough, i.e., having a trust value higher than the credibility threshold. The system run starts from year 2012. Subsequently, users seek to make transactions with businesses as exists in the original dataset which brings the distribution of transactions happening in the real word. The decision to initiate a transaction with a business is made by the user and it is entirely based on information about the business received from the user's advisers. The user calculates a reputation value for the business using the information he gathers from his advisers.

To evaluate the success of the transaction we use the following rule: the value calculated using advisers feedback differs more than 0.02 from what the actual user experience with the business, we consider it as unsatisfactory transaction. The real transaction outcome (experience) exists in the dataset as a value between one and five (the users rating of the business), which we normalize between zero and one. At the end of each month, users report the number of their satisfactory and total number of interactions in the system to the central server. And TRM uses the Eqs. 6, 7, 8 to measure the performance of the system. After doing so, it employs the Eqs. 9, 10, 11 to calculate the new value of β for the next time slice.

We compare the outcome of the PID approach with the system which uses fixed credibility threshold of 0.55, the best credibility threshold introduced in the literature [5].

5.2   Experimental Results

The following graphs show the performance of the marketplace during the 30 month period, from 2012-01-01 until 2014-07-16.

Figure 1 illustrates the changes of β throughout the whole period of the experiment when the system uses the PID-based approach compared to when it uses fixed β which is set to 0.55. The credibility threshold of the PID approach starts from the pre-defined β as 0.55 and it almost reaches to 0.7 by the end of the experiment. In the following graphs we will see the effect of this increase of the credibility threshold.

First we measure the transaction rate of the system in both settings, where the TRM uses fixed and PID-based credibility threshold. As we can see in Fig. 2, initially the transaction rate for both cases are the same and this value is 0.788.

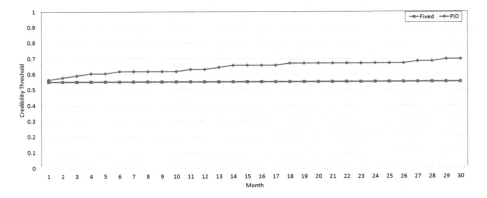

Fig. 1. Credibility threshold value in two settings with fixed and PID-based β

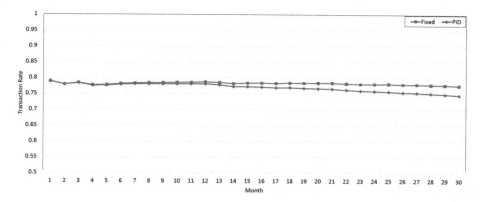

Fig. 2. Transaction rate of marketplaces when users adopt fixed or PID-based β

After the seventh month we can observe a decrease in transaction of the marketplace which uses PID-based credibility threshold. This decrease continues until the end of the experiment period. The transaction rate of the marketplace when a fixed β is used stays at 0.775 while this value for PID-based β becomes 0.745. However, this decline was anticipated. As mentioned in the background section, as we increase the credibility threshold we are limiting the number of advisors. We can see this increase in β in Fig. 1. In other words, users filter out more advisers. As a result, the user may not have enough information about a seller to carry out an intended transaction with that seller, which in turn decreases the transaction rate in the marketplace.

From Fig. 3 we notice that the throughput of the marketplace increases when the TRM uses a PID-based β compared to the time it uses fixed β. Both cases initially have the same value of 0.228 for throughput. Again the changes happen after the seventh month. But this time the throughput increases more for the PID-based approach as it rises to 0.263 while this value for the fixed β approach increases only to 0.243.

As mentioned before, the system tries to improve the harmonic mean of transaction rate and throughput. As we can see in the following graph, the PID approach is successful at increasing this variable in comparison with the fixed approach. Figure 4 shows that this value for both approaches are 0.354 at the beginning of the experiment and then the PID approach starts to increase more that fixed one from the sixth month. By the end of the experiment, 30th month, the PID approach reaches the value of 0.389 while the fixed approach gains the harmonic mean of 0.370.

As can be seen, determining the credibility threshold using PID increases the accuracy of the model and the throughput of the system. On the other hand, it decreases the transaction rate. This was expected as each user filters out a fraction of its advisers by increasing the value of credibility threshold. And it results in less knowledge about a potential business. That is, in this case users do not know much about a business and they may not begin a transaction with that business which will result in lower value of coverage and transaction rate.

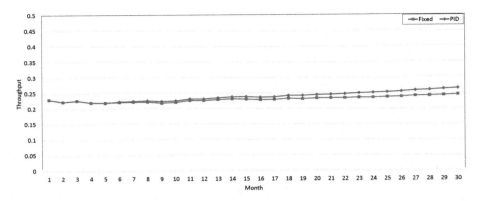

Fig. 3. Transaction success rate of marketplaces when users adopt fixed or PID-based β

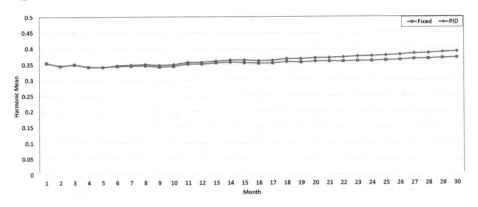

Fig. 4. Harmonic mean of throughput and transaction rate in marketplaces when users adopt fixed or PID-based β

To measure the performance of the two approaches in addition to the metrics discussed above two other metrics are used.

1. Prediction Accuracy: Measured by the Mean Absolute Error (MAE) each approach generates.
2. Prediction Coverage: Number of reviews (items) predicted by the model out of all reviews in the dataset.

In order to measure the accuracy of both approaches we calculate the absolute error of the predictions for each approach. The lower the error, the higher the accuracy.

As we can notice from Table 1, PID approach outperforms fixed approach in terms of accuracy. However, it has a lower coverage. This was expected as each user filters out a fraction of its advisers by increasing the value of credibility threshold, which results in less knowledge available at the decision point about

Table 1. Prediction accuracy of TRM systems when fixed or PID-based β is used

	Fixed	PID
MAE (Mean Absolute Error)	0.1191	0.1150
Coverage	0.9986	0.9980

a potential business. That is, in this case users do not know much about a business and they may not begin a transaction with that business which will result in lower value of coverage and transaction rate.

As can be seen, having a dynamic thresholding management help users find more helpful advisers and therefore have more successful transactions. In addition, this approach results in more accurate predictions for the TRM system used in the marketplace.

6   Conclusion and Future Works

This paper pinpoints a common problem of existing trust and reputation systems in electronic commerce systems. Existing TRM systems have the assumption that a default honesty threshold exists, and most of the times the choice of this value for this "magic" threshold is left to the designers implementing a particular system. Moreover, the advances of the field of trust and reputation management systems have mostly been in the ways to determine the trust values of users in an environment. However, what should be done afterwards has always been lacking.

The credibility threshold used in social networks of buyers should be determined in a dynamic manner and relative to the status of the environment. A low value of credibility threshold results in large number of advisers which might have little or even negative contribution to buyers decision making. On the other hand, having a high level of honesty threshold eliminates more advisers from the social network of buyers- which restricts buyer to acquire sufficient information about sellers.

In this study, an adaptive credibility threshold is introduced which used a controller that monitors the quality of e-marketplace and uses a PID feedback controller technique to determine new values for the honesty threshold to adapt to the changing marketplace. The proposed threshold adjustment works independent of the trust model used in the system, and this makes it well-suited to be incorporated with different credibility evaluation mechanisms and filtering models for electronic marketplaces.

Experimental results show the advantages of adaptive evaluation on the honesty threshold. In particular, we demonstrate that credibility evaluation mechanism guided by PID-based threshold management techniques can increase the performance of the marketplace in terms of satisfactory interactions. It also improves the TRM accuracy in terms of predicting the trust values in the system.

An interesting direction for future work would be to improve the feedback controller method by adopting different dynamic performance metrics supported in the market microstructure literature [17], in addition to those considered here. Furthermore, since the buyers' contribution in providing feedback is an essential elements in the performance monitoring of the marketplace, a useful direction for future work would be the incorporation of an incentive mechanism to promote more participation (in terms of providing honest feedback) from the buyers.

References

1. About yelp. http://www.yelp.ca/about. Accessed on 12 December 2014
2. Barnes, S.J., Vidgen, R.: Measuring web site quality improvements: a case study of the forum on strategic management knowledge exchange. Ind. Manage. Data Syst. **103**(5), 297–309 (2003)
3. Delone, W.H.: The delone and mclean model of information systems success: a ten-year update. J. Manage. Inf. Syst. **19**(4), 9–30 (2003)
4. Fleming, M.: Measuring treasury market liquidity. FRB of New York Staff report, 133 (2001)
5. Gorner, J., Zhang, J., Cohen, R.: Improving trust modeling through the limit of advisor network size and use of referrals. Electron. Commer. Res. Appl. **12**(2), 112–123 (2013)
6. Gorner, J.M.: Advisor networks and referrals for improved trust modelling in multi-agent systems. Master's thesis, University of Waterloo (2011)
7. Haghpanah, Y., Desjardins, M.: PRep: a probabilistic reputation model for biased societies. In: Proceedings of the 11th International Conference on Autonomous Agents and Multiagent Systems, AAMAS 2012, vol. 1, pp. 315–322 (2012)
8. Herlocker, J., Konstan, J.A., Riedl, J.: An empirical analysis of design choices in neighborhood-based collaborative filtering algorithms. Inf. Retr. **5**(4), 287–310 (2002)
9. Irissappane, A.A., Jiang, S., Zhang, J.: A framework to choose trust models for different e-marketplace environments. In: IJCAI (2013)
10. Jøsang, A., Golbeck, J.: Challenges for robust trust and reputation systems. In: Proceedings of the 5th International Workshop on Security and Trust Management (SMT 2009), Saint Malo, France (2009)
11. Josang, A., Ismail, R.: The beta reputation system. In: Proceedings of the 15th Bled Electronic Commerce Conference (2002)
12. Jurca, R., Faltings, B.: An incentive compatible reputation mechanism. In: Proceedings of the Second International Joint Conference on Autonomous Agents and Multiagent Systems, AAMAS 2003, pp. 1026–1027. ACM, New York (2003)
13. Liu, X.: Towards context-aware social recommendation via trust networks. In: Lin, X., Manolopoulos, Y., Srivastava, D., Huang, G. (eds.) WISE 2013, Part I. LNCS, vol. 8180, pp. 121–134. Springer, Heidelberg (2013)
14. Liu, X., Aberer, K.: SoCo: a social network aided context-aware recommender system. In: Proceedings of the 22nd International Conference on World Wide Web, pp. 781–802. International World Wide Web Conferences Steering Committee (2013)
15. Luca, M.: Reviews, reputation, and revenue: the case of yelp. com. Technical report, Harvard Business School (2011)
16. Luca, M., Zervas, G.: Fake it till you make it: reputation, competition, and yelp review fraud. Harvard Business School NOM Unit Working Paper, 14–006 (2013)

17. Madhavan, A.: Market microstructure: a survey. J. Finan. Markets **3**(3), 205–258 (2000)
18. Mukherjee, A., Venkataraman, V., Liu, B., Glance, N.: Fake review detection: classification and analysis of real and pseudo reviews. Technical report UIC-CS-2013-03, University of Illinois at Chicago (2013)
19. Noorian, Z., Marsh, S., Fleming, M.: Multi-layer cognitive filtering by behavioral modeling. In: The 10th International Conference on Autonomous Agents and Multiagent Systems, AAMAS 2011, vol 2, pp. 871–878 (2011)
20. Noorian, Z., Ulieru, M.: The state of the art in trust and reputation systems: a framework for comparison. J. Theor. Appl. Electron. Commer. Res. **5**, 97–117 (2010)
21. Ozbay, H.: Introduction to Feedback Control Theory. CRC Press, Boca Raton (2000)
22. Parasuraman, A., Zeithaml, V.A., Malhotra, A.: ES-QUAL: a multiple-item scale for assessing electronic service quality. J. Serv. Res. **7**(3), 213–233 (2005)
23. Qian, X., Feng, H., Zhao, G., Mei, T.: Personalized recommendation combining user interest and social circle. IEEE Trans. Knowl. Data Eng. **26**, 1763–1777 (2013)
24. Regan, K., Poupart, P., Cohen, R.: Bayesian reputation modeling in e-marketplaces sensitive to subjectivity, deception and change. In: Proceedings of the National Conference on Artificial Intelligence, vol. 21, p. 1206. AAAI Press (2006)
25. Castelfranchi, C., Falcone, R.: Socio-cognitive model of trust. In: Encyclopedia of Information Science and Technology (V) (2005)
26. Sabater, J., Sierra, C.: Review on computational trust and reputation models. Artif. Intell. Rev. **24**(1), 33–60 (2005)
27. Saxton, G.D., Anker, A.E.: The aggregate effects of decentralized knowledge production: financial bloggers and information asymmetries in the stock market. J. Commun. **63**(6), 1054–1069 (2013)
28. Smith, M.J., et al.: Learning to trust in the competence and commitment of agents. Auton. Agent. Multi-Agent Syst. **18**(1), 36–82 (2009)
29. Teacy, W.L., Patel, J., Jennings, N.R., Luck, M.: TRAVOS: trust and reputation in the context of inaccurate information sources. Auton. Agent. Multi-Agent Syst. **12**(2), 183–198 (2006)
30. Visioli, A.: Practical PID Control. AIC. Springer, London (2006)
31. Wang, Y., Singh, M.P.: Formal trust model for multiagent systems. In: IJCAI, pp. 1551–1556 (2007)

XCuteKIP: Support for Knowledge Intensive Process Activities

Ednilson Veloso Moura[✉], Flávia Maria Santoro, and Fernanda Araujo Baião

Department of Applied Informatics,
Federal University of the State of Rio de Janeiro (UNIRIO), Rio de Janeiro, Brazil
{ednilson.moura,flavia.santoro,fernanda.baiao}@uniriotec.br

Abstract. The century of information puts the organizational processes of which the work highlights knowledge as the main asset into perspective, as well as an engine generator of competitive advantage. The nature of processes that include intensive use of knowledge points out several features that can be exploited to assist in adding value to products and services supported by organizations. These processes are known as Knowledge-intensive Processes. This article presents the XcuteKIP architecture that aims to support the participants of these processes. Particularly, the proposal assists in the execution of knowledge-intensive collaborative activities by providing semi-automatic recommendations of collaborative services. The approach applies the concepts of a service-oriented architecture subsidized by WGWSOA and a semantic modeling Ontology supported by KIPO.

Keywords: Knowledge-intensive process · Collaboration ontology · Service oriented architecture

1 Introduction

The heterogeneity of consumer goods and services has significantly expanded the markets and its multiplication factor has been the breakneck competition among companies. Thus, for a company to surpass, it is necessary to expand its competitive advantage. Differently from the mechanistic nineteenth century theory, organizations have included creativity and innovation in their decision-making processes in order to achieve this increased capacity. It is possible to observe the intensive use of knowledge of workers who perform those processes. Consequently, Knowledge Management (KM), which delivers the production, dissemination and accessibility and use of information, has grown in importance. It points to the increase of interest in a particular type of business process, which is known as Knowledge-Intensive Process (KIP) [7]. In order to achieve its objectives, the implementation of the activities inherent to the KIP depends on the knowledge that each participant in the process has.

This new dynamic pushes organizations and academia to turn their attention to the characteristics of KIP considering their critical success factor. Accordingly, the literature indicates several perspectives, derived from those characteristics: decisions taken in the processes, collaboration between participants; business rules that are applied to

N. Baloian et al. (Eds.): CRIWG 2015, LNCS 9334, pp. 164–180, 2015.
DOI: 10.1007/978-3-319-22747-4_13

constrain the activities and participants involved; and the coordination of activities to provide a structural basis to support processes that make intensive use of knowledge [5]. Explore these perspectives helps to understand the nature of these processes and allows organizations to improve them and maximize their results.

The making of decisions, creation of new products, improvement of existing products, specification of steps and modeling of information systems, among others are KIP examples. However, due to the unpredictability of these scenarios, the most important activities of the KIP are usually carried out with insufficient or inappropriate computer support [13]. Additionally, KIP are collaborative by nature [10]. In scenarios where the processes are collaborative, activities are carried out collectively, for better productivity. In this sense, the computational support for collaborative work can contribute to achieving more significant results to organizations [1].

Moura et al. [8] argue that there is not an adequate computing infrastructure to help individuals perform their activities in KIP although such infrastructure would play the role of recovering important pieces of knowledge of the participants' communicative work. The authors present the XcuteKIP a service-oriented approach to support KIP execution, focusing on collaborative activities among its participants. XcuteKIP is able to identify relevant pieces of information necessary for the participants to perform their knowledge intensive activities. The proposed approach recommends collaborative services based on mapping underlying collaborative services available in a repository and the KIP. This paper presents a set of axioms that formally define the concepts necessary to do the matching among services and activities in a KIP. Besides it discusses the results obtained in a case study. The aim of this paper is to present the results of the case study and demonstrate the advantages of the approach.

This paper is organized as follows: Sect. 2 details the part of the proposal with focus on the concepts formalization; Sect. 3 discusses the results from a case study; Sect. 4 compares related work; and Sect. 5 presents our conclusions and points the future perspectives of the research.

2 XCuteKIP: Computer Support for Collaborative KIP

Business process consists of various activities performed by agents within an organizational environment, the data flow specifications and control between them. Companies do business through their processes [14]. There is a kind of process that differs from the traditional structured ones by having participants' knowledge as the core for activities performance. These processes are known as Knowledge Intensive Processes (KIP) [10].

The intensity of knowledge demanded in a KIP is recognized by the complexity of the activities that are carried out, and how much these activities depend on the knowledge of its participants. Processes involving collaboration, creativity [4], innovation, decision making and constant interventions of experts require much knowledge [6].

Because of its dynamics and complexity, KIP has little or no support from computational applications [12]. However, Papavasiliou et al. [9] stated that KIP can be supported by groupware, which is the technology specifically designed to support group work with features for collaboration and knowledge management to support the recovery and access to information.

In this context, recommendation of collaborative services adequate to support collaborative activities in KIP would be particularly relevant. With this goal in mind, Moura et al. [8] present an architecture based on services to support the implementation of KIP tasks, performing automatic discovery of collaborative applications based on an ontology. We present XcuteKIP composed by: (a) a formal specification that is able to map collaborative activities to collaborative services using a semantic of KIP; (b) a taxonomy for classifying collaborative activities; (c) a method for semi-automatic recommendation of collaborative services to support collaborative activities in knowledge intensive processes; and (d) semi-automatic discovery mechanisms of collaborative requirements of these activities. The architecture is briefly explained and the formalisms proposed are detailed in the next sub-sections.

2.1 Collaboration/Communication Semantic Applied to KIP

França [5] proposed an ontology to organize the concepts involved in KIP, called Knowledge-Intensive Process Ontology (KIPO). The overall objective of the work of França [5] was to build a conceptual model which, when instantiated, would be able to make explicit a knowledge intensive process, promoting its understanding within an organization.

The KIPO aims to organize the concepts related to several aspects in a KIP, among them: motivational factors, social interactions, feelings, beliefs, mental images, socialization, informal exchanges, innovation and decisions. According to the authors, KIPO is a composition of four sub-ontologies and a core ontology that integrates several concepts of the others that together present in the semantics of their classes the characteristics that define a knowledge-intensive process. The four ontologies from the literature are: Collaboration Ontology (CO), Decision Ontology (DO), Business Rules Ontology (BRO) and Business Process Ontology (BPO).

The semantics provided by KIPO enables the identification of relevant pieces of information that participants in the KIP need to perform their knowledge intensive activities, having CO as the basis for modeling the collaboration. Some of the elements in CO represent the communication among participants involved in the process. Among others, there are the concepts of Contribution Material, Communicative Acts, Perception, Messages, Idiomatic Language, Sender and Receiver as depicted in Fig. 1.

A Communicative Interaction (Fig. 1) is a Complex Action composed of at most a Communicative Act and Perception. To illustrate a communicative interaction, consider the case of a writer assuming the role of Sender, who publishes a book. This is an Action Contribution that is conducting a Communicative Act (publication of information). When the book is read by another agent who assumes the role of Receiver, a Perception (of this information) is observed. It completes the communication chain cycle, and therefore a Communicative Interaction was generated. The propositional content of the communicative act is a Message. The message may be coded in an Idiomatic Language.

Agents assume the role of Sender when performing (performance of) a Communicative Act in a Communicative Interaction. But when performing (performance of) the Perception of a message, they assume the role of Receiver. The Idiomatic Interactions are subtypes of a Communicative Interaction and represent communication through

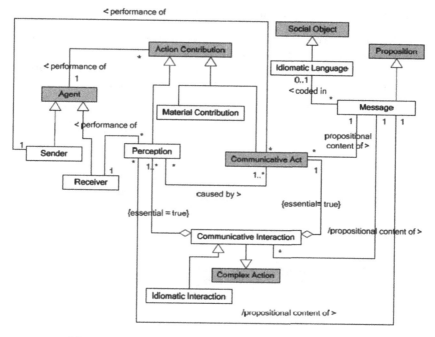

Fig. 1. Communication ontology (Oliveira apud França [5])

dialogues, newspapers, magazines, television, books, etc. Another type of Communicative Interaction that is not idiomatic is by gestures such as a handshake, an ok signal, among others.

KIPO, more specifically the CO Ontology, provides the foundational concepts for XcuteKIP proposal.

2.2 Classification of Collaborative Services

KIPO provides the semantic collaboration concepts required on a KIP. But in order to enable the matching of communication features to those concepts, we used the Communication Taxonomy of [2].

The taxonomy prescribed by [2] assembles a decision tree where the leaves point to one or more set of tools (features) able to meet a requirement of communication. The criteria for choosing features are: synchronization of interlocutors, number of participants, relationship between participants, communication language, discourse structuring, and message size. These criteria point directly to one or more group conversation features. Each criterion generates a decision tree. This taxonomy can be applied in different scenarios; both to specify the communication features to be implemented in a collaborative system, and also to support the characterization and understanding of the different communication features [2].

In XcuteKIP, the collaborative services to be recommended are classified according to this taxonomy.

2.3   Semi-automatic Recommendation of Services

The XcuteKIP approach comprises a method (previously presented in [8]) and an architecture (Fig. 2) in order allow the automation of choosing among the collaborative services to support KIP. Therefore, it is possible to automatically recommend appropriate services to support collaborative activities of a knowledge intensive process.

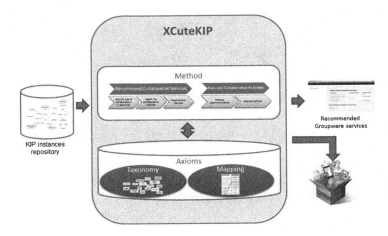

Fig. 2. XCuteKIP architecture [8]

To properly match the collaborative activities with collaborative services, XCuteKIP proposes a framework with a service-oriented architecture and method for semi-automatic discovery and invocation of services [8]. It is assumed that the activities are represented as instances of KIPO classes. The relationships between the instantiated activities of KIPO with the collaborative services are defined through a mapping, which uses the taxonomy proposed in [2] to categorize the groupware services.

The set of collaborative services used in our proposal is provided by WGWSOA [3]. Building groupware services from scratch is very complex by several factors, including their evolutionary nature. In collaborative environments, the context in which interactions arise is constantly changing, so the participants' object of interest and the requirements for interaction of the activities and the environment need to be represented through dynamic and flexible elements. Therefore, the main issue addressed by WGWSOA [3] is flexibility to adapt to the dynamic context in which collaborative applications are inserted. The goal of WGWSOA is to support the construction of distributed groupware and offer them as collaborative services.

The taxonomy of [2] is used in XcuteKIP for the classification of collaborative services provided by WGWSOA. The taxonomy acts as a filter to categorize each service. This categorization is useful primarily for services other than common sense, as in the case of a map of discussion. For example, using the taxonomy as a filter we observe that a map of discussion is an asynchronous service, which has many stakeholders and its message structure is carried out as a graph. Consequently, the collaborative services

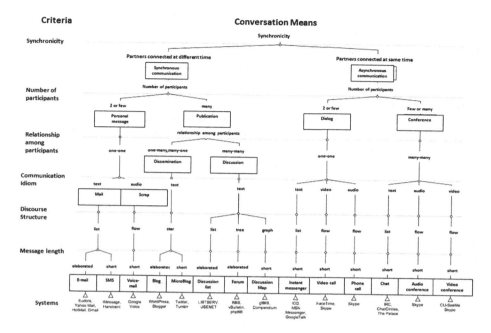

Fig. 3. Calvão taxonomy [2]

developers should classify every new service developed and register this service with one of the categories defined in the taxonomy.

2.4   Axioms for Collaboration Service Discovery

Collaborative Activities that are part of a KIP should be identified by XCuteKIP; thus, they must be precisely specified. Hence, its concept is formalized through axioms, described as follows. We also show another parts of KIPO to support the clarification of the concepts.

In this proposal, it is assumed that a KIP is modeled based on the KIPO meta-model and therefore the concept of collaborative activity makes use of classes and relationships provided in the KIPO. According to KIPO, Socialization is a type of Communicative Interaction composed by Communication and Perception, developed by an Agent. Communication is a type of Communicative Act which has a Message as propositional content that makes up the KIP message flow. Socialization is also a type of Collaborative Session.

From this conceptualization, it is possible to derive the following definition for Collaborative Activity, formalized through the axiom A1.

Axiom A1. All communicative acts performed in a Socialization are collaborative activities.

CollaborativeActivity(ca) ← CommunicativeAct(ca) ∧ CommunicativeInteraction(ci)

∧ Socialization(ci) ∧ composed_by(ci, ca) ∧ happens_in(ca, ci)

A Collaborative Session is an Interaction between agents ruled by Collaborative Agreements. Within the collaborative sessions, agents perform Collaborative Roles that are characterized by a Closed Commitment Universal, which have signed with each other to perform their collaborative activities. The activities of the agents in the Collaborative Session are called Action Contribution (Fig. 4) and they should have at least two participants by definition. Axiom A2 defines this.

Axiom A2. All activities carried out in a Collaboration Session are collaborative.

CollaborativeActivity(cs) ← CollaborationSession (cs) ∧ ActionContribution(ca) ∧

composed_by(cs, ca)

Each Knowledge Intensive Activity may involve a Decision and is responsible for an Innovation Agent. The making of a decision considers several Alternatives. The alternatives are associated with Specialty of Innovation Agent. Axiom A3 formalizes that.

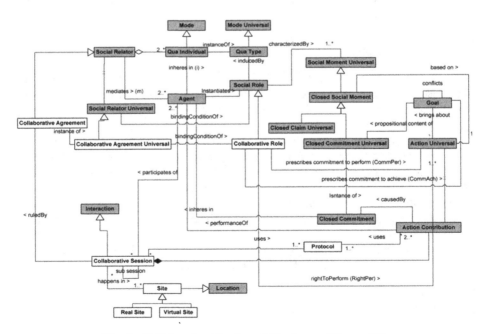

Fig. 4. Collaboration Ontology (Oliveira apud França [5])

Axiom A3. Each knowledge intensive activity is a collaborative activity when it involves decision and the innovation agent responsible for the activity is not an expert in the domain of the alternatives associated with the decision.

> CollaborativeActivity(kia) ← KnowledgeIntensiveActivity(kia) ∧ Decision(d) ∧
>
> Alternative(a) ∧ Speciality(s) ∧ InnovationAgent(ia) ∧ InnovationAgent(ia') ∧
>
> involves(kia, d) ∧ considers(d, a) ∧ associated_with(a, s)   ∧ has(ia', s)   ∧ ia < > ia'
>
> is_discussed_in(a, s)

Once the axioms of collaborative activities in a KIP modeled on KIPO were defined, the criteria to identify the collaboration requirements related to these activities should also be stated. Such requirements are also formalized through axioms for a precise ambiguity-free definition and. The axioms specified here follow the hierarchical order defined by the taxonomy of [2] (depicted in Fig. 3).

Synchronicity. According to KIPO, a Communicative Interaction consists of at least a Communicative Act and Perception. Both of them act as communicative perception and are treated as events. The event contains the property "synchronized with", and defines a self-relationship with another event. When this property is valuable, it means that the two related events occur simultaneously. Then, we define Axiom A4. With this axiom is also possible to infer the asynchrony, assuming that whenever two activities are not synchronous, they are necessarily asynchronous. When the knowledge intensive process is instantiated, its collaborative activities should set the attribute "synchronized with" with other event.

Axiom A4. Let two activities a and a' within the same instance of a KIP. Knowing that an activity is a specialization of an event, meaning that every event is also an activity, a and a' are considered synchronous activities if a has the property "synchronized with" configured with a reference to a'.

> synchronous (e, e') ← Event(e) ∧ Event(e') ∧ KowledgeIntensiveProcess(kip) ∧
>
> composed_by(kip, e) ∧ composed_by(kip,e') ∧ synchronized_with(e, e')

Number of Participants. The cardinality of the interlocutors relates to how many agents can perform communicative acts within a communicative interaction (Fig. 5). A Communicative Act is performed by an Agent in a Communicative Interaction assuming the role of Sender. Another agent in the same communicative interaction assumes the role of Receiver when performing the Perception of the message sent by the sender. Agents can be individual or social. A single agent can be, for example, a football player, a counter, a requirements analyst. The social workers refer to a group, an organization or a society. Social agent examples are the football clubs and the United Nations.

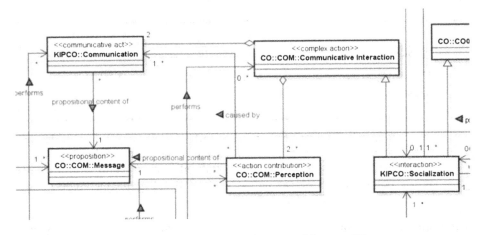

Fig. 5. Collaboration Ontology – social agents [5]

In this research, we define cardinality "one" for individual agents and cardinality "many" for social workers. Based on these premises we specify the following axioms.

Axiom A5. A communicative interaction has cardinality of interlocutors "one" if an individual agent (other than a social) is participating in this communicative interaction.

interlocutorCardinality(ci, "um") ← ComunicativeInteraction(ci) ∧ part_of(ci, ca) ∧

communicativeAct (ca) ∧ performanceOf(ca,a) ∧ agent(a) ∧ not socialAgent(a)

Axiom A6. A communicative interaction has cardinality of interlocutors "many" if a social worker is participating in this communicative interaction.

interlocutorCardinality (ci, "muitos") ← ComunicativeInteraction(ci) ∧ part_of(ci, ca)

∧ communicativeAct (ca) ∧ performanceOf(ca,a) ∧ agent(a) ∧ socialAgent(a)

Relationship Among Participants. The taxonomy [2] defines that parties can relate to in a communication noting the following relationships with each other: one-one (person-person), one-many (person-people) and many-many (people-people). Based on the definition already mentioned in the axioms A5 and A6 it is possible to compose the relationship between interlocutors by analyzing communication that takes place between the participants of the communicative interactions (Figs. 6 and 7). So, we define Axioms A7, A8 and A9.

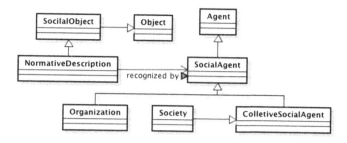

Fig. 6. Collaboration Ontology – social agents (Oliveira apud França [5])

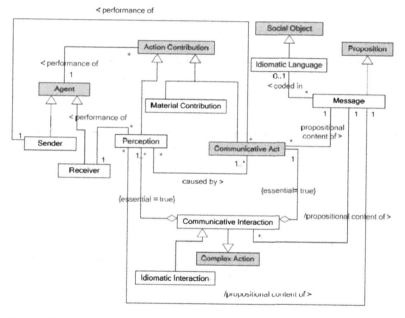

Fig. 7. Collaboration Ontology – communication act (Oliveira apud França [5])

Axiom A7. A communicative interaction is a relationship "one-one" between parties if an individual agent, which is present in a communicative interaction, has an interlocutor another agent that is also an individual agent.

interlocutorRelator(ci, "um-um") ← ComunicativeInteraction(ci) ∧ part_of(ci, ca) ∧ communicativeAct (ca) ∧ performanceOf(ca,a) ∧ agent(a) ∧ not socialAgent(a)

∧ part_of(ci, p) ∧ Perception (p) ∧ performanceOf(p,a′) ∧ agent(a′) ∧ not socialAgent(a′)

Axiom A8. A communicative interaction is a relationship "one-many" of parties if a single agent that is present in a communicative interaction has as interlocutor an agent that is a social agent.

interlocutorRelator(ci, "um-muitos") ← ComunicativeInteraction(ci) ∧ part_of(ci, ca) ∧ communicativeAct (ca) ∧ performanceOf(ca,a) ∧ agent(a) ∧ not socialAgent(a) ∧ part_of(ci, p) ∧ Perception (p) ∧ performanceOf(p,a′) ∧ agent(a′) ∧ socialAgent(a′)

Axiom A9. A communicative interaction is a relationship "many-many" between parties if a social agent is present in a communicative interaction and its interlocutor is another social agent.

interlocutorRelator(ci, "muitos-muitos") ← ComunicativeInteraction(ci) ∧ part_of(ci, ca) ∧ communicativeAct (ca) ∧ performanceOf(ca,a) ∧ agent(a) ∧ socialAgent(a) ∧ part_of(ci, p) ∧ Perception (p) ∧ performanceOf(p,a′) ∧ agent(a′) ∧ socialAgent(a′)

Communication Language. The taxonomy [12] defines the following types of communication idioms: video, audio and text. Messages are associated with the Communicative Act, which are their propositional content. Messages are encoded in an Idiomatic Language. In this research we assume the communication language as a property of a message, and define three constants ("VIDEO", "AUDIO" and "TEXT") to compose the domain of possible values of this property, as formalized in the axioms A10, A11 and A12.

Axiom A10. A message is encoded in the text, when the contents of its idiomatic language inform so.

communicationLanguage(m,"TEXT") ← Communicative Act (ca) ∧ Message (m) ∧ IdiomaticLanguage(il) ∧ proposicional_content_of(m,ca) ∧ coded_in(m,il) ∧ content_of(il,"TEXT")

Axiom A11. A message is encoded in the audio, when the contents of its idiomatic language inform so.

> communicationLanguage(m,"AUDIO") ← Communicative Act (ca) ∧ Message (m) ∧ IdiomaticLanguage(il)   ∧   proposicional_content_of(m,ca)   ∧   coded_in(m,il)   ∧ content_of(il,"AUDIO")

Axiom A12. A message is encoded in the video, when the contents of its idiomatic language inform so.

> communicationLanguage(m,"VIDEO") ← Communicative Act (ca) ∧ Message (m) ∧ IdiomaticLanguage(il)   ∧   proposicional_content_of(m,ca)   ∧   coded_in(m,il)   ∧ content_of(il,"VIDEO")

Discourse Structure. Taxonomy of [2] states that groupware can be classified regarding its discourse structure as flow, list, tree, star and graph. The structure of speech is related to sequencing of messages structure. This research sets an attribute to inform the discourse structure (Message Structure) in a Communicative Interaction, in which the domain of possible values are (LIST, TREE, STAR and GRAPH), assigned according to the axioms A13, A14 and A15.

Axiom A12. The format of discourse structure of a communicative interaction is list when the contents of its Message Structure attribute inform so.

> communicativeInteraction(ci, "LIST") ← messageStructure(ci, "LIST")

Axiom A13. The format of discourse structure of a communicative interaction is tree when the contents of its Message Structure attribute inform so.

> communicativeInteraction(ci, "TREE") ← messageStructure(ci, "TREE")

Axiom A14. The format of discourse structure of a communicative interaction is star when the contents of its Message Structure attribute inform so.

> communicativeInteraction(ci, "STAR") ← messageStructure(ci, "STAR")

Axiom A15. The format of discourse structure of a communicative interaction is graph when the contents of its Message Structure attribute inform so.

> communicativeInteraction(ci, "GRAPH") ← messageStructure(ci, "GRAPH")

Message Length. This property could be automatically inferred if the process had already been performed, calculating the size of the messages exchanged. However, the recommendation services in XCuteKIP are made at design time, so it was necessary to define an attribute for the class Message (MessageSize). The possible values for this attribute are defined in the variables contained in the axioms A16 and A17: SHORT and ELABORATED.

Axiom A16. A message will be short when the contents of its attribute MessageSize inform so.

```
message(m, "SHORT") <- messageSize(m, "SHORT")
```

Axiom A17. A message will be elaborated when the contents of its attribute Message-Size informs so.

```
message(m, "ELABORATED") <- messageSize(m, "ELABORATED")
```

The recommendation of collaborative services results in a set of collaborative services tailored to support the implementation of the KIP activities. This goal is achieved when they run the steps of the method as proposed in [8]. After the execution of algorithms based on the axioms in this section that identifies each type of activity where collaboration is needed, collaborative groupware services layer are identified to support the collaborative needs of these activities. We evaluated preliminarily the proposal in a case study presented in next section.

3   Preliminary Case Study

A scenario where a knowledge intensive process has a strong need for collaboration among agents is the software requirements elicitation process [11]. The aim is to find a set of functions for the system, find out the performance characteristics, hardware restrictions and other information relating to this project. The techniques and methods to support such requirements elicitation activities are diverse, and the team is generally composed by analysts and software engineers, besides customers and end-users.

Aiming to evaluate XcuteKIP, a case study based on this process was conducted within a Brazilian oil exploration company. The group that participated in the case study uses agile approaches to software development. Basically, demands for applications from customers arise by one of their representatives. Several meetings are held to define the scope of the application, risks and technical feasibility of the solution. Often, these activities bring together a large group of collaborators to decide the best technical solution. Several techniques of requirements engineering are applied to list the requirements for the application. For the case study, a group consisting of professionals working in different areas was set, being distributed as follows in relation to its main occupation: six developers (analysts and programmers); one professional from quality area (tests, standards, etc.); three solution architects; two project managers. The list of tasks in requirements elicitation process and a list of collaboration services present in WGWSOA, as well as the description of activities and collaboration tools for equalizing the knowledge were given to the group.

The participants performed the following tasks: (1) Assess and respond which activities performed by them are collaborative; (2) Recommend one or more collaborative services for each activity that was classified as collaborative; and (3) Assess the recommendation obtained by XCuteKIP.

The set of data collected in the case study showed a large dispersion in the answers. Analysts diverged about how many activities and recommendation of the collaborative services for these activities. The smallest amount of collaborative activities identified was 5 (28 %). Four analysts have identified a similar number of collaborative activities in relation to the XCuteKIP tool. Two analysts (6 and 8) have identified 72 % of the activities as being collaborative, and two other analysts (5 and 10) pointed out that there 83 % of them were collaborative (Fig. 8).

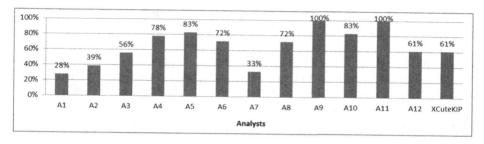

Fig. 8. Amount of recommendations of collaborative services for collaborative activities

Regarding the first task, identifying collaborative activities, it was found that the XcuteKIP pointed the activities that most analysts also have pointed. The second task was to indicate which collaborative service would be best suited to each activity. XcuteKIP recommended collaborative services that most analysts also recommended. When analysts assessed the responses of XcuteKIP, even those who previously did identified the same services, replied that would adopt the suggestions given. The high percentage of matching recommendations from XCuteKIP in relation to manual recommendations pointed to a suitability of the services recommended in scenario investigated.

4 Related Work

Böhringer [15] applied the ideas of social software to address the collaborative tasks in KIP, such as combining a microblog with tagging rules. The approach was to create a lightweight architecture to support collaborative activities that can be found on a KIP, such as conversations through audio and video, group chats, among others. According to the author, ad hoc activities of the processes are created using microblog posts and relate the process instance by a hashtag.

Although its architecture has been successful in organizing collaborative activity engaged in KIP, this approach is not successful in supporting the execution of all types of collaborative activities. Microblogs have, in general, message size restrictions and limitations in their communication structure. The size of message content is short and primarily text-oriented.

Supporting collaborative activities requires compliance with a wide range of requirements. Some activities need video capabilities, others need audio; some are carried out at distance, while others are face-to-face.

It is increasingly common to find software development teams working remotely and quite often the necessity of alignment meetings. Videoconferencing is a recurrent tool used by such teams.

In this context, finding out the requirements for choosing the most appropriate groupware tools to support the implementation of collaborative activities is a precondition for better support KIP. The systematization proposed by Calvão [2] lists relevant criteria to characterize collaborative services such as: sync interlocutors, number of partners, relationships between partners, communication language, speech structure and size of message. These criteria point directly to one or more systems in a group conversation.

The goal of Stoitsev et al. [12] is to support collaborative activities in performing end-to-end business process. The motivation is that it is not usually easy storing and retrieving KIP instances, and so, best practices exchange are not adopted. Their proposal is based on the development of a tasks management tool integrated to email and associated to the task list. While emails and task list are very common among end users, offering low resistance in its acceptance as a solution, it is limited to the scope of collaboration in knowledge intensive processes. To achieve their goals, knowledge workers need other tools that explore various other communication features.

Building some collaborative tools to support KIP activities is a recurring approach to this category of problem. However, as discussed by Maciel et al. [3], the development of systems with these characteristics without a framework to abstract complexities is a laborious and error prone task. Indeed, the authors propose the WGWSOA framework, and established a reliable and robust base to provide groupware services for XcuteKIP.

Papavassiliou et al. [9] uses an ontology to provide the context for the creation of the specification and use of knowledge in knowledge intensive processes and touches the purpose of this article. In their approach, Papavassiliou et al. [9] present a tool for modeling weakly structured processes (KIP) and focus on knowledge management involved in these processes. Although the approach provides a method for modeling processes driven by an ontology and a engine for automation of processes intensive activities in knowledge, he does not focus on the collaboration between the participants of the processes.

The advantage of XcuteKIP over the proposals in literature is that it applies a rational that classifies collaborative services and maps them directly to the activities to be performed by groups, being more effective to recommend the groupware that is more suitable for a specific collaborative activity.

5   Conclusion

This work has researched aspects of knowledge-intensive processes which are, by nature, dynamic, complex, constantly changing in objectives and, in most cases, conducted collaboratively. This paper focused on the collaborative aspect, by recommending groupware services for supporting the process activities.

The approach includes a method that was based on process instances that were created following the structure of KIPO, the knowledge-intensive processes ontology. A service-oriented architecture was used to provide collaborative services. This architecture performs the method steps to recommend services within WGWSOA.

The results achieved through the approach allow us to affirm that the services recommendation facilitates collaborative activities in KIP. In this way, the collaborative service recommendations provided by XcuteKIP are very close to those manually obtained by a groupware expert. The way to achieve these results was to instantiate knowledge-intensive processes with the use of KIPO and map collaborative activities to services.

The contributions of this paper are three-fold. First, we specify a method to identify the type of collaboration for each activity of a KIP based on a conceptualization of the domain of collaboration; second, we define an approach that makes the features of a knowledge intensive process and its collaborative aspects explicit and recommends collaborative services to more appropriately assist the collaborative activities within it; finally, we formally specify the concepts of collaboration within KIPs. This research also contributes to the literature of KIPs when assessing how the elements of the KIPO support collaboration in KIP and set axioms that describe formally the collaboration in KIP activities.

Acknowledgements. Fernanda Araujo Baião and Flávia Maria Santoro are partially funded by the CNPq Brazilian research council, respectively under the projects 309069/2013-0 and 307377/2011-3.

References

1. Andersson, B., Bider, I., Perjons, E.: Business Process Support System as a Tool for Communication/Collaboration. IbisSoft AB – Internal Report (2004)
2. Calvão, L., Pimentel, M., Fuks, H.E., Gerosa, M.A.: A taxonomy for computer-supported conversation. In: Proceedings of SBSC, IX Simpósio Brasileiro de Sistemas Colaborativos. São Paulo, SP, pp. 29–34 (in Portuguese) (2012)
3. Maciel, R.S.P., David, J.M.N., Bispo, C.P., Ribeiro, I., Conceição, R.P.: From Groupware Requirements to Services Design: Supporting the Development Process of a Pre-meeting Application. VII Simpósio Brasileiro de Sistemas Colaborativos, pp. 25–31 (2010)
4. Eppler, M.J., Seifried, P.M., Röpnack, A.: Improving knowledge intensive processes through an enterprise knowledge medium. In: Proceedings of the 1999 ACM SIGCPR Conference on Computer Personnel Research. April 08–10. New Orleans, Louisiana, United States, pp. 222–230 (1999)
5. França, J.B.S., Netto, J.M., Carvalho, J.E.S., Santoro, F.M., Baião, F.A., Pimentel, M.: KIPO: The Knowledge-Intensive Process Ontology. Software and Systems Modeling, Springer, pp. 1–31 (2014). doi:10.1007/s10270-014-0397-1
6. Hagen, C.R., Ratz, D., Povalej, R.: Towards self-organizing knowledge intensive processes. J. Univ. Knowl. Manage. **2**, 148–169 (2005)
7. Isik, O., Van Den Bergh, J., Mertens, W.: Knowledge intensive business processes: an exploratory study. In: System Science (HICSS) 45th Hawaii International Conference on IEEE, pp. 3817–3826 (2012)

8. Moura, E.V., Santoro, F.M., Baião, F.A.: Collaborative support for knowledge-intensive processes through a service-based approach. In: IEEE International Conference on Computer Supported Cooperative Work in Design, 2013, Whistler. 17th IEEE International Conference on Computer Supported Cooperative Work in Design (CSCWD 2013), pp. 319–324 (2013). doi:10.1109/CSCWD.2013.6580982
9. Papavassiliou, G., Ntioudis, S., Adreas, A., Mentzas, G.: Managing knowledge in weakly structured administrative process. In: The Third European Conference on Organization Knowledge, Learning and Capabilities (2002)
10. Singularity, W.P.: Case Management: Combining Knowledge with Process. Singularity, Ltda (2009)
11. Sommerville, I.: Software Engineering. Addison-Wesley, Berlin (2007)
12. Stoitsev, T., Scheidl, S., Flentge, F., Mühlhäuser, M.: Enabling end users to proactively tailor underspecified, human-centric business processes: "programming by example" of weakly-structured process models. In: Filipe, J., Cordeiro, J. (eds.) Enterprise Information Systems. LNBIP, vol. 19, pp. 307–320. Springer, Heidelberg (2009)
13. Van Elst, L., et al.: Weakly-structured workflows for knowledge-intensive tasks: an experimental evaluation. In: Proceedings of the Twelfth IEEE International Workshops on Enabling Technologies: Infrastructure for Collaborative Enterprises WET ICE 2003. IEEE, pp. 340–345 (2003)
14. Weske, M.: Business Process Management – Concepts, Languages Architetures. Springer, Heidberg (2007)
15. Barnes, S.T., Böhringer, J.M.: Modeling use continuance behavior in microblogging services: the case of twitter. J. Comput. Inf. Syst. **51**(4), 1 (2011)

BESIDE: Immersive System to Enhance Learning Within a Museum

Ryuichi Yoshida[1(✉)], Haruya Tamaki[1], Tsugunosuke Sakai[1], Ryohei Egusa[2,3],
Machi Saito[4], Shinichi Kamiyama[3], Miki Namatame[5], Masanori Sugimoto[6],
Fusako Kusunoki[5], Etsuji Yamaguchi[2], Shigenori Inagaki[2], Yoshiaki Takeda[2],
and Hiroshi Mizoguchi[1]

[1] Tokyo University of Science, 2641 Yamazaki Noda, Chiba, Japan
drive.g3.x@gmail.com, {7515636,7515624}@ed.tus.ac.jp,
hm@rs.noda.tus.ac.jp
[2] JSPS Resarch Fellow, 5-3-1, Koujimachi, Chiyoda, Tokyo, Japan
etuji@opal.kobe-u.ac.jp,126d103d@stu.kobe-u.ac.jp,
{inagakis,takedayo}@kobe-u.ac.jp
[3] Kobe University, 3-11, Tsurukabuto, Nada, Kobe, Hyogo, Japan
s-kamiyama@people.kobe-u.ac.jp
[4] Tama Art University, 2-1723, Yarimizu, Hachioji, Tokyo, Japan
Okame0904@gmail.com
[5] Tsukuba University of Technology, 4-3-15, Amakubo, Tsukuba, Ibaraki, Japan
miki@a.tsukuba-tech.ac.jp,kusunoki@tamabi.ac.jp
[6] Hokkaido University, Kita 15, Nishi8, Kita-Ku, Sapporo, Hokkaido, Japan
sugi@ist.hokudai.ac.jp

Abstract. We are developing an immersive learning support system for a paleontological environment within a museum. The system measures the physical movement of a learner using a Kinect sensor and provides a sense of immersion in the paleontological environment by modifying the surroundings according to these movements. As the first stage of this project, we have developed a prototype system that enables learners to experience paleontological environments. We evaluated the operability of the system, the degree of learning support, and the sense of immersion for primary schoolchildren. This paper summarizes the current system and describes the evaluation results.

Keywords: Kinect sensor · Museum · Full-body interaction

1 Introduction

Museums represent important places of scientific learning for children [1]. They also operate as centers for informal education that enhance the effectiveness of scientific education conducted in schools [2]. However, the main learning method within museums typically involves the study of the specimens on display. As a result, there are few opportunities for learners to experience the environment about which they are learning. In particular, it is impossible to experience the ecological environment of

© Springer International Publishing Switzerland 2015
N. Baloian et al. (Eds.): CRIWG 2015, LNCS 9334, pp. 181–189, 2015.
DOI: 10.1007/978-3-319-22747-4_14

extinct animals and plants in the real world [3]. Furthermore, it is difficult for children to learn using only fossil displays and their descriptions. Overcoming this problem would qualitatively improve scientific learning within museums. One possible solution would be to reproduce the paleontological environment artificially using video content displayed in a booth. However, most museums cannot accommodate such an exhibit owing to space and cost issues. Similarly, standard video typically does not provide a realistic body experience.

Hence, we are developing BESIDE (Body Experience and Sense of Immersion in a Digital paleontological Environment), an immersive learning system that will enable learners to explore a virtual paleontological environment in any museum. During development, we decided to incorporate the learner's physical movements into the system to impart a sense of immersion. In a related study, PCs and tablets were used to provide a sense of immersion for a learning support system [4]. However, systems such as this do not provide realistic body experiences because they are operated using interfaces such as a mouse or touch panel. Owing to these limitations, it is difficult to enhance knowledge and understanding because the learner does not experience a true sense of immersion. Accordingly, we focused on full-body interaction in order to provide this immersive experience. In addition, it has been suggested that full-body interaction improves the sense of immersion, which promotes knowledge and understanding [3]. The BESIDE system acquires information about the learner's movements using a Kinect sensor and operates according to the measured information. Our system uses multiple screens spread across the learner's entire field of vision. Because they are reflected within this real virtual space, the learner can use physical movements as an observation action. We anticipate that full-body interaction will be implemented, which will engender a sense of immersion in the virtual space. Because BESIDE consists of only a commercial image sensor, projector, and control PC, we can provide a low-cost immersive learning experience within a small space. As the first step toward realizing an immersive learning support system for museums, we developed and evaluated a BESIDE prototype. In this paper, we summarize the current system and describe the evaluation results for supporting learning and sense of immersion in the paleontological environment.

2   Beside

2.1   Body Experience and Sense of Immersion

The BESIDE system consists of various sensors and digital learning content. The sensors measure the learners' location, pose, and actions; the learning content is then controlled according to these measurement results.

Figure 1 illustrates the overall concept of the BESIDE system. Learners walk around a space containing a screen that displays a virtual environment, and observation objects such as animals move in synchronicity with them. In this manner, the learners obtain a sense of immersion in the paleontological environment. Synchronizing the movement of the paleontological animals with that of the learners makes it possible to consider the animals as being, in some sense, real rather than imaginary.

Fig. 1. Conceptual picture of BESIDE.

Furthermore, by introducing near-real observation activities such as "approaching the observation object" or "diving into water," the level of interest and learning effects are significantly enhanced, compared with watching a typical exhibition and video. At present, we are developing a prototype system that displays the figure of the virtual learner on the screen, allowing them to experience the paleontological environment. In this system, the learner stands in front of the screen, and an image of the learner is displayed with the background removed. The learner can change the background by moving their hand and manipulating the content. The system then allows the learner to select animals associated with the geological period represented by the background. From this, the learner enters a virtual paleontological environment on the screen and can enjoy a simulated experience in this environment.

2.2 Configuration of the System

The system must be able to acquire real-time knowledge about the learner's location and movements. We utilize Microsoft's Kinect sensor for this purpose. The Kinect sensor is a range image sensor, originally developed as a home videogame device. Although inexpensive, the sensor can provide advanced measurements that delineate a user's location [5]. Additionally, this sensor can recognize humans and the human skeleton using libraries such as the Kinect for Windows SDK. The Kinect can measure the locations of human body parts such as hands and legs and can identify the user's pose or status by using this function along with location information. We use these functions of the Kinect sensor and the Kinect for Windows SDK library to recognize humans and detect the human skeleton.

Figure 2 shows the setup of the current system. The system consists of a Kinect sensor, control PC, and projector. The paleontological environment is reproduced by placing a suitable animal from one of three geological periods [Paleozoic, Mesozoic, or Cenozoic] into the display. The animals associated with each period are listed in Table 1. We also prepared four fossil types that are typical of these animals; the fossils can be observed at the museum. In this system, the Kinect sensor provides the necessary frame and depth information. This information is transmitted to the control PC, which generates the various images that are displayed on the screen. Figure 2 shows an example of a paleontological environment background and illustrations of extinct animals. The system contains the following functions:

Table 1. Eras and related animals.

Era	Paleozoic	Mesozoic	Cenozoic
Animals	Elrathiakingi (Trilobite)	Triceratops	Mammoth
	Peronopsis (Trilobite)	Perisphinctina (Ammonoidea)	Merycoidodon
	Orthoceras	Hadrosaurus	Shark
	Crinoidea	Mosasaurus	Capreolinae

(a) displays images on the basis of sensor information,
(b) operates using the learner's body motion, and
(c) enables observations of animals as GIF animations.

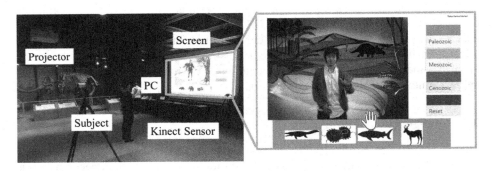

Fig. 2. Current system setup and example background and extinct animal illustrations.

Function (a) displays the learner on the screen by recognizing their outline. Using this function, the learner is merged into the paleontological environment. Function (b) allows the system to operate according to user hand movements. The learner can click a button by pushing their hand toward the Kinect sensor. The learner selects one of the three geological periods; the screen is then replaced by an image representing that time. Icons of animals are displayed at the bottom the screen. If the learner selects an animal from that geological period, the animal is displayed on the screen. If the selected animal is from the wrong geological period, a warning sounds and the learner is prompted to reselect the animal. Therefore, the system is able to depict which animals lived in which period, which supports learning and provides a sense of immersion. Function (c) enables the displayed animal to move around the screen as a GIF animation. As a result, learners can observe extinct animals as if they were real.

3   Evaluation Experiments

3.1   Purpose

We conducted a qualitative study to assess the effectiveness of the prototype BESIDE system for supporting learning and a sense of immersion in paleoecology immersion learning activities conducted in museums. For learning, the effectiveness of the system in supporting the acquisition of paleoecology knowledge was examined. For a sense of immersion, we examined the effectiveness of the virtual experiences created with the system of prior eras in which ancient creatures existed.

3.2   Methods

Participants: Twenty-eight fifth- and sixth-grade students (ages 10 to 12) at a national university-affiliated elementary school.

Procedure: First, the participants were divided into groups of three or four, and they were shown designated fossils that were on display in the museum. The fossils were of living creatures that were prepared by the prototype system. Next, each participant was given an individual experience with the system. During these experiences, the participants selected the proper geological era (Paleozoic, Mesozoic, or Cenozoic) that corresponded to each of the fossils they had viewed earlier. Then, the paleoecosystems of these geological eras were recreated by the system. The individual experiences with the system lasted for approximately 5 min per student. Finally, the system was evaluated by interviewing the students.

Evaluation Process: For the interview, 21 individuals were randomly selected from among the 28 participants and questioned about learning and a sense of immersion. The questions about learning were related to the effectiveness of the system in supporting paleoenvironmental learning and any possible improvements needed in this regard.

Fig. 3. Use of the BESIDE system.

Table 2. Number of participants making learning- and immersion-related positive and negative statements

Perspective	Positive statements	Negative statements Or no statements
Learning**	19	2
Sense of immersion*	16	5

$N = 21.$ **$p < 0.01.$ *$p < 0.05.$

The questions about the sense of immersion addressed the virtual experiences of the past eras created by the system and any possible improvements needed in the virtual experiences. The interview durations were approximately 5 min per student.

Date of Study: November 29, 2014
Location: Hyogo Prefectural Natural Sciences Museum (Fig. 3)

3.3 Results

The interview responses of each participant were classified as positive, negative, or no response. Table 2 summarizes the numbers of participants whose responses were classified as positive, negative, or no response. The differences in the numbers of responses between the two groups were tested for significance with 1×2 direct probability calculations. For both learning and a sense of immersion, the number of positive responses was significantly higher than the number of negative or no responses.

Table 3 summarizes an example of a positive response to learning. With respect to recreating paleoecosystems through body movements during the system experience, this participant said, "It's more fun to take quizzes with my body than by writing on paper" and "In the direct exhibits, there were places where the Cenozoic landscape was not recreated, so it helped me think about them together." This indicated that the system helped this student enjoy learning about the connections between ancient plants and animals and their environment, which are difficult to observe in the museum's general exhibits.

An example response of a suggestion for a learning-related improvement is summarized in Table 4. This participant said, "It would be good to know not just where the plants and animals are but also a little bit more about how they are connected (to other ancient plants and animals and to their environment)." This response was related to the amount of information that was provided by the system.

Table 5 summarizes an example of an immersion-related positive response. This participant said, "Today only four (ancient plants and animals) appeared, so I'm curious about the ones that come next" and "It felt like I was in that world too. I didn't live during the Mesozoic era, but it was like I got to experience that era just a little bit." This indicated that the student had a sense of actually experiencing an era in which ancient creatures lived and felt a sense of closeness to those creatures.

Table 3. Example of a learning-related positive response

E1:	If you had to pick between taking a quiz with your body and taking one on paper using a pencil, which one would be more fun?
S1:	The one with my body.
E1:	Why would that be?
S1:	Basically, the same reason as before. It is more fun to take quizzes with my body than by writing on paper.
E1:	When you answered something on the quiz, animals appeared with the landscape of the Cenozoic period drawn around them, I believe. Thus, the landscape and the animals were shown together. In terms of learning about them, were there any good things about having them shown together?
S1:	In the direct exhibits, there were places where the Cenozoic landscape was not recreated, and so, it helped me to think about them together.
E1	Think about them together in what ways?
S1:	I saw what type of environment they lived in and how they lived.

Note. E1 = Experimenter 1. S1 = Student 1.

Table 4. Example of suggestions for learning-related improvements

E2:	Please tell me if there are things about this system that should be modified.
S2:	It would be good to know not just where the plants and animals are but also a little bit more about how they are connected (to other ancient plants and animals and to their environment). In addition, for example, when you get the answer wrong, I think it would be easier to understand if it would tell you which era those plants and animals lived in.

Note. E2 = Experimenter 2. S2 = Student 2.

Table 6 summarizes an example of a response suggesting immersion-related improvements. This participant said, "It would be good if creatures are represented as not just silhouettes completely in black but instead some color is added, and they are made more realistic." This suggests the necessity of making the images more realistic in order to heighten the sense of immersion.

Table 5. Example of an immersion-related positive response

S3:	Today only four (ancient plants and animals) appeared, so I'm curious about the ones that come next.
E3:	Curious about things like where they live?
S3:	Yeah. I think about finding out stuff like what family they are in, what they look like, what they eat, and their special features.
E3:	So it sounds like it would be good to see more and more of them. You also appeared in those screen images. How did that feel?
S3:	It felt like I was in that world too. I did not live during the Mesozoic era, but it was like I got to experience that era just a little bit.

Note. E3 = Experimenter 3. S3 = Student 3.

Table 6. Example of suggestions for immersion-related improvements

E1:	You and the living beings from the past appeared together on that screen, I believe. Did you feel anything when you saw that?
S4:	It would be good if creatures are represented as not just silhouettes completely in black but instead some color is added, and they are made more realistic. It would be good if they made things like the sizes more realistic too.
E1:	So it would be good if things like that were fixed, right?

Note. E1 = Experimenter 1. S4 = Student 4.

4   Conclusion

In this paper, we summarized the current system and described the evaluation results for supporting learning and a sense of immersion in a paleontological environment. From the results of evaluation for both learning and a sense of immersion, the number of positive responses was significantly higher than the number of negative or no responses.

In our future work, we intend to enhance the immersive experience of the paleontological environment by making the images more realistic and using a technique to change the background according to the movement of the learner.

Acknowledgment. This work was supported in part by Grants-in-Aid for Scientific Research (B). The evaluation experiment was supported by The Museum of Nature and Human Activities, Hyogo.

References

1. Falk, J.H., Dierking, L.D.: Museum Experience Revisited, 2nd edn. Left Coast Press, Walnut Creek (2012)
2. Stocklmayer, S.M., Rennie, L.J., Gilbert, J.K.: The roles of the formal and informal sectors in the provision of effective science education. Stud. Sci. Educ. **46**(1), 1–44 (2010). Routledge Journals, Taylor and Francis Ltd. (2010)
3. Adachi, T., Goseki, M., Muratsu, K., Mizoguchi, M., Namatame, M., Sugimoto, M., Kusunoki, F., Yamaguchi, E., Imagaki, I., Takeda, Y.: Human SUGOROKU: full-body interaction system for students to learn vegetation succession. In: Interaction Design and Children 2013, pp. 364–367 (2013)
4. Deguchi, A., Inagaki, S., Kusunoki, F., Yamaguchi, E., Takeda, Y., Sugimoto, M.: Development and evaluation of a digital vegetation interaction game for children. In: Natkin, S., Dupire, J. (eds.) ICEC 2009. LNCS, vol. 5709, pp. 288–289. Springer, Heidelberg (2009)
5. Shotton, J., Fitzgibbon, A., Cook, M., Sharp, T., Finocchio, M., Moore, R., Kipman, A., Blake, A.: Real-time human pose recognition in parts from a single depth image. In: 2011 IEEE International Conference on CVPR, pp. 1297–1304 (2011)

Secure Collaboration in Public Cloud Storages

Aram Jivanyan[1]([✉]), Roland Yeghiazaryan[2], Armen Darbinyan[2],
and Azat Manukyan[2]

[1] American University of Armenia, Yerevan, Armenia
ajivanyan@aua.am
[2] SkyCryptor, Yerevan, Armenia
{roland,armen,azat}@skycryptor.com
https://www.skycryptor.com

Abstract. Public cloud storages such as Box, Dropbox, Google Drive or
OneDrive provide a great services of file storing, sharing and collaboration. But these services are provided at the cost of storage providers
having access to all users data. This is a very serious security issue
and is an obstacle which discourages many individuals and businesses
from using these services. Many security solutions have been emerged in
recent years to allow using the cloud storages in a secure way. However
the design of advanced cloud encryption gateway which will secure users
data in clouds without compromising their usability and convenience is
a hard scientific and technical problem. In this paper we will review the
existing solutions and will briefly introduce our own solution called Skycryptor which provides a perfect secrecy for users without compromising
other advantages offered by cloud storage providers.

Keywords: Cloud encryption gateway · Secure file sharing · Dropbox
security · Google drive security · Encrypted drive · Encrypted dropbox ·
Skycryptor

1 Introduction

Cloud storage services are used in ubiquitous ways for both individual and business purposes. They provide easy access to users data from anywhere and any-
time, affording the sharing of data with friends or colleagues, and providing
free storage space for all. But this great service is provided at the price of the
cloud storage providers having access to all the users data. Dropbox or Google
Drive take and can read all information we store there. This means there is
a risk they may give or even sell the data to third parties (e.g. NSA). This
is a very serious security issue [1] and for all individuals and organizations
caring about their data security but still wanting to benefit from public cloud
storages, the only solution is using some encryption tool which will help to
encrypt user information before uploading it to the cloud. The design of advanced
security solution for public cloud storages and for distributed file storages in
general is a hard scientific and technical problem [2–6]. From the other hand,

© Springer International Publishing Switzerland 2015
N. Baloian et al. (Eds.): CRIWG 2015, LNCS 9334, pp. 190–197, 2015.
DOI: 10.1007/978-3-319-22747-4_15

there is a tradeoff between security and usability, as encryption eliminates the easy access to data via search and also makes the sharing/collaboration harder. Various special cloud encryption gateways had been emerged in recent years aiming to secure users data in public cloud storages without compromising the sharing and collaboration features provided by the storage providers. In this paper we will review the main solutions existing in this domain showing what level of security is provided by each of them and their main advantages and disadvantages from both the security and usability points of view. Next we present our own cloud encryption gateway called Skycryptor which provides highest-level security for users and has certain competitive advantages over other solutions.

1.1   Existing Cloud Encryption Gateways

In this section we will review three most famous cloud encryption gateways which all aims to secure users data in main public cloud storages such as Dropbox and Google Drive. Among them only one provides a perfect security for users at the price of affected usability although all of them had have a great business importance.

Sookasa. Many organizations can not use public cloud storages because of specific law regulations. Good examples are the HIPAA and FERPA acts in USA, which prohibit the healthcare organizations and educational institutions sharing their patients and students data with third parties including cloud storage providers. Sookasa [7] is a new emerged cloud encryption gateway specially designed to help the companies from regulated industries and facilitate compliance with six federal standards such as HIPAA, FERPA, PCI DSS, GLBA,FINRA,SOX. It helps such organizations to store their data in cloud in encrypted form and also have full visibility on how the data was used or shared. However Sookasa does not provide a perfect secrecy as its lightweight cryptographic architecture is relied on the fact that Sookasa itself should handle all user secret key management. Sookasa secures the users files in Dropbox in the following manner:

1. Sookasa creates a special folder in user's Dropbox.
2. The user put sensitive files in that folder which are seamlessly encrypted with AES-256 encryption with unique file key randomly generated for that file
3. Sookasa encrypts the file encryption key with the Sookasa's public key. The encrypted file key is stored at the beginning of the file
4. The encrypted files are synced among all devices and users having access to the sookasa's secure folder.
5. When Alice shares some file with Bob and Bob wants to access Alice's encrypted file, Sookasa's server takes the file key encrypted with the server's public key, decrypts it and sends the file key to Bob.

As can be seen Sookasa owns all encryption keys used for securing the users files. This is a serious security drawback as the powerful adversary can always access the users sensitive files by compromising Sookasa to get the file encryption keys and then compromising the storage provider to get the encrypted files.

Such solution may satisfy specific companies but it can not be a reliable security solution for companies which want to fully exclude the chance of their data appearing into third-parties hands. Sookasa provides also a solution for securely sending files to non-sookasa users. Again this is possible only because of sookasa handles all the encryption keys meaning he always can decrypt the required file and preview it to any user. It is worth to mention that Sookasa works now only with Dropbox.

nCryptedCloud. nCryptedCloud [8] is another cloud encryption gateway working with most cloud storage providers such as Dropbox, Google Drive, OneDrive and Egnyte. It provides a rich functionality of file/folder sharing and unlike Sookasa allows securing any file in any folder. However from the security point of view there is still a little difference between Sookasa and ncryptedcloud. The later provide perfect security for individual files meaning the user does not need to share the file encryption keys with nCryptedCloud as far as the file should not be shared with others users. But for securely collaborating on cloud files, the user again needs to share the file encryption keys with nCrypteCloud's server. The following examples highlight the main file storing and sharing functionality.

1. Encrypting and Decrypting Private Files.
   File encryption works as follows:
   - Create a secure unique password for the file.
   - Encrypt the plaintext data using AES-256 Zip encryption by using the generated password.
   - Encrypt the file password with the user's public key.
   - Store the encrypted password in the encrypted Zip file.
   File decryption works as follows:
   - Decrypt the file password using the user's private key.
   - Decrypt the encrypted data using the file password.
2. Shared File encryption:
   - Bob wants to share some documents with other users.
   - When Bob encrypts his files using nCryptedCloud Share Securely method, nCryptedCloud creates a unique key for the folder and stores it locally on Bobs machine.
   - nCryptedCloud sends the key to nCryptedCloud server, and it is encrypted and stored on our server.
   - All the files in the shared folder are encrypted with unique passwords which are derived from the symmetric folder key value and additional entropy.
   - The file password is also encrypted with the Bob's public key.
   - The encrypted file password and symmetric folder key ID are stored with the encrypted data in the Zip file.
   - Bob shares the folder with Sue and Joe.
   - Sue receives the shared folder request from Bob and accepts the request.
   - When Sue needs to access the files on her machine, nCryptedCloud verifies that Sue has access to the folder key and distributes it to her.
   - If Bob removes Sues access to the folder, the folder key is removed from Sues local key store and she can no longer decrypt the files

Again the main drawback of nCryptedCloud is the fact that it can learn the secret keys and/or passwords used for file encryption. Although they claim that they never can access the cloud encrypted files, theoretically they can do it having the cloud storage access token for each user as well as the secret keys generated by user for securing data.

Boxcryptor. Boxcryptor [9] is the only cloud encryption gateway among the existing solutions providing a zero-knowledge service to users which means it never can learn any secret information of users including their encryption keys. Its secure key management is based on asymmetric RSA cryptosystem and all files are encrypted with AES-256 block cipher. Each user has own private and public keys where private key is always storing at server's side encrypted with the user's password. Every file has its own unique random file key generated at file creation. The file key is used to encrypt and decrypt the contents of the file as follows:

1. Create a secure random file key.
2. Encrypt the file using the file key.
3. Encrypt the file key with the user's public key.
4. Store the encrypted file key next to the encrypted data in the encrypted file.
5. If multiple users have access to a file, the file key is encrypted multiple times with different user public keys and each result is stored in the encrypted file.

The boxcryptor encryption algorithm requires the user to re-encrypt each file with different file key every time the group of people having access to the file is changed. Also the file size is growing linearly with number of people having access to it as for each new user having access to that file a new ciphertext should be stored at the beginning of the file. The situation becomes more complicated when multiple files are shared among multi-member groups within large corporations. Boxcryptor allows to create groups in the following manner [9].

1. A group is a list of users that has group keys. Additionally every group has a membership key which is used to manage group memberships.
2. The group keys are generated on a user's device when a user creates a new group. Before the keys are submitted to the Boxcryptor Key Server, the sensitive information is encrypted so that only the user who created the group has access to it.
   - The group's private RSA key is encrypted with the membership key so that access to the membership key is required to decrypt the private RSA key.
   - The wrapping key is encrypted with the membership key so that access to the membership key is required to decrypt the wrapping key.
   - All other AES keys are encrypted with the wrapping key so that access to the wrapping key is required to decrypt any other AES key.

- The membership key is encrypted with the user's public RSA key so that access to the user's private RSA key is required to decrypt the membership key.
- In order to speed up the sign in process, the membership key will be additionally AES encrypted with the user's group key on the first occasion.

When the user Alice wants to share a file with some group where Bob is a member, Boxcryptor executes the following steps:

1. Alice requests the group's public key from the Boxcryptor Key Server.
2. Alice encrypts the file key with the group's public key.
3. Alice writes the new encrypted file key to the encrypted file.
4. The cloud storage provider syncs the modified encrypted file.
5. Bob uses his private key to decrypt the group's membership key.
6. Bob uses the group's membership key to decrypt the group's private key.
7. Bob uses the group's private key to decrypt the file key.
8. Bob uses the file key to decrypt the file.

Imagine a situation where thousands of files are shared among some group and one member of that group leaves the organization. In order to protect the secrecy of old files as well as the secrecy of all new files have to be shared with that group, Boxcryptor should generate different group key, change all file keys and re-encrypt all files shared with that group.

2   SkyCryptor

Skycryptor is a novel cloud encryption gateway which goal is to secure public cloud storages without compromising any of the advantages the clouds have to offer. It concerns not only to the collaboration features, but also to the easy cloud data access via search and device-level access control. Skycryptor will provide search functionality over user's encrypted data via own patent-pending searchable encryption technology. Below we cover only some details about the secure collaboration features provided by Skycryptor. Skycryptor provides a zero-knowledge service meaning it never can learn any sensitive information of user including his files, encryption keys or even search queries. On the basis of Skycryptor's key management technique lies the so-called proxy encryption schemes [10–12] which allows the semi-trusted proxy server to transform a ciphertext computed under Alices public key into one that can be opened by Bobs secret key
Basically Skycryptor's file encryption and sharing works as follows (Fig. 1).

1. Alice creates a secure unique key for the file fk.
2. Alice encrypts the plaintext data using AES-256 encryption by using the file key fk.
3. Alice encrypts the file key with the her public key and stores it at the beginning of the encrypted file.

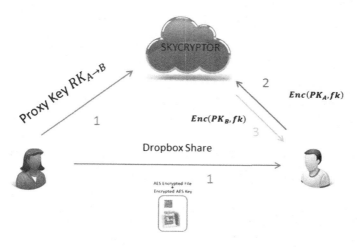

Fig. 1. File sharing.

When Alice wants to share his encrypted file with Bob, she does the following.

1. Alice generate a proxy key for Bob and gives the proxy-key to Skycryptor server which acts as the proxy server.
2. Alice create a permission object indicating that the given file is allowed to be opened by Bob.

When Bob wants to open a file owned and shared by Alice, he makes the following steps

1. Extracts the encrypted file key from the beginning of the file. The file key is encrypted via Alice's public key.
2. Sends the encrypted file key to Skycryptor server asking it to be re-encrypted.
3. Skycryptor server checks whether Bob was given permission for that file and re-encrypt the encrypt file key with help of the corresponding proxy-key given by Alice. The resulted ciphertext is sent back to Bob.
4. Bob decrypts the re-encrypted ciphertext via his private key. The content of the file is decrypted already with the revealed file key.

When Alice needs to share his files with many users, she just creates corresponding proxy-keys and the permission objects indicating which user can access the given file. There is no need to encrypt the file encryption key with all users public keys. The other most important aspect is there is no need to re-encrypt the file in case the file's accessors domain has been changed. In case the file is shared within some group where Chris is a member, proxy keys are created for all group members and permission objects are created for the given file. When Chris leaves the group, Alice should only delete the permission object indicating Chris is not allowed to access the file anymore.

Skycryptor's unique key management technology allows to enable device-level key management allowing the user's private keys to be device specific instead

Table 1. Competitive analysis

	Sookasa	nCryptedCloud	Boxcryptor	Skycryptor
Personal files security	False	True	True	True
Shared files security	False	False	True	True
Zero-knowledge security	False	False	True	True
Easy group/Team sharing	True	True	False	True
Search	False	False	False	True
Device-level access control	False	False	False	True

of being user specific. This allows to preserve user's files security even when some of his devices get fully compromised, as the user can always revoke the compromised device's access from his Skycryptor account.

The next fundamental security advantage of Skycryptor is it will allow the users to securely search over their encrypted data. This is possible via proprietary patent-pending searchable encryption algorithm. The client application which is responsible for all encryption/decryption functionality, also creates a special encrypted index which is uploaded to Skycryptor's server. Next during search the user's query is encrypted properly in client side so the server after getting the encrypted query will be able to return the files containing the user's searched keyword. Note that again skycryptor does not learn either the index's content or the searched queries (Table. 1).

3   Competitive Analysis

Below we describe the most important metrics related to the security and usability aspects of cloud encryption gateways which should be considered while providing general comparative analysis and to demonstrate the competitive advantages of our solution.
Security Metrics:

1. Personal file Security.
2. Shared file security.
3. Zero-Knowledge security.

Usability Metrics:

1. Easy Group Management and Group Sharing.
2. Search over encrypted data.
3. Device-Level Access Control.

Boxcryptor provides highest security at the price of usability. SkyCryptor provides highest security without compromising the cloud usability and user experience.

4   Conclusion

Public cloud storages thoroughly changed the way we work and collaborate together on digital data. But this should not be done at the price of compromised personal or corporate privacy. In this paper we have shown what solutions can be applied to ensure privacy in insecure clouds by representing also our solution Skycryptor which is specially designed to transform public cloud storages to privately secure environments without compromising their usability and convenience. Skycryptor allows to manage the encrypted content in more efficient way which in turns brings to more user-friendly experience. Skycryptor is in the development phase now. The full-flow testing and benchmarking is subject of future work when the service will be publicly launched. It is worth to mention that numerous secure cloud storage providers such as [13–15] also exist providing end-to-end encrypted cloud storage for users, although non of them gained the popularity that Dropbox or Google Drive have.

References

1. Mather, T., Kumaraswamy, S., Latif, S.: Cloud Security and Privacy: An Enterprise Perspective on Risks and Compliance. OReilly media, Sebastopol (2009)
2. Fu, K.E.: Group sharing and random access in cryptographic storage file systems, Masters thesis, MIT (1999)
3. Goh, E.-J., Shacham, H., Modadugu, N., Boneh, D.: SiRiUS : securing remote untrusted storage. In: Proceedings of NDSS, no. 0121481, ISOC, Geneva (2003)
4. Harrington, A., Jensen, C. Cryptographic access control in a distributed file system. In: Proceedings of 8th ACM Symposium on Access Control Models and Technologies (2003)
5. Fu, K.: Integrity and access control in untrusted content distribution networks. Ph.D. thesis, Massachusetts Institute of Technology, Cambridge, MA (2005)
6. Kallahalla, M., Riedel, E., Swaminathah, R., Wang, Q., Fu, K.: Plutus: scalable secure file sharing on untrusted storage. In: USENIX (2003)
7. http://www.sookasa.com
8. https://www.ncryptedcloud.com
9. http://www.boxcryptor.com
10. Ateniese, G., Benson, K., Hohenberger, S.: Key-private proxy re-encryption. In: Fischlin, M. (ed.) CT-RSA 2009. LNCS, vol. 5473, pp. 279–294. Springer, Heidelberg (2009)
11. Green, M., Ateniese, G.: Identity-based proxy re-encryption. In: Katz, J., Yung, M. (eds.) ACNS 2007. LNCS, vol. 4521, pp. 288–306. Springer, Heidelberg (2007)
12. Blaze, M., Bleumer, G., Strauss, M.J.: Divertible protocols and atomic proxy cryptography. In: Nyberg, K. (ed.) EUROCRYPT 1998. LNCS, vol. 1403, pp. 127–144. Springer, Heidelberg (1998)
13. Ag, L.: Wuala - secure online storage (2010). http://www.wuala.com
14. www.tresorit.com
15. www.mega.co.nz

Sketchpad: A Learning Tool Supporting Creativity in Collaborative Learning Activities

Gustavo Zurita[1], Catalina Cárdenas[1], and Nelson Baloian[2(✉)]

[1] Management Control and Information Systems Department,
Faculty of Economics and Business, Universidad de Chile,
Diagonal Paraguay 257, Santiago, Chile
{gzurita,ccardenasb}@fen.uchile.cl
[2] Department of Computer Sciences, Universidad de Chile, Beauchef 851, Santiago, Chile
nbaloian@dcc.uchile.cl

Abstract. There is consensus among curriculum developers of Business Schools around the world that along with technical knowledge students should be trained to also acquire soft skills. Communication, collaboration, creativity, critical thinking and problem solving are mentioned by some authors as the most important for professionals of the 21st century to be successful. In order to develop these skills learners have to perform learning activities where they need to apply them. In the literature we found many works about learning activities designed for training creativity which have been used in Business Schools. They do not make use of technology. On the other hand, there are many works about learning activities which make use of technology to train collaboration and problem solving skills. In this work we present a learning activity which makes use of a technologic tool for supporting it, which promotes collaboration, creativity and critical thinking. A first experiment shows that the perception students get from the activity and the ability of the tool for supporting these factors is positive.

Keywords: Creativity · Collaboration · Business schools · Mobile devices · Brainsketching

1 Introduction

In today's globalized world, there is an increasing need that professionals develop not only technical competences but also the so called "soft skills" in order to perform their activities in an effective and efficient way. This is especially true for professionals of the business and economics sphere, who need to perform tasks in a high competitive, changing and demanding environment, in order to adapt themselves to the constant changes and generate strategies which convey added value to the diverse business processes. In order to achieve this goal it is necessary to include pedagogical activities, methods and tools in their university curricula.

Griffin et al. [1] presented the KSAVE (Knowledge, Skills, Attitudes, Values, Ethics) model which defines ten key competences professionals of the 21st century should have

© Springer International Publishing Switzerland 2015
N. Baloian et al. (Eds.): CRIWG 2015, LNCS 9334, pp. 198–209, 2015.
DOI: 10.1007/978-3-319-22747-4_16

in order to be successful. The KSAVE model categorizes creativity as part of the *Ways of thinking* competences, along with others, like critical thinking, problem solving, decision making, learn to learn, and meta-cognition. The operational definition of creativity provided by the KSAVE model includes knowledge, skills, and attitudes related to thinking and working creatively, individually and collaboratively. In the same way, KSAVE highlights the relevance of collaboration and communication skills, which are classified as *Ways of Working* skills.

According to Schlee & Harich [2] and Fekula [3], creativity and the ability of working in teams are the most relevant and required skills in professionals of the business area in order to be successful. Moreover, the AACSB (Association to Advance Collegiate Schools of Business) highlighted the importance of considering various competences, among these creativity and the ability of working in teams, when designing curricula for business schools students [4] which is in line with the KSAVE model. In 2015, the AACB held various seminars on Curriculum Development Series. One of them was called *Teaching Design for Creativity and Innovation* [5], which again highlights the importance of creativity as the way to cope with the requirements of the modern business environment. The Harvard Business Review also shows the importance of creativity by publishing many articles on that subject [6].

The literature reports about many works on how to support the development of creativity in university students, presenting learning activities introduced in courses in business schools. However, we have not found pedagogical practices supported by recent technologies among them. On the other hand there are some works reporting on successful pedagogical activities supported by technology in order to promote creativity but applied to other learning scenarios. Thus we want to take these works as example, adapt and extend them, in order to be used for the business school curricula.

This work presents a pedagogical activity designed to help the development and application of skills and attitudes related to collaborative work and creativity in pregraduate students of a business school. The activity, which is performed inside the classroom, is supported by a collaborative application called Sketchpad, which runs on tablets wirelessly interconnected among them. Sketchpad was designed based on the principles of collaboration and externalization using brainsketching, promoting the development and practice of creativity according to previous research works on this subject reported by the literature. Compared with previous works, the contribution of Sketchpad is that it promotes considering various points of views when students work on a creative task. This is done by incorporating rotation among the members of various groups working on the same task. Sketchpad was tested in a real classroom in order to formally evaluate its contribution to creativity.

Based on the ideas described above, this research work has been guided by the following questions: (1) According to the students' perception, to what extend the provided tool (Sketchpad) contributes to the development of creativity?; (2) which is the perception the students get about the contribution of Sketchpad to promote collaboration; and (3) is there a difference in this perception when students work in groups where members have to rotate among the various groups and when they do not?

The results obtained show that Sketchpad enhances creativity in teams working with rotation compared to those working without rotation. There was also positive evidence on the perception students had about the ability of Sketchpad supporting collaboration and externalization.

2   Supporting Creativity Development

The complexity about teaching students to be creative lies in the fact that we cannot teach that skill but to foster its development through educational activities that include specific design principles, pedagogical practices that generated positive previous experiences based on theories explaining how to generate creativity [7].

The design principles of the pedagogical activity, and consequently of the tool supporting it, presented in this work is based on a pedagogical frame that incorporates mainly two elements: collaboration and externalization. Regarding collaboration, Fisher [8] proposes that creativity emerges from the interactions between individuals and the world, and between the individual and others; in the same way, Csikszentmihalyi emphasizes human interaction as the place where creativity emerges [9]. Egeström adopts a similar approach when proposing that creativity lies in interactions between persons' thoughts and their socio cultural context, [8, 10]. Sawyer [11] proposes that creativity breakthroughs occur during the dialog among persons when they answer to each other; this contrasts with the myth of individual inspiration, which represents the idea that creative inspiration comes from the individual. Similarly, Wegerif and others [11, 12], identify that the base of creativity lies in the tension between different perspectives. Therefore, interactions among people having different point of views, which are in opposition (tension), can be the base for a suitable activity where creative ideas may arise. From the importance of collaboration we can derive the convenience of designing activities that include intensive and varied interaction with other persons, allowing the sharing and discussion of ideas, and observing new points of views.

The second element of creativity we consider, externalization, refers to "taking out of her/himself" the ideas and thoughts in order to translate them in concrete artifacts which represents them, in order to make them accessible for working and reflect about them [13]. This attribute of externalization is based on what Schön calls the *"back-talk"*. The meaning is that the process of externalizing ideas can unveil questions about them which were initially ignored, facilitate the emergence of new perspectives, show new possibilities or obstacles, as well as new relationships to other ideas [14]. Sketching, drawing and diagramming are good examples of externalization processes, which can facilitate creative work and foster the development of this competence. From the advantages of externalization we can derive the usefulness of designing activities which include the elaboration of sketches or other forms of graphic expression. [15, 16].

2.1   Pedagogical Practices and Technological Tools Supporting Creativity

The literature reports on a number of pedagogical practices that make no use of technology which are aimed at fostering expressiveness and externalization in order to stimulate creativity. Some of them make use of diverse methods which combine the collaborative exchange of ideas [17] based on drawing and sketching [18–20].

The most simple case is the *brainsketching* [21] technique, in which students first draw their ideas individually and then exchange them, so that other participant can complement or modify them, either silently or explaining them at the moment they pass them to other participants [22]. C-sketch was conceived to foster collaboration in industrial design. Five persons work individually on a problem simultaneously proposing a solution by drawing a sketch. After this, they pass their sketches to the following person who complements, modifies or deletes parts of the original design. Sketches are passed among the members of the group until each participant has worked on each proposal once, thus incorporating the aspect of rotation of the ideas to implement collaborative work [23].

There is positive evidence about the use of technology for supporting brainstorming processes using sketches and drawings, although not precisely focused on creativity support: Inkboard [24], Collboard [25], Magic Paper [24], y Co-lab [26] are some examples.

Inkboard, was designed to be used along with videoconferencing, where participants synchronously can draw sketches over a shared workspace (a virtual board) [24]. Collboard, incorporates collaborative elements and freehand sketches using digital pens and interactive boards with private and public spaces; sketches first drawn on private workspaces can be then shared in public ones in order to continue working collaboratively [25]. Magic paper was developed by the MIT and allows teacher and students to draw physical model on a virtual board working collaboratively [24].

All mentioned applications use technology to support creativity. A common aspect to all of them is that participants first develop ideas individually and then share them, in order to converge to a single idea collaboratively; therefore we incorporate this aspect in the design of Sketchpad. Another common aspect to all mentioned applications is that working groups remain static from the beginning to the end of the activity.

Regarding pedagogical practices in business schools' curricula for developing creativity skills in students, the literature reports some research works made on pedagogical methodologies introduced in the curses of their curricula. For example in the year 2007, the *Creative Marketing Breakthrough* (CMB) presents a reference frame for the development of creativity in lectures through specific activities related to Marketing [27]. The CMB model defines creativity as the process through which disruptive ideas are generated, and considers five theoretical concepts as its key elements: (1) *task motivation,* (2) *cognitive flexibility,* (3) *disciplinary knowledge,* (4) *serendipity* and (5) *uncertainty* [27]. In the year 2008, Aylesworth [28] propose to develop creativity in the business classroom through the *improve-mindset* based on the use of techniques of theater improvisation applied to discussion of case analysis. For this, students must follow five steps of theater improvisation: (1) *"Yes, and..."* they have to accept what their classmates say and add something to it. They cannot deny or reject what others previously said. (2) *"Deny, order, repeat and question"*, none of these actions is permitted. (3) *"Driving in the rearview mirror"*, they have to build on the context proposed at the beginning. (4) *"Take Care of yourself ... by Taking Care of Everyone Else"*, collaboration instead of competition is promoted. (5) *"Mistakes are good offers in disguise"*, there are no mistakes during the discussion since all ideas can lead to new perspectives and better understanding of the case. [28]. The *improve-mindset* is meant to generate a collaborative and highly participative atmosphere in the classroom, which leads to spontaneity and creativity [28].

We think it is worthwhile to explore which is the role technology can play for developing creativity in students of a business school, like for example, using tablets for supporting externalization through brainsketching.

2.2 Evaluating the Creativity Factor in Technological Tools

Carroll et al. [29] proposed a questionnaire called Creativity Support Index (CSI), which evaluates the contribution of a technological tool to creativity. CSI identifies six factors which are considered relevant when designing such a tool: (1) *exploration* of the various ideas, concepts or proposals; (2) *collaboration* among participants; (3) *engagement* with the activity being performed; (4) the *effort/reward* of the task must be adequate; (5) *tool transparency*, which means the tool be a mean and not the center of the task; (6) *expressiveness*, (or *externalization*) of ideas must be supported by the tool [29].

The collaboration and externalization factors identified by [29], are relevant aspects for designing a computational tool. Additionally exploration and tool transparency should also be considered. In our opinion engagement and effort/reward result from the perception the user has from the tool.

3   Sketchpad Design

Sketchpad is a collaborative tool running on tablets (specifically iPads) designed to support pedagogical activities which are aimed at developing creativity in undergraduate students of the fourth year in the Business School of the Universidad de Chile. It has been implemented using HTML5 and the Coupled Object technology (described in [30, 31]) so it can be run using web browsers Chrome, Mozilla, or Safari regardless from the operative system of the computational device. Its main interface, shown in Fig. 1, consists of a workspace, which can be private or shared, where the user create sketches by freehand drawing and text typewriting, including basic edition functionalities like deleting, copy and paste, undo, redo, changing colors, zooming in and out, etc.

Students can make their contributions through brainsketching to several individual and/or shared pages but they can work on one only at a time. Icons with a small view of the page content are shown at the right hand side of the interface, separated in a private ("Personal") and a public ("Grupal"). The page that is currently edited is highlighted with a blue frame (see Fig. 1). In order to share a private page the user has simply to drag and drop its icon from the private to the public area. A copy of the page will appear in the public area, keeping the original in the private one. After this, all users participating in the session will see this page as a new icon in the public area. They can start working collaboratively by selecting it, clicking on the icon. Figure 1 shows that the user has created two private pages; one of them has been copied to shared area and has received another icon of someone else who shared a page. The second public page highlighted with a blue frame indicating that the user is currently working on it, thus it is shown in

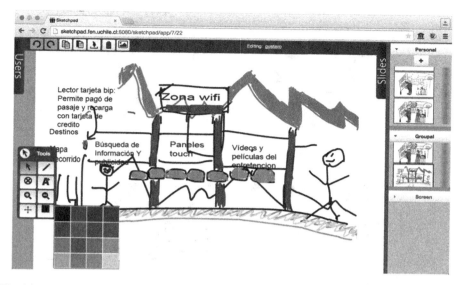

Fig. 1. Main interface of Sketchpad showing in the main workspace a proposal for the design of "technological bus stop"; that is being edited collaboratively. The selected page (highlighted with a blue frame) is in the public ("Groupal") area (color figure online).

the main workspace at the center of the interface. By sketching, students can externalize ideas and proposals, thus promoting creativity [13, 15, 16]. Bruner [13] and Schön [14] mention the advantages of translating ideas into sketches in order to gain new points of views.

Collaborative work using Sketchpad promotes creativity according to what was stated by Fisher, Csikszentmihalyi, Egeström [8] and Sawyer [11], who says that the base for creativity lies in the interaction with others. The easy way that students can access the working pages in the collaborative area contributes to the *tool transparency*, (see Sect. 2.2). Since Sketchpad can be used on tablets it is easy to perform rotations of students among the groups. We think the more students can contribute to one idea or proposal, the better will be the *exploration* factor described in Sect. 2.2, since various points of views can defy the thinking and knowledge structures previously built.

4   Evaluation Methodology

Sketchpad was preliminary evaluated in an exploratory way, through an experiment which consisted of a pedagogical activity in which students had to work in teams each one with three members. Students had to rotate, that means, go from one group to another, in order to work with other teams.

The activity consisted of students proposing ideas through sketches and texts about how to implement technological bus stops that could help solve diverse problems related to the waiting time. First, students had to work individually and then they had to share their ideas with the members of the group and reach consensus on a single proposal for

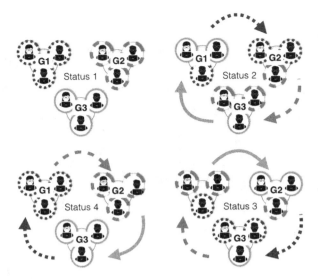

Fig. 2. Descriptive schema of the collaborative activity during rotations of members among groups. The four statuses show the composition of the groups after the rotations indicated by the arrows.

each group. Once the groups have reached consensus they had to rotate in the following way: two members of each group (previously defined) had to leave the group and join the next one, in order to analyze and discuss the idea previously proposed by the group they join. After a while, they rotate to the next group where they see the solution of the new group they join. This rotation is performed until the students reach their original group, where they prepare the final proposal for this group. Figure 2 shows schematically how rotations were performed. There were three working groups G1, G2 and G3, each one with three students. The first sketch (upper right) shows status 1, where participants are in the original arrangement. The second sketch (upper right, status 2) shows the groups after two of them have moved to the next group. The third sketch (bottom right, status 3) shows the groups after the second rotation. The fourth sketch (bottom left, status 4) shows the group after the final rotation where students return to their original groups. It is important to highlight that sketches do not rotate, but only the students. So when students arrive to a new group they have to join the new group by joining the public session in which the sketch corresponding to that group is being worked out. After all rotations are performed, students have seen all the ideas proposed by all groups when they reach their original one. They had also the opportunity to contribute to them. This activity shares some similarities with brainsketching, Gallery method and C-sketch, because it involves sketching and the possibility of having various perspectives on them. The main difference lies in the interaction with other group members before producing the final proposal of the group.

In order to have a control group against which we can compare results, the course was divided in two groups, one working with rotation and the other without.

The universe of students for the experiment consisted of fourth year students of the Faculty of economics and Business of the Universidad de Chile studying during the second semester of 2014. The sample consisted of students enrolled in the Informatics Technology course. Therefore the sample was not probabilistic and was defined by convenience, because it was possible to perform the activity without being disruptive to the course planning. In total, 19 students participated in the experiment, 9 of which performed the activity with rotation divided in three groups of three students each. The rest was divided in two groups of three students and one group with four. The groups were formed randomly. In order to collect information about the experiment we used a closed questionnaire based on the on the Creativity Factor Evaluation (CSI) proposed by Carroll et al. [29]. Additionally we used an open questionnaire in order to evaluate the interaction among participants, and their opinion about the possibility of approaching the problem from different points of views. We also included an external viewer who registered aspects about collaboration and externalization. The CSI questionnaire consisted of two parts. In the first one, students answered questions from the Likert type, assigning values from "totally disagree" to "totally agree" to five assertions, each one expressing positively that the tool was able to support one of the five factors (*collaboration, exploration and expressiveness (externalization), effort/reward, tool transparency, and engagement) according* to their opinion. In the second part they were presented with a list of all possible factor pairs. Since there are five factors the list consisted of 10 pairs. From each pair they had to select which factor they considered more important than the other one for performing the activity.

The obtained data were analyzed in two steps. First, the data collected with the modified CSI questionnaire were processed according to what the authors propose in [29] in order to generate values from 0 to 100 for each factor. Second, the data was processed for obtaining descriptive statistical information using a standard software application (SPSS). On another hand, the data obtained by the observations were analyzed manually.

The activity was performed during a normal class, which lasted for one hour and thirty minutes, after which the questionnaires were applied.

5   Results

Results associated to the CSI questionnaire are shown in Table 1. According to them, Sketchpad favors creativity on a 67,85 level, from 0 to 100. Students who participated in the activity with rotation evaluated better the support of the technological tool with a CSI of 75,07, compared with a CSI of 58,96 from the students who participated in the activity without rotation. However, this difference is still not statistically significant and cannot be generalized. Now we will analyze the CSI factors applied to Sketchpad, this is the pair wise comparison of the factors: (a) the *collaboration* was the factor which was perceived as the most relevant by the students who worked with rotation as well as by the students who worked without rotation; (b) *exploration and expressiveness (externalization)* are the factors which come next, and are within the 53,2 % of the total relevance of the factors, therefore, we can consider that Sketchpad supports the expression and exploration of the proposed ideas; (c) although *effort/reward* factor received a good evaluation (VP = 6,97), it was seldom selected as the most relevant factor for performing the activity (d) Also the *tool transparency* was good evaluated but was seldom regarded as important for the activity; (e) *engagement* was the factor with the lowest evaluation and at the same time the less important for performing the activity.

Table 1. Results of the first part of the questionnaire

FACTOR	Total			Group without rotation			Group with rotation		
	ANF	VP	Rate	ANF	VP	Rate	ANF	VP	Rate
Collaboration	5	6,40	21,33	5	5,32	17,73	5	7,60	25,33
Exploration	4	6,68	17,82	4	5,86	15,63	3	7,60	15,20
Expressiveness (Externalization)	3	7,16	14,32	3	6,58	13,16	3	7,80	15,60
Effort/reward	2	6,97	9,29	1,5	6,58	6,58	3	7,40	14,80
Tool transparency	1	6,21	4,14	1	6,22	4,15	1	6,20	4,13
Engagement	0	5,64	0,94	0,5	5,14	1,71	0	6,20	0,00
	Rate:		67,85	**Rate:**		58,96	**Rate:**		75,07

ANF = mean number of times this factor was selected as the more important in the pair wise comparison; VP = Average score assigned by the students to each factor computed as (number of times the factor was selected *ANF)/1,5. Rate = the rate of the factor according to the answers to the Lickert scale evaluation, modified according to the CSI to obtain values between 0 and 100.

From the analysis of the answers given to the open answers questionnaire related to the aspects of interaction among participants, approaching the problem from various points of views and having them included in the final proposal, the possibility to approach the solution we can conclude the following remarks: (a) regarding the ability of the activity and the tool to support interaction among participants, students in general responded with totally agree, or strongly agree; they said they could discuss with their classmates various ways to approach the problem and the ideas that were proposed. Only 5 % of the answers were negative. (b) Regarding the ability for approaching the solution through various points of view the perception of the students was also positive and most answers were totally agree, strongly agree or agree. Again only 5 % were negative. (c) Regarding the ability to contribute from various points of view to the final result, students said they could know ideas from other participants and this helped to refine the final proposal. Most answers to this assertion were totally agreed, strongly agree or agree. Only 7,9 % of the answers were negative.

The analysis of the observation guideline has shown that actively interacted with their classmates, sharing their ideas and explaining them to the rest. Then students proceeded to merge the individual proposals. In this way, new solutions emerged from the elements of the initially proposed ideas and the discussion. In this way we can consider that the activity fosters creative products collaboratively. During the discussion the individual ideas complemented each other and disagreements were part of the merging process. New ideas emerged when individual proposals were challenged transforming the original ones in new contributions. Sketches made individually helped students to explain their proposals promoting discussion among students. We observed that the number of ideas proposed by the groups which worked with rotation were higher.

6   Discussion

The obtained results allow us to answer positively to the research question about the perception students got from the contribution of Sketchpad to the collaborative activity. They expressed they could interact with the rest of the participants during the activity and that this interaction was fruitful. This assertion is backed by the 67,85 over 100 score they assigned to the creativity factor of the tool. In the same way, we can conclude that students had a positive perception about working with rotations, since students who worked with this modality evaluated all factors better than those working without rotations. Performing the activity with rotations gave students the opportunity to get acquainted with various points of view, often different from their own ones, in a short period of time and consider them when preparing the final proposal. In this way, we wanted to shape a pedagogical activity with a strong collaborative component, a key element for the emergence and development of creativity, based on the approaches proposed by Fisher [8] Csikszentmihalyi, Egeström (described also in [8]) and Sawyer, 2006 [11]. This has been backed by the observations of a collaborative activity performed by students, where we identified that new ideas emerged from discussions among participants. Another key element considered for shaping the activity was externalization, proposed by Bruner [13] and Schön [14], which was achieved incorporating sketching which students have to elaborate and share, which gave students the opportunity to know new perspectives, thus promoting creativity. During the activity sketches were used to explain ideas, being a central element for discussion.

Results obtained about collaboration during the collaborative activity let us believe that the proposed tool, Sketchpad, can be successfully used to support pedagogical activities in classroom that promote creativity skills. The difference between the results obtained with participants who worked with rotations and without them let us think that Sketchpad could be more effective when is used for supporting collaborative activities, as well as in activities requiring a tool for sharing ideas.

Students who worked in both groups, with and without rotation mentioned collaboration as the faction which Sketchpad supports most, which indicates this is perhaps the most relevant factor of the tool. Although the expressiveness (externalization) was the third one selected by the students as the most important factor, was the best evaluated. This let us consider that Sketchpad is successful for supporting an activity based on collaboration and externalization for promoting creativity through brainsketching.

As future work we consider important to make more experiments with a higher number of students to validate these preliminary results.

References

1. Griffin, P., McGaw, B., Care, E.: Assessment and Teaching of 21st Century Skills. Springer, Dordrecht (2011)
2. Schlee, R.P., Harich, K.R.: Teaching creativity to business students: how well are we doing? J. Educ. Bus. **89**(3), 133–141 (2014)
3. Fekula, M.J.: Managerial creativity, critical thinking, and emotional intelligence: convergence in course design. Bus. Educ. Innov. J. **30**(2), 92–101 (2011)
4. AACSB.: Standard 9. Curriculum content is appropriate to general expectations for the degree program type and learning goals (2013) http://www.aacsb.edu/accreditation/standards/2013-business/learning-and-teaching/standard9.aspx
5. AACSB.: Teaching Design for Creativity and Innovation (2015). http://www.aacsb.edu/en/events/Seminars/curriculum-development-series/design-thinking.aspx
6. Harvard Business Review. Harvard Business Review Search: Creativity (2015). https://hbr.org/search?term=creativity
7. Rotherham, A.J., Willingham, D.: 21st century. Educ. Leadersh. **67**(1), 16–21 (2009)
8. Fischer, G.: Social creativity: turning barriers into opportunities for collaborative design. In: Proceedings of the Eighth Conference on Participatory Design: Artful Integration: Interweaving Media, Materials and Practices, ACM (2004)
9. Amabile, T.: Creativity in Context. Westview press, Boulder (1996)
10. Vyas, D., et al.: Collaborative practices that support creativity in design. In: Wagner, I., Tellioğlu, H., Balka, E., Simone, C., Ciolf, L. (eds.) ECSCW 2009, pp. 151–170. (2009)
11. Wegerif, R., et al.: Exploring creative thinking in graphically mediated synchronous dialogues. Comput. Educ. **54**(3), 613–621 (2010)
12. Hennessy, S.: The role of digital artefacts on the interactive whiteboard in supporting classroom dialogue. J. Comput. Assist. Learn. **27**(6), 463–489 (2011)
13. Bruner, J.S.: The Culture Of Education. Harvard University Press, Cambridge (1996)
14. Schön, D.A.: The Reflective Practitioner: How Professionals Think in Action, vol. 5126. Basic Books, New York (1983)
15. Zurita, G., Baloian, N., Baytelman, F.: A collaborative face-to-face design support system based on sketching and gesturing. Adv. Eng. Inform. **22**(3), 340–349 (2008)
16. Zurita, G., Baloian, N., Baytelman, F.: A face-to-face system for supporting mobile collaborative design using sketches and pen-based gestures. In: 2006 10th International Conference on Computer Supported Cooperative Work in Design CSCWD 2006, IEEE (2006)
17. Guzdial, M., Rick, J., Kehoe, C.: Beyond adoption to invention: Teacher-created collaborative activities in higher education. J. Learn. Sci. **10**(3), 265–279 (2001)
18. Van der Lugt, R.: Brainsketching and how it differs from brainstorming. Creativity Innov. Manage. **11**(1), 43–54 (2002)
19. Van der Lugt, R.: How sketching can affect the idea generation process in design group meetings. Des. Stud. **26**(2), 101–122 (2005)
20. Lane, D., Seery, N., Gordon, S.: Promoting creative discovery and mental synthesis through freehand sketching. In: Visualizing Change–Graphics on the Horizon ASEE Engineering Design Graphics Division 65th Mid-Year Conference October (2010)
21. Pickens, J.: Brainsketching. University of Oklahoma, Norman (1980)
22. Linsey, J.S., et al.: An experimental study of group idea generation techniques: understanding the roles of idea representation and viewing methods. J. Mech. Des. **133**(3), 031008-1–15 (2011)

23. Shah, J.J., Vargas-Hernandez, N.O.E., Summers, J. D., Kulkarni, S.: Collaborative sketching (C-Sketch)—An idea generation technique for engineering design. J. Creative Behav. **35**(3), 168–198 (2001)
24. Beavers, J., et al.: The Learning Experience Project: Enabling Collaborative Learning with Conference XP. Microsoft Research (2004)
25. Alvarez, C., et al.: Collboard: fostering new media literacies in the classroom through collaborative problem solving supported by digital pens and interactive whiteboards. Comput. Educ. **63**, 368–379 (2013)
26. van Joolingen, W.R., et al.: Co-Lab: research and development of an online learning environment for collaborative scientific discovery learning. Comput. Hum. Behav. **21**(4), 671–688 (2005)
27. Titus, P.A.: Applied creativity: the creative marketing breakthrough model. J. Mark. Educ. **29**(3), 262–272 (2007)
28. Aylesworth, A.: Improving case discussion with an improv mind-set. J. Mark. Educ. **30**(2), 106–115 (2008)
29. Carroll, E.A., et al.: Creativity factor evaluation: towards a standardized survey metric for creativity support. In: Proceedings of the Seventh ACM Conference on Creativity and Cognition, pp. 127–136 (2009)
30. Frez, J., Baloian, N., Zurita, G.: Software platform to build geo-collaborative systems supporting design and planning. In: 2012 IEEE 16th International Conference on Computer Supported Cooperative Work in Design (CSCWD), IEEE (2012)
31. Baloian, N., Gutierrez, F., Zurita, G.: An architecture for developing distributed collaborative applications using HTML5. In: 2013 IEEE 17th International Conference on Computer Supported Cooperative Work in Design (CSCWD), IEEE (2013)

A Subscription Overlay Network for Large-Scale and Efficient File Parallel Downloading

Patricio Galdames[(✉)], Claudio Gutierrez-Soto, and Cristopher Barrientos

Departamento de Sistemas de Informacion, Universidad del Bio-Bio,
Av. Ignacio Collao 1202, Concepcion, Chile
{pgaldames,cogutier,crbarrie}@ubiobio.cl

Abstract. This paper presents a subscription-based overlay network that supports file parallel downloading for cloud collaboration. First, our system lets users to register to a central server and allows this server to incrementally build a topology graph containing the network connections among the subscribers. With this topology graph in place, we plan to address the challenges of minimizing network traffic and choosing the best set of nodes storing a chosen file for parallel downloading. When a subscriber wants to access a chosen file stored in the cloud, our system obtains for her a list of nodes having this file. Nodes in this list, are sorted considering both their network distance to the subscriber and their workloads. Second, selecting those top nodes, a bandwidth-aware parallel downloading technique is executed. Finally, our proposed system also features leveraging idling nodes for file downloading. More specifically, the subscribers who are on-line but not participating in downloading are recruited to reduce both network traffic and average latency.

Keywords: Subscription-based overlay networks · File parallel downloading · Idling nodes

1 Introduction

File Parallel Downloading (PD) is a technique proposed to disseminate large files across the network. In this scheme, a client opens concurrent connections to several mirror nodes and downloads different part of the file from each one. Since several downloads are executed in parallel, PD can shorten the download time experienced by client nodes, especially for large files [23]. A scenario where PD can be useful since users desire to access their files promptly is in cloud collaboration. This is an emerging way of sharing co-authoring computer files through the use of a cloud computing [20]. In a cloud, files can be automatically disseminated and duplicated in several nodes in order to guarantee their availability and low delay access [12]. These nodes can be servers of a CDN (Content Distribution Network) [25] or computers conforming a P2P (Peer-to-Peer) Network [18].

This work was supported by the Universidad del Bio-Bio, grant no. GI 150115/EF.

© Springer International Publishing Switzerland 2015
N. Baloian et al. (Eds.): CRIWG 2015, LNCS 9334, pp. 210–218, 2015.
DOI: 10.1007/978-3-319-22747-4_17

The initial research in PD focuses in proving that PD can reduce the download time compared to a single downloading [22]. Subsequently, [9] studies the scenario where multiples users are performing PD but they focused on finding an optimal size of a file part, called as *chunk*, to be downloaded from every mirror node. If chunks are too small, client will waste too much time just waiting for the execution of the file transfer. On the contrary, if a chunk size is too large, the download process will take longer since it is more difficult to balance workload among the selected mirror nodes. To overcome this trade-off, several works have suggested that a mirror can pipeline several byte range requests [6, 22]. However, in a P2P scenario where nodes may leave ungracefully at any time, the client downloader can lose the proper synchronization, ending the download with a corrupted file. Other works [6, 13] have studied the impact of multiple PDs over the network performance. These studies show it is necessary to limit the number of client a server can serve and the number of concurrent downloads a client can maintain.

In this work, we propose a bandwidth-aware PD technique that can be used for cloud collaboration. Without loss of generality, we assume the cloud computing is mainly supported by a P2P network. While downloading, our technique periodically adjusts the size of a chunk for every server node based on estimates of the download rate. The size of a chunk is computed as a function of the network congestion and each the state of each server. Second, we take topology and mirror capabilities into account to rank a pool of mirror nodes. Only those nodes with highest rank are considered for downloading. Third, in addition to being topology-aware, the proposed system leverages idling nodes, which are on-line but not participating in downloading/uploading to reduce network traffic and delay. We show how our algorithm is able to find appropriate idling nodes for file sharing.

The remainder of this work in progress is organized as follows. In Sect. 2, we discuss some closely related works. In Sect. 3, we give an overview of the proposed system and assumptions. Then, we discuss how our bandwidth-aware PD works in Sect. 4 and how to incorporate appropriate idling nodes for file sharing in Sect. 5. Finally, we discuss the future work on this paper in Sect. 7.

2   Related Work

PD was first introduced by Rodriguez et al. who proposed two schemes [22]. The first one computes the size of the file chunk to be downloaded from each mirror based on the historic performance of each mirror. The second scheme, called the dynamic one, consists in dividing the file in small disjoint chunks of equal size. When a chunk is completely downloaded from a mirror, a new one is immediately requested. To minimize the amount of time between download requests; the proposed technique requires the server to pipeline several http byte range requests. However, these approaches have some problems. First, the pipeline feature is not recommendable to be used because clients may lose synchronization with the server and they can finally end up producing a corrupted file. According to Bernstein [4] the RFC 959 prohibits the use of pipeline for FTP. Second, the pipeline approach requires knowing beforehand the size of the chunks, which is not possible in a dynamic environment like a P2P network. In our case, our approach does not use pipelining and customizes the size of the chunks on-the-fly according to the network conditions of each mirror node. Later, Funasaka et al. [9] proposed an improvement of the dynamic scheme by replacing the worst performance mirror.

Al-Jaroodi et al. [3] presented a dual-direction FTP (DDFTP) technique that performs the download of a chunk from different directions. This feature allows DDFTP to show high resilience against a mirror failure since the same chunk is being downloaded from another mirror but in the opposite direction. Few other PD techniques ([6] and [5]), require either a new implementation of the operation of the server or a new modification in the content encoding method. Grid-FTP [6] is designed for grid environments by extending the basic FTP to support pipeline of byte range transfer requests in grid systems. On the contrary, our current PD implementation works with standard FTP and therefore it does not require any changes at traditional FTP servers.

The previously mentioned schemes do not take into account network and server resources as a parameter to select the mirror servers. On the contrary, Sohail et al. [23] proposed a parallel FTP that uses the standard FTP. This technique chooses the mirror nodes based on the available bandwidth and end to end delay. In the research area for multi-path forwarding, Zinner [26] and Haitao [7] provide selections of paths for transmissions in a static way, where nodes can eventually decrease their performance. Different to the previous works, we area planning to take into account the dynamic nature of network stress to provide a better selection of transmission paths on-the-fly.

Koo et al. [14] presents analytical and simulation results to show that parallel downloading approaches impact servers and the network significantly. Gkantsidis et al. [11] compares the performance of three parallel downloading techniques in large scale deployment scenario with simulation. This work shows that the introduction of many simultaneous parallel downloading clients in the network can degrade the performance experienced by other clients. To our knowledge none of the aforementioned techniques take advantage of the available resources of those idling nodes to improve the network performance in file parallel downloading. In many file sharing applications, like cloud collaboration, there may exist many registered users, but at any time point, only a few of them could be actively uploading/downloading. Galdames et al. [10] propose the idea of using incentive nodes to leverage an overlay communication network for multi-source multicasting.

3   System Model and Assumptions

When a user C logs into our cloud storage system storage to access a file F, our system checks the freshness of F maintained by C. If F is either not locally maintained or is tainted, our system automatically triggers a file lookup scheme to find out the latest version of F. In this work, we are not concern on how the file lookup technique is implemented [19,21,24] but we assume that our cloud storage service can be either supported by traditional servers [25] or P2P users [18]. In either case, we simply assume our system can call a primitive called as *Search(F)* to locate a set of mirror nodes caching F. We denote this set as *Mirrors(F,C)*. In addition, when C logs into our system, she reports her IP address, current available downlink and uplink bandwidth, the number of active uplink connections and the network path from its Internet location to our server. A simple approach for discovery of network topology is using *tracepath* [16], which is ICMP-based and has been used extensively for Internet topology discovery. Although, our system can operate with any topology discovery tool, we have decided to use *tracepath* due to its simplicity and low bandwidth overhead. Thus, we assume that most of the time the downloading traffic is forwarded through the paths discovered with this technique. The paths obtained may be at router level or coarse-grained AS level. Without loss of generality, we assume router-level path. If only AS information is available, we treat each AS as a router. When a set *Mirrors(F, C)* is retrieved, then it is sorted according to both the network distance of each mirror to C and the available network resources of these nodes. Then C establishes a TCP connection with a few selected nodes in *Mirrors(F,C)*. From each chosen node, a different portion of the file is requested and downloaded concurrently. In addition, C will monitor periodically the downloading rate obtained from each mirror and it will adjust the portion of the file being downloaded. If C detects the download rate obtained for a node is below a pre-defined threshold, the connection is close and the pending data is downloaded later from another node selected from *Mirrors(F,C)*. Also, C informs our system to keep updated details of the historic performance of every mirror. When a file is completely downloaded, C also informs the amount of data downloaded from each node.

When the cloud service storage is supported by a P2P network, we assume its members can be reimbursed (e.g., on-line discount coupons) according to the amount of data they uploaded. Many incentive approaches have been developed [8,17] and we assume that any of them can be used.

In the following sections, we will explain how our PD works and how idling nodes can be used to improve the network performance.

4   Parallel Downloading

We have developed our own parallel downloading technique that we simply named as *APD*. To facilitate its discussion we have divided it in three stages:

Stage 1: Initialization

1. Let n be the cardinality of the ranked subset of *Mirrors(F)*.
2. File F is divided in k blocks of equal size. The value k is a predefined value that controls the chunk size adjustments done during the process of file downloading. The default value for k is n.
3. In addition, each block is divided in n chunks of equal size.

Stage 2: Chunk Downloading

1. For each mirror node i, the client sends a request for a chunk and it begins the process of downloading the flow of bytes from that mirror.
2. When the download of a block is finished, C computes the download rate obtained for each node i, by dividing the size of the chunk downloaded from that node and the downloading time incurred for that mirror. Let r_i be the download rate computed for mirror node i, let l_i be the size of the chunk for mirror i and t_i the download time obtained for chunk i. Then $r_i = (1 - \gamma) * l_i/t_i + \gamma * r_i - 1$ where γ is a constant value equals to $1/8$ [15].
3. A new pending block is chosen and divided into n chunks, where the i-th chunk has a size proportional to r_i.
4. Go back to step 1.

Stage 3: File Verification

1. If any mirror provides a checksum of the file computed with MD5 or SHA-1, then this is compared to the one computed by the client. Otherwise a simple verification of the file size is done.

5   Incentive Forwarding

Users can access our cloud storage service to share their files at any moment. In order that a our system works effectively for users it must be on-line 24 hours a day, 7 days a week. Our system may have a large number of registered users, but at any time chances are that only a small percentage of them are actively using PDs while others are on-line (for activities such as Internet browsing) but not participating in file sharing. We refer to these two types of nodes as active nodes and idling nodes, respectively.

In this section, we first show that recruiting idling nodes (e.g., using some monetary incentive as a motivation) for data forwarding can dramatically reduce the network traffic and latency incurred in data transferring. We will then propose an algorithm that can find appropriate idling nodes.

Figure 1 shows four subscribers, A, B, C, and I, and their underlying network topology. Suppose A, B and C are active and I is idling. If A needs to upload a data packet, we can let it send to B and C directly. In this case, the network

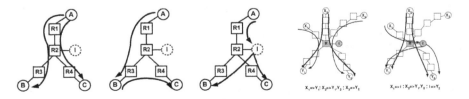

Fig. 1. Motivation example   **Fig. 2.** Traffic bundling

traffic on link R_1 and R_2 will be duplicated. Alternatively, A can upload data packets to B directly and ask B to forward it to C. This approach creates duplicate traffic on link R_2 and R_3. In addition, the data arriving at C experiences a longer latency, since it flows through $A \to R_1 \to R_2 \to R_3 \to B \to R_3 \to R_2 \to R_4 \to C$. Similar problems exist if A sends to C directly and asks C to forward to B. Now suppose node I, an idling node, has the capacity and can be recruited for data forwarding. Then A can send data to I first and let I forward to A and B. Apparently, this approach minimizes the network traffic over the Internet backbone and also ensures a promptly packet delivery.

When an idling node is recruited to forward data, we say this node becomes an incentive node I. A major challenge of implementing such incentive forwarding is to find and incorporate appropriate idling nodes in constructing an overlay flow graph. Unlike an active node, an idling node does not need downloading/uploading data for its own. Thus, an idling node should be recruited only when its assistance in data forwarding can reduce the network costs in file sharing services.

In our design, recruiting idling nodes happens when an off-line node I become on-line, it reports to the server that it is available. When the server is asked to download the same file for two or more clients, the server will find out if one of the recruited idling nodes can be beneficial for data forwarding. We follow a similar idea as it is suggested by [10] to decide whether or not to recruit an idling node in data forwarding. Suppose the server obtains the mirror sets for different clients requesting the same file F. Based on a flow graph generated from nodes in these mirror sets, the server estimates the most probable routes that data will follow from each mirror until it arrives to the client. Given an idling node I, the system first finds out the router R to which I is connected directly and retrieves all connections go through R. If two connections have different sources, say, X_1 and X_3 and different destinations, say Y_1 and Y_2 as shown in Fig. 2, then I can be recruited to assist X_3 in data forwarding. That is, we can replace $X_1 \to Y_1$ and $X_3 \to Y_2$ with $X_1 \to I$, $I \to Y_2$, and $I \to Y_1$. We call this process *bundling*. The benefit of recruiting I to bundle $X_1 \to Y_1$ and $X_3 \to Y_2$ can be computed as $Benefit(X_1, X_3, Y_1, Y_2, I) = Hop(X_1, Y_1) + Hop(X_3, Y_2) - Hop(X_1, I) - Hop(I, Y_1) - Hop(I, Y_2)$. Where $Hop(X, Y)$: is the

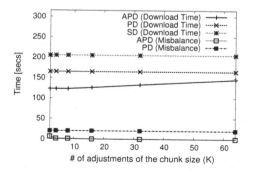

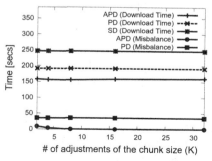

Fig. 3. Test 1   Fig. 4. Test 2

number of hops between nodes X and Y. So if there are multiple candidates for bundling, we bundle the pair that can result in the maximum positive benefit but preventing that a helped client can establish a second connection with node I for a file F and repeat this process until cannot be recruited either a new I that achieves a positive benefit or all the recruited "Is" runs out of its uplink or downlink bandwidth.

6   Performance Evaluation

First, we evaluated the effectiveness of PD technique. To do so, we have implemented a detailed Java parallel downloader that works with FTP. For simplicity, we call this implementation APD. We compare it against two adversary approaches: A single downloading (SD) and a static Parallel Downloading technique (PD) that divides a file into n chunks of equal size and each one is downloaded from a different mirror.

Two performance metrics are measured. The first one is the *download time* which is the time elapsed since the application starts receiving the first byte until the last byte of the file is received. The second one is the *misbalance* which is the time elapsed since the downloading from the fastest mirror finished until the downloading from the slowest mirror has finished.

We have prepared a network testbed with four computers connected to an Ethernet switch of 100 Mbps. Three of these computers act as FTP servers running FileZilla FTP server (version 0.9.42)[1] and the last one runs our Java PD downloader. We performed several tests downloading a file of 1 GB. In our first test, all servers have homogeneous resources and the network bandwidth is divided equally among them. Figure 3 shows the results obtained when chunk-size adjustments (k) are executed during the download process.

As we expected APD achieves the lowest download time in almost all scenarios ($2 < k < 64$). The increasing of the download time is caused by the increasing of the idling time elapsed during the chunk transfer requests. This time becomes higher when the chunk size becomes smaller. We observe our APD gets the highest misbalance when k =2, because APD has just a few (only two) opportunities to equilibrate the workload of each server. As we expected by increasing k (more chunk adjustments) we gets a better balance.

In our second test, we study how APD behaves when servers change abruptly their network resources. We set two mirrors having the same bandwidth but the third one has twice the bandwidth of the first two mirrors. When the download achieves 50 % of the file size, the bandwidth of the third server is reduced to 14 of its initial bandwidth. Figure 4 shows the results obtained when chunk adjustments (k) are executed during the download process. We observe APD can reduce the misbalance without compromising excessively the download time. The above results are promising but we still need to perform more testing to prove the soundness of APD specially when multiple APDs compete for network resources. We plan to study if the recruiting of idling nodes is beneficial. We are currently preparing a testbed on NS-3 [2].

7   Conclusion

We have presented a service for cloud collaboration based on a subscription-based overlay network. Our system supports cloud storage and file parallel downloading for large files. Our system distinguishes itself from existing systems with three unique features. First, it takes into consideration the physical network topology and the network resources of the mirror nodes to select a few of them from which a file will be downloaded through several concurrent connections. The proposed system allows the server to incrementally build a topology graph that reflects the network connections among the subscribers. This topology graph allows minimizing the network traffic and delay incurred in downloading/uploading large files. Second, the proposed PD scheme is able to customize the size of a chunk for every chosen mirror according to its current network and hardware resources.

As future work, we plan to show that the recruiting of idling nodes can indeed give a boost to the overall system performance by reducing link stress and without compromising user latency. We are currently discussing new scenarios where idling nodes can be recruited. For instance, when an idling node becomes online, it can be recruited to reduce network stress and latency for active users performing file downloading. We also are studying the impact of caching portions of popular files in idling nodes. Finally, we plan to extend our Java PD downloader to support http and to improve the robustness of our scheme against ungrateful leaving of nodes.

References

1. FileZilla Server. http://filezilla-project.org/download.php?type=server
2. Ns-3. http://www.nsnam.org
3. Al-Jaroodi, J., Mohamed, N.: Ddftp: dual-direction ftp. In: Proceedings of the International Symposium on Cluster, Cloud and Grid Computing, pp. 504–513 (2011)
4. Bernstein, D.J.: Pipeling. http://cr.yp.to/ftp/pipeling
5. Byers, J.W., Luby, M., Mitzenmacher, M.: Accessing multiple mirror sites in parallel: using tornado codes to speed up downloads. In: Proceedings of IEEE International Conference on Computer Communications, pp. 275–283, 21–25 March 1999
6. Chang, R.S., Guob, M.H., Lina, H.C.: A multiple parallel download scheme with server throughput and client bandwidth considerations for data grids. Future Gener. Comput. Syst. **24**(8), 798–805 (2008)
7. Chen, H., Gong, Z., Huang, Z.: Parallel downloading algorithm for large-volume file distribution. In: Proceedings of the 6th International Conference on Parallel and Distributed Computing, Applications and Technologies, pp. 745–749, December 2005
8. Feldman, M., Lai, K., Stoica, I., Chuang, J.: Robust incentive techniques for peer-to-peer networks. In: Proceedings of the Conference on Electronic Commerce, pp. 102–111 (2004)
9. Funasaka, J., Nakawaki, N., Ishida, K., Amano, K.: A parallel downloading method of coping with variable bandwidth. In: Proceedings of the IEEE ICDCS Workshop on Assurance in Distributed Systems and Networks, pp. 14–19, 19–22 May 2003

10. Galdames, P., Zheng, Q., Cai, Y.: A subscription overlay network for large-scale and cost-efficient any source multicast. In: Proceedings of the IEEE on Performance Computing and Communications Conference, pp. 1–8, 17–19 November 2011
11. Gkantsidis, C., Ammar, M., Zegura, E.: On the effect of large-scale deployment of parallel downloading. In: IEEE Workshop on Internet Applications, pp. 79–90, 23–24 June 2003
12. Kolodner, E.K., Tal, S., Kyriazis, D., et al.: A cloud environment for data-intensive storage service. In: Proceedings of the International Conference on Cloud Computing Technology and Science, pp. 357–366, 29 November - 1 December 2011
13. Koo, M., Rosenberg, C., Dongyan, X.: Analysis of parallel downloading for large file distribution. In: Workshop on Future Trends of Distributed Computing Systems, pp. 128–135, 28–30 May 2003
14. Koo, S., Lee, C., Kannan, K.: A genetic-algorithm-based neighbor-selection strategy for hybrid peer-to-peer networks. In: Proceedings of the International Conference on Computer Communications and Networks, pp. 469–474 (2004)
15. Kurose, F., Ross, K.: Computer Networking: A Top-Down Approach, 6th edn. Pearson, US (2012)
16. Kuznetsov, A.: Tracepath. http://linux.die.net/man/8/tracepath
17. Lai, K., Feldman, M., Stoica, I., Chuang, J.: Incentives for cooperation in peer-to-peer networks. In: Workshop on Economics of Peer-to-Peer Systems (2003)
18. Li, J.: Erasure resilient codes in peer-to-peer storage cloud. In: Proceedings of the International Conference on Acoustics, Speech and Signal Processing, 14–19 May 2006
19. Lv, Q., Cao, P., Cohen, E., Li, K., Shenker, S.: Search and replication in unstructured peer-to-peer networks. In: Proceedings of ACM International Conference on Supercomputing, New York City, NY, U.S.A, 22–26 June 2002
20. Ning, K., Zhou, Z., Zhang, L.J.: Leverage personal cloud storage services to provide shared storage for team collaboration. In: Proceedings of the International Conference on Services Computing, pp. 613–620, 27 June - 2 July 2014
21. Ratnasamy, S., Francis, P., Handley, M., Karp, R., Shenker, S.: A scalable content-addressable network. In: Proceedings of ACM SIGCOMM, pp. 161–172, San Diego, CA, U.S.A (2001)
22. Rodriguez, P., Kirpal, A., Biersack, E.: Parallel-access for mirror sites in the internet. In: Proceedings of the IEEE on Computer Communications, pp. 864–873 (2000)
23. Sohail, S., Jha, S., Kanhere, S., Chun, T.: Qos driven parallelization of resources to reduce file download delay. IEEE Trans. Parallel Distrib. Syst. **17**, 12 (2006)
24. Stoica, I., Morris, R., Karger, D., Kaashock, M., Balakrishman, H.: Chord: a scalable peer-to-peer lookup protocol for internet applications. In: Proceedings of ACM SIGCOMM, pp. 149–160. San Diego, CA, U.S.A (2001)
25. Zhang, Z.L.: Feel free to cache: towards an open cdn architecture for cloud-based content distribution. In: Proceedings of the International Conference on Collaboration Technologies and Systems, pp. 488–490, 19–23 May 2014
26. Zinner, T., Tutschku, K., Nakao, A., Tran-Gia, P.: Using concurrent multipath transmission for transport virtualization: analyzing path selection. In: International Teletraffic Congress, pp. 1–7. IEEE (2010)

Synchronizing Dining Progress in Video-Mediated Time-Shifted Table Talk Induces More Engagement

Tomoo Inoue[1]([✉]) and Yasuhito Noguchi[2]

[1] Faculty of Library, Information and Media Studies, University of Tsukuba,
1-2, Kasuga, Ibaraki, Tsukuba 305-8550, Japan
inoue@slis.tsukuba.ac.jp
[2] Graduate School of Library, Information and Media Studies,
University of Tsukuba, 1-2, Kasuga, Ibaraki, Tsukuba 305-8550, Japan
noguchi@slis.tsukuba.ac.jp

Abstract. To the people who are difficult to have a meal together with their families or close partners because of the time-zone difference or the life-rhythm difference, asynchronous video messaging is one way to achieve time-shifted communication. This paper studies the influence of adaptive video speed control in such a video message. We propose synchronization of the video with its user in that the dining progress matches between the video person and the user. Experimental study was conducted and found that the proposed synchronization increased speech frequency, and decreased the duration of switching pauses of the user. Moreover, higher ratio of eating actions immediately after verbal responses was observed in the proposed video condition, which indicated more active commitment of the user. In total, the synchronized video induced the user become more active in the conversation with the video person.

Keywords: Video-mediated communication · Time-shifted co-dining · Remote co-dining · Synchronization effect · Table talk

1 Introduction

Remote video-mediated communication has been one of the major topics of CSCW to date. Video-mediated communication in daily life has become widely accepted recently after decades of office use by professionals. New demands then have been raised. Remote video-mediated co-dining is one of them. With a video chat tool such as Skype and FaceTime, people can connect each other through video easily. They can enjoy eating together in front of the always-on video chat tool. However such video chat tools are not versatile. All of them only support real-time communication. To the close friends and families who are geographically far apart and/or who have living time difference, those tools cannot provide communication opportunity. Instead rather conventional video messaging is the best way to choose for this time-shifted (asynchronous) environment. Thus they suffer from enjoying remote co-dining experience with conversation.

© Springer International Publishing Switzerland 2015
N. Baloian et al. (Eds.): CRIWG 2015, LNCS 9334, pp. 219–231, 2015.
DOI: 10.1007/978-3-319-22747-4_18

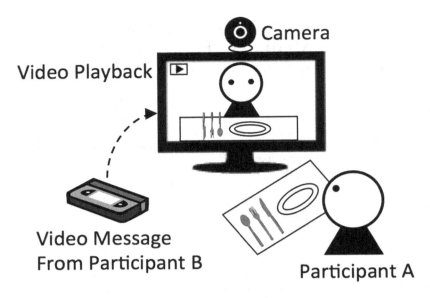

Fig. 1. Conceptual diagram of time-shifted co-dining

To ease this situation, a video-mediated time-shifted co-dining method called KIZUNA has been proposed. The method is as follows. While a person is having a meal, he/she is videotaped in eating and talking knowing that the video will be sent to the partner. When the other person has a meal in different time, the video is played back in front of him/her. This way the basic environment of video-mediated time-shifted pseudo communication, which is a simple exchange of video messages, is established. In this proposed method, the playback speed of the video is adaptively controlled so that the dining progress of the video person is about the same with the one of the viewer in front of the video (Fig. 1) [1].

The method was confirmed to make improve subjective impression on the video person's speak timing and the feeling of co-dining [2], and make increase the viewer's utterance and turn taking frequency [3]. The method is rather simple but seems to produce interesting effects on the user. Yet the analysis of the user's behavioral change was in its initial stage only from a few simple measures. We do not know why the user's subjective impression was improved for instance. Thus in this paper we further investigate what is going on with the user.

2   Related Work

2.1   Conversation over a Meal

A few studies analyzed conversation during a meal. Equalization tendency of utterance and gesture was observed when multiple participants were talking over meal compared with one without meal. This study suggested co-dining was useful when various opinions are called for from diverse people, especially from non-talkative people [4]. Another study investigated the table talk with multiple participants focusing on their roles as a speaker and a hearer. This study suggested the participant decided when to eat depending on the degree of engagement with the conversation, resulting cooperative and fluent table talk. In the study it was observed that the speaker tended to eat soon after his/her utterance whereas the hearer tended to eat soon after his/her response, and this way the table talk was coordinated [5]. These studies analyzed communication behavior in face-to-face conversation over meal.

We can think of a situation where table talk occurs remotely with mediated technology, but fewer studies are found perhaps because this situation is emerging very recently. One such study investigated the difference of face-to-face co-dining and remote co-dining. In the study it was suggested the visibility of a meal in remote co-dining was effective to make it closer to face-to-face [6].

All the studies address conversation over a meal in the same time. No study except our proposal that was described in the introduction is found that address conversation over a meal in different time.

2.2   Co-dining Support System

The development of co-dining support systems seems to have been rather advanced compared to the analysis of co-dining or table talk. Accenture introduced a tele-dining prototype called the Virtual Family Dinner that would allow a remote family to dine together through a video connection. The prototype was essentially a videoconferencing system which was highly automated and easy to operate by targeting people with limited knowledge of technology, such as the elderly. The system monitors the site and when it detects a meal dish on the table, it goes through a list of contacts, trying to reach one who is available for a chat [7]. The advertising agency Wieden+Kennedy's Amsterdam office produced a web site called Virtual Holiday Dinner, enabling scattered friends and family to have a dinner party of up to five people via Skype. Guests can call into the dinner, and their faces are shown on the displays placed at the heads of models physically sitting around a dining table. The models are equipped with video cameras, so each guest can look around the dining table from the respective model's viewpoint by moving his/her head from the web site [8]. A system called CoDine consists of a dining table embedded with interactive subsystems that augment and transmit the experience of communal family dining. CoDine connects people in different locations through shared dining activities, such as gesture-based screen interaction, mutual food serving, ambient pictures on an animated tablecloth, and the transmission of edible messages [9]. These systems only achieve co-dining experience in the same time.

2.3   Video-Mediated Time-Shifted Communication Support System

There are systems for supporting video-mediated time-shifted communication. They essentially exchange video messages in different settings. VideoPassage was one of such systems in the different-time and same-place setting. This enabled asynchronous exchange of video messages by overlaying new video recordings on the replayed old video message [10]. Asynchronous video messages was also employed to support interpersonal relationships in separated families. The recipient viewed the video messages asynchronously, creating a non-stressful, continuous line of communication. This was believed to enhance the connectedness and intimacy between separated family members [11]. Tang et al. introduced a system enabling a distant person to contribute to a workplace meeting by pre-recording comments to be played during the meeting when needed. The conducted field experiment showed that most of the recorded messages were played in the meetings, while a lesser percentage of the messages generated in the meeting were reviewed by the distant person [12]. All these systems however only used the video without processing. The possibility of media processing for enhancing communication have not been explored. In contrast our proposal explores the media processing for enhancing communication.

3   Experiment

To investigate the effect of synchronizing the dining progress of the video person in time-shifted co-dining, an experiment was conducted that compared the pseudo co-dining in adaptive video playback speed (synchronizing condition) with the one in normal video playback speed (control condition).

3.1   Video Message for the Experiment

In the experiment the video message from the dining partner should be the same, and thus it was recorded while an actor (experiment cooperators) ate and talked according to the predetermined scenario shown in Table 1. Because the assumed co-dining situation, which is the most common situation, is with close people such as family members, friends, and colleagues, the participant of the experiment should be a friend of the actor. As this constraints the number of participants, 3 video messages by 3 different actors were prepared. All 3 videos were with the same scenario but with different languages (Japanese, Chinese and Arabic) by 3 males. Each video included a single person that was watched by a single participant in this experiment. The actors were instructed to have a meal just like in the daily life. The sentences of the scenario were from questions and answers, the time between was set considering the time to respond. a 400 g plate of curry with rice and a soft drink was used as the meal in the videos. The video lengths resulted in about 9 min. The meal progress in the each video was measured and recorded in every minute before the experiment.

3.2   Video Control

The video playback speed was set to 0.7 times for slow playback and 1.5 times for fast playback compared to 1 for standard playback. These were determined

Table 1. Scenario of the recorded video message

(mm:ss)	Questions and Comments
Begin	Q) Hello, how are you today?
00:45	The weather here is so nice today, I like the summer season
01:30	Q) Do you like your meal?
02:15	Delicious, I like curry rice
03:00	Q) By the way, What's your favorite food?
03:45	Personally, I like the (Italian) food a lot
04:30	Q) Where do you live?
05:15	I like (Tsukuba) city. It's safe, clean and the people are so friendly
06:00	Q) Do you have any plan for the summer vacation?
06:45	I like the sea a lot, so most probably I will go to a beach and have some relaxed time
07:30	Q) Which country would you like to visit?
08:15	Nice, I like to visit (Italy). I want to go there to eat (Italian) food
End	Thank you. I am looking forward to meeting you again in the next video

by the impression survey in advance so that the video could be watched without any serious problem. In the experiment, the meal progress was looked up every minute. When more than 5 % difference between the food remain in the video and of the user was found, the playback speed was changed to decrease the difference.

3.3 Setup

The experimental session was conducted in the booth of our lab so that the environment was controlled across the conditions. Actual scene is shown in Fig. 2. The USB Camera 1 was used to record the viewer's facial expressions, gestures, and responses, which could become a response video message. The USB Camera 2 was used to read the weight of the meal, which the experimenter used for controlling the video. This means that we used WOZ (Wizard of Oz) method in this experiment. The experimenter was outside of the booth and hidden from the participants. He read the meal progress from weight of the meal, compared it with the one in the video, and control the video playback speed according to the difference in dining progress every minute.

3.4 Participant

Twenty-four university students, 9 males and 15 females, participated. They were divided in 2 groups where one group participated in the synchronizing condition and the other in the controlled condition. None of the participants experienced this experiment before.

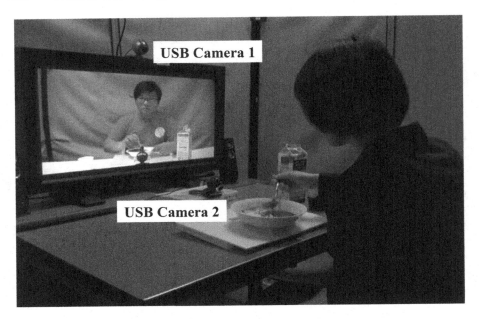

Fig. 2. Actual scene of the experiment

3.5 Meal

A plate of curry with rice and a soft drink was used as the meal, which was the same in the videos. Each participant chose the size of the meal from 300 g or 500g, which was different from 400 g in the videos. This was intended to represent the meal difference in the real world within the limitation of controlled experiment. The weights were determined after looking around similar commercial products. Com-pared with 400g, 300g is 25 % decrease and 500 g is 25 % increase. 300g was chosen by 11 and 500 g was chosen by 13 participants.

3.6 Procedure

After the briefing and the information consent for the experiment, the participant was guided to the booth and was instructed the use scenario of the setup. He/she was instructed that the person in the video would talk, that his/her dining and talking was recorded and would be watched by the video person later. He/she was asked to behave just like in their daily lives. He/she was not informed of the experimental conditions. The experimenter then left the booth and started the video playback which was the indication of the beginning of the session. After the session he/she was asked to fill out a questionnaire.

4   Result

The recorded video was analyzed in terms of the participant's communication and eating behavior. The analyzed part of the video was from the beginning of the video message to the end of the video message or to the time the participant finished a meal. The average length of the video was 8.8 min (s.d. = 1.2). 28.2 % of the total playback time was not in the standard speed, where 15.4 % was in slow playback and 12.8 % was in fast playback.

Figure 3 is an example of the actual dining progress with and without synchronization. Here x-axis is the time past from the beginning of the experiment and y-axis is the percentage of the food remains. Participant line shows the food remains of a participant. Actor Sync. line shows the food remains of the video person in the synchronizing condition. Actor Non-Sync. line shows the simulated food remains of the video person if it was in the control condition. The value on the plot is the subtraction of the participant's food remain from the video person's food remain, which means the difference in dining progress (DDP).

In this example where the participant chose 500 g meal, the average difference in dining progress was -8 %. DDP from the beginning to 3 min. was within -5 % to 5 %, and the video was played in the standard speed. DDP was -9 % which was below -5 % when checked on 4 min., the playback speed was set slow. As DDP kept below -5 % after this, the playback speed kept slow. The difference of each finishing meal was about 1 min. If the speed had not been changed the video person would have finished his meal in 9 min., resulting 4 min. finishing time difference. Slow playback speed in the synchronizing condition helped decreasing DDP.

4.1   Descriptive Values

The video was labeled in terms of speech and eating using a video annotation tool. The measures were:

- Speech frequency: The number of speech in a minute
- Speech length: The average length of speech
- Switching pause of the participant: The time needed for the participant respond to the video person's speech
- Switching pause of the video person: The time until the video person speak after the participant's speech
- Overlapping frequency: The number of overlapping speech between the video person and the participant in a minute
- Response rate: The rate of the participant's response to the video person's speech
- Eating frequency: The number of eating in a minute

Here the utterance longer than 1.5 second was identified as speech, and the action of taking the food and bringing it to the mouth was identified as eating.

The result of each measure for both conditions and the statistical significance of those differences were shown in Table 2. The speech frequency was marginally

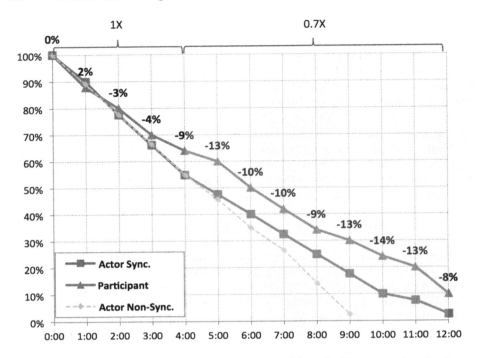

Fig. 3. An example of the actual dining progress with and without synchronization

Table 2. The average data per condition result.

Measures	Synchronizing	Control	p-Value of Mann-Whitney U test
Speech frequency (times/minute)	3.45	2.43	*0.083
Speech length (sec.)	3.49	3.11	0.908
Switching pause (Participant) (sec.)	1.57	2.89	***0.004
Switching pause (Video person) (sec.)	16.9	20.6	0.386
Speech overlap (times/minute)	0.40	0.27	0.885
Response rate (%)	85.2	78.7	0.487
Eating frequency (times/minute)	3.07	2.81	0.436

***: $p < 0.01$, *: $p < 0.1$

significantly larger in the synchronizing condition than in the controlled condition (U=42, Z=-1.732, p=0.083). The switching pause of the participant was significantly shorter in the synchronizing condition than in the controlled condition (U=22.5, Z=-2.859, p=0.004).

4.2 Relation Between Speech and Eating

The time-shifted communication in this setup is pseudo communication where the participant responds to the message of the video person. Because of the

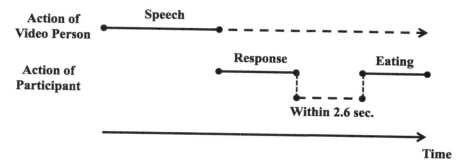

Fig. 4. Adjacent eating

style that the participant watches the video, it was common that the participant became a hearer of the video person.

In a study that addressed the behavior of a hearer in face-to-face triad table talk, it was reported that the hearer adjusted the eating timing according to the degree of engagement to the conversation, which contributed to bring cooperative table talk. When the hearer was directly addressed from the speaker, it was defined that the degree of engagement to the conversation of the hearer was high. In this situation, it was observed that the hearer responded to the speaker before eating. In other words, the conversation gained the priority to eating. This eating action adjacent to the response was regarded as distinctive action of attentive listening of the hearer [5].

The degree of engagement could be measured by investigating the eating action adjacent to the response according to this study (Fig. 4). As our experimental setting was dyad table talk, the participant was always the direct addressee of the speech. We assumed however there could be the different degree of engagement to the conversation in different dyad conversations.

We compared this "adjacent eating" between the conditions. All the first eating actions the participant took during or after the video person's speech were investigated whether it was the adjacent eating or not. The adjacent eating is the eating action after the response within certain limited time.

As for the response, verbal response such as answering to the video person's question and back-channeling is included. Nonverbal response such as turning head, gazing, and nodding is not included on the other hand because this measure intends to see the case where speech takes priority to eating. Whether the response was corresponding to the video person's speech and thus was acceptable as response or not was determined by the two experimenters independently.

As for the certain limited time within which eating action should follow after the response, adequate maximum time is regarded as twice the standard deviation of the stroke action of eating, which can be acceptable as the time-lag between intention and behavior of eating [5]. In this experiment the stroke action was from scooping the food by a spoon to carrying it to the mouth. The total number of eating actions was 706. The average stroke length was 1.6 second with

Table 3. Adjacent eating rate.

	Synchronizing		Control		p-Value of Mann-Whitney U test
	Adjacent	Non-Adjacent	Adjacent	Non-Adjacent	
Number of samples	114	28	87	39	
Rate	82.6 %	17.4 %	66.0 %	34.0 %	**0.034

**: p < 0.05

the standard deviation 0.5 second. Thus the limited time in this experiment was 2.6 second (=1.6+2*0.5).

Therefore the precedence of the response within 2.6 second was examined for all the above sampled eating. Table 3 shows the result. In the synchronizing condition, the number of all the sampled eating was 142 where the number of adjacent eating was 114. The rate of adjacent eating was 83 %. In the control condition, the number of all the sampled eating was 126 where the number of adjacent eating was 87. The rate of adjacent eating was 66 %. Significant difference was found in the rate of adjacent eating between the conditions by Mann-Whitney's U test (U=35.5, Z=-2.115, p=0.034). The adjacent eating was taking place more often in the synchronizing condition. This suggested higher degree of engagement to conversation in the synchronizing condition.

5 Discussion

5.1 Behavioral Change in Synchronizing Dining Progress

Synchronizing dining progress had effect of increasing speech frequency and decreasing the length of switching pause of the participant as shown in Table 2. It indicates that the participant involves in conversation more actively when the dining progress is synchronized. Synchronizing dining progress also induced more adjacent eating after the response to the video person as shown in Table 3. This behavior indicates that the participant feels more engagement with the conversation with the video person.

5.2 Unaware Behavioral Change Causing Better Subjective Feeling

It was reported that synchronizing dining progress increased the feeling of eating together in the same room, and the feeling of naturalness of the video person's speech timing [2], despite the fact that video person's speech timing was not controlled. In the beginning we had no idea what caused this subjective feeling. First we hypothesized that this might be related to the difference of speech overlaps between the video person and the participant. If there happens very frequent speech overlaps, it could be recognized as unnatural. The result was however negative to this hypothesis. We found no significant difference regarding the speech overlap as in Table 2. We then hypothesized that this might be related to the difference of switching pause of the video person. If the switching pause of the video person happened to be shorter in the synchronizing condition as a result of video playback speed control, it could be recognized as more natural because the switching pause in face-to-face conversation is shorter. The result was again negative to this hypothesis. We found no significant difference regarding the switching pause of the video person as in Table 2.

In contrast with these initial hypotheses that were turned down, significant difference between the conditions was found in the switching pause of the participant, not the video person. The switching pause of the participant was significantly shorter in the synchronizing condition. This shorter switching pause could make the participant feel more natural of the speech timing. Also more adjacent eating, which was also the behavior of the participant, was observed in the synchronizing condition. This could make the participant feel more engaging to the conversation. Surprisingly these results revealed that the participant himself/herself adjusted when to talk and when to eat cooperatively with the video person's recorded behavior. Thinking together with the subjective feeling obtained in the previous study, the participants were not aware of this their own behavior.

5.3 Switching Pause of the Participant

The average switching pause of the participant in this experiment was 1.6 second in the synchronizing condition and 2.9 second in the control condition. Compared with the reported median switching pause in face-to-face dialogue which was about 0.4 second [13], the synchronizing condition was closer to face-to-face conversation in this aspect. Although these switching pauses were both longer, considering that the reported switching pause with meal was longer than one without meal [14], the result was in line with the previous studies.

5.4 Synchronization Effect

It is well known that various synchronization occurs when people take cooperative action consciously or unconsciously. Spontaneous synchronization of body movement which is also called entrainment is one of this synchronization effect. In general this can be interpreted as reciprocity. Interesting phenomenon observed in this research is that a small synchronization from the video induced the viewer's synchronizing reaction unconsciously. Even the matching of meal progress, which seems indirect synchronization, causes rather surprising effect.

As a similar video control of changing playback speed, other matching or synchronization could be possible with the development of human behavior recognition technology. For example talking speed in the video might be matched with the user's talking speed if they are different. If the behavior matching between the video person and the user can work as the synchronization between the video person and the user in the same way of matching the meal progress, meal might not be necessary for improving communication and other synchronization can be used for improving interpersonal communication.

5.5   On the Limitation of Synchronizing Target

In this study the video person is a human, but we can think of changing he/she to other object. We can easily think of replacing the video person with a human-like interface agent, an avatar, or a robot. It is possible that similar synchronization effect is observed when the replaced object is human-like. We can also think of other animals, creatures, and even inorganic objects, but how far it could be from human appearance to have synchronization effect is another issue.

5.6   On the Different Number of Participants

This study is on person-to-person table talk, but it is common that more than two persons have meal together when talking. We can think of the case where a video person is watched by multiple persons around a table. It is probable that the multiple persons may somehow adjust meal progress each other in this face-to-face setting. So the meal progress of the video person can be synchronized with these persons. This also applies to the case where multiple video persons are around a table with multiple persons. The meal progress of all the video persons can be synchronized with these persons. We can think of yet another case where multiple video persons are watched by a single user, but this is not a problem because all the video can be synchronized with the user.

6   Conclusion

In long pursuit of better remote communication in CSCW, video-mediated time-shifted communication has not been explored very much. Our proposal of synchronizing the video with its viewer may be one way to improve this communication category. In this study we applied meal as a key for synchronization and successfully produced synchronization effect, besides meal effect which brings other improvement to communication. The synchronization induced more engagement with conversation. The behavioral evidence was observed by deliberate investigation although the participant was not always aware of the behavior.

Acknowledgment. We thank Fumihiro Yoshizawa for helping the analysis of this study. Thanks also goes to JSPS Grant-in-Aid for Scientific Research 26330218 and 15K00888 for financial support of this study.

References

1. Otsuka, Y., Nawahdah, M., Inoue, T.: Development of KIZUNA system capable of time-shifted co-dining communication. Technical report of The Institute of Electronics, Information and Communication Engineers, **112**(75), 85–90 (2012)
2. Nawahdah, M., Inoue, T.: Virtually dining together in time-shifted environment: KIZUNA design. In: Proceedings of the 2013 ACM SIGCHI Conference on Computer Supported Cooperative Work (CSCW 2013), pp. 779–788 (2013)

3. Inoue, T., Nawahdah, M.: Influence of dining-progress synchrony in time-shifted tele-dining. In: Proceedings of the CHI 2014 Extended Abstracts on Human Factors in Computing Systems, pp. 2089–2094 (2014)
4. Inoue, T., Otake, M.: Effect of meal in triadic table talk : equalization of speech and gesture between participants. Trans. Hum. Interface Soc. **13**(3), 19–29 (2011)
5. Tokunaga, H., Mukawa, N., Kimura, A.: Structure of cooperative communication behavior during table talk: when do hearers eat and when do they respond. J. Jpn Soc. Fuzzy Theory Intell. Inform. **26**(4), 793–801 (2014)
6. Furukawa, D., Inoue, T.: Showing meal in video-mediated table talk makes conversation close to face-to-face. IPSJ **54**(1), 266–274 (2013)
7. http://gizmodo.com/accenture-virtual-family-dinner/
8. http://www.virtualholidaydinner.com/
9. Wei, J., Wang, X., Peiris, R.L., Choi, Y., Martinez, X.R., Tache, R.J. Koh, T.K.V., Halupka, V., Cheok, A.D.: Codine: an interactive multi-sensory system for remote dining. In: Proceedings of the 13th International Conference on Ubiquitous computing, pp. 21–30 (2011)
10. Takada, T., Harada, Y.: Citation-capability of video messages and its supporting system. Comput. Softw. **16**(6), 562–570 (1999)
11. Zuckerman, O., Maes, P.: Awareness system for children in distributed families. In: Proceedings of the Conference on Interaction Design and Children (2005)
12. Tang, J., Marlow, J., Hoff, A., Roseway, A., Inkpen, K., Zhao, C., Cao, X.: Time travel proxy: using lightweight video recordings to create asynchronous, interactive meetings. In: Proceedings of the 2012 ACM Annual Conference on Human Factors in Computing Systems (CHI 2012), pp. 3111–3120 (2012)
13. Nagaoka, C., Komori, M., Nakamura, T.: The interspeaker influence of the switching pauses in dialogue, Japan Ergonomics Society (JES). Ergonomics **38**(6), 316–323 (2002)
14. Furukawa, D., Higaki, Y., Inoue, T.: The effect of the appearance of meal in dyadic video-mediated table talk. Technical report of The Institute of Electronics, Information and Communication Engineers, **112**(176), 37–41 (2012)

Contrasting People's Attitudes Towards Self-disclosure in Online Social Networks and Face-to-Face Settings

Maria L.B. Villela[1,2,3(✉)], Simone I.R. Xavier[1], Raquel O. Prates[1], Marcos O. Prates[1], Frank Shipman[2], Antônio A.P. Prates[1], and Alexandre A. Cardoso[1]

[1] Universidade Federal de Minas Gerais, Belo Horizonte, Brazil
{mvillela,simone.xavier,rprates}@dcc.ufmg.br
marcosop@est.ufmg.br, aaprates@oi.com.br,
alexcard@fafich.ufmg.br
[2] Texas A&M, Texas, USA
shipman@cse.tamu.edu
[3] Universidade Federal dos Vales do Jequitinhonha e Mucuri, Unaí, Brazil

Abstract. While Online Social Networks (OSNs) allow closer interaction among their users, they trigger users' privacy concerns related to self-disclosure. The reason for is that individual's information and online activities are easily traced, collected and stored in OSNs when compared to face-to-face settings. In this context, this work aims at understanding how similar or different are people's concerns and attitudes about self-disclosure in both OSNs and face-to-face settings, focusing on investigating what information people consider personal and with whom they feel comfortable in sharing which pieces of their information within these two contexts. Our analysis shows that people associate different degrees of "personalness" to different pieces of information. Furthermore, our data shows that people have different attitudes regarding which information they share in which world and how they share it. This indicates that people understand that OSN and face-to-face settings require different behaviors and that they take into account how personal they perceive a piece of information to be, in deciding if and how to share it.

Keywords: Self-disclosure, privacy · Online social networks · Facebook · Face-to-face settings · Survey · Self-disclosure attitudes, contrast

1 Introduction

Over the past few years, online social networks (OSNs) have experienced a growth in their number of participants, as well as having been integrated into people's daily lives [1]. Such remarkable presence of OSNs in people's lives is because they offer their users the opportunity to interact with each other in a fast and easy way.

In OSNs, users are encouraged to post photos and videos and to share personal information about their interests, hobbies, beliefs and others, fostering self-disclosure, (i.e., the process through which we share information about ourselves with others [2]). Thus, as one of the goals of OSNs is to foster interaction, self-disclosure becomes a necessary requirement for this interaction to take place [3]. However, while these

© Springer International Publishing Switzerland 2015
N. Baloian et al. (Eds.): CRIWG 2015, LNCS 9334, pp. 232–247, 2015.
DOI: 10.1007/978-3-319-22747-4_19

systems allow for a closer interaction among their users, they trigger users' privacy concerns, given that one's information and online activities can be easily traced, collected and stored in OSNs when compared to face-to-face settings [4, 5].

Considering privacy as a desirable state that people strive towards by keeping personal information private according to their context [6], and given that self-disclosure implies a major threat to privacy [3, 7], we might get a broader understanding of how similar or different are people's concerns and attitudes about privacy in OSNs and face-to-face settings, by analyzing and contrasting people's concerns and attitudes related to self-disclosure in these two contexts. Understanding this difference is important in order to evaluate how OSNs support users' needs, as well as how they change the way people interact and create new needs. In this direction, the present study focuses on investigating the following two questions: (1) what information do people consider personal and to what degree? and (2) who do they feel comfortable in sharing their information with in both OSN and face-to-face settings?

In order to collect data about people's attitudes that would allow us to investigate these questions, we have conducted a survey through Mechanical Turk of US participants. The survey requested users to rate how personal several pieces of information were to them, and to report with whom they would feel comfortable sharing them in face-to-face settings (which we will refer to as "physical" or "offline" world) and OSNs (which we will refer to as "virtual" or "online" world), among other things. To probe about the virtual world we chose Facebook as the representative system, since it is the most popular OSN in the United States and globally, having in March 2015 over one billion active accounts.[1]

Our analysis shows that people associate different degrees of how personal different pieces of information are and that they have different concerns and attitudes regarding self-disclosure in virtual and physical worlds. This understanding about online and offline self-disclosure might contribute to research, design and evaluation of privacy mechanisms in OSNs.

This paper is organized as follows: at the outset, we summarize related work and describe the survey designed and its application. Then we describe the respondents, their experience on Facebook and discuss the findings on the different levels of "personalness" they consider a piece of information to be, and with whom they share some pieces of information according to how personal they have rated them. We conclude by discussing implications of these findings and by outlining future work.

2 Related Work

Several studies have explored self-disclosure online and shown that contexts play an important role in how people share their private information. We expand on prior work by examining self-disclosure of content clustered according to how personal participants rated each piece of information that compose it, aiming to understand the connection between self-disclosure in both online and offline contexts.

---

[1] http://newsroom.fb.com/company-info/ Last visited in May, 2015.

2.1   Sharing Different Kinds of Information with Different People

A number of works have found that when sharing specific types of elements, who it is being shared with is an important factor in deciding whether or not to share it [4, 8–11]. Kolimi et al. [9] analyzed with whom and why people want to share (or not) some private information elements and found that people share their private information with people who they trust and are close to them. In the same direction, Olson et al. [10] studied the disclosure of some types of private information (e.g., age, phone number, credit card number, email content, income, health, current location, etc.) to different types of people, in a general context not restricted to online or offline worlds. They found that an individual's willingness to share depends on who they are sharing the information with, besides they also found clusters of information that are treated similarly with respect to how such information is (or not) shared (with a specific audience). In the opposite direction, Sleeper et al. [4] examine what kinds of content people do not want to share on Facebook and why; and their most interesting finding was that participants could have potentially shared a relatively large subset of their self-censored content if they could have exactly targeted the desired audiences.

On another direction, a number of studies have explored users' sensitivity towards sharing different kinds of information with a broad audience in an online environment [5, 12–17]. Stutzman et al. [5] conducted a longitudinal study to understand how Facebook users' disclosure behavior related to some profile elements changed over a period of time and found a robust decreasing trend in public disclosure between the years 2005 and 2009 and a smaller but significant trend reversal in the years of 2010 and 2011, due to continual changes in policy and interface settings. Day [13] investigates the use of Facebook to self-disclose and found that people were aware of personal privacy issues and tended to be cautious about the types of information they reveal, posting mainly positive statements about themselves. Bevan et al. [12] examined how Facebook users prefer to share important positive and negative life events related to romantic relationships, health, and work/school information. They found that users preferred to share positive life events indirectly, via photos with no caption or relationship status changes without context or explanation, whereas negative life events were more likely to be disclosed directly, through status updades. Atrill and Jalil [14] found that people disclose their personal information online aiming to form relationships in these environments and such self-disclosure occurs mainly for superficial self-information relating to personal matters and interests, indicating a selective categorical disclosure, which was later confirmed for the domain of OSNs [17].

Like these previous studies, our results also show a selective categorical disclosure on SNS. However, different from them, we categorize information according to their level of personalness rated by participants themselves. Such clustering is important to understand the connection between people's sharing attitudes in face-to-face settings and on OSNs, considering that how personal a piece of information is may determine or influence the sharing attitudes towards it.

2.2 Sharing in Online and Offline Contexts

Several studies have explored how online and offline contexts are intertwined. For example, Cranshaw et al. [18] investigated relationships between the users' mobility patterns and structural properties of their underlying social network, providing a model for predicting friendship between two users by analyzing their location trails. Grieve et al. [19] investigated offline social connectedness derived from the use of Facebook and concluded that it may act as a separate social medium in which to develop and maintain relationships, providing an alternative social outlet associated with a range of positive psychological outcomes. Rosen et al. [20] addressed the impact of offline social network characteristics on online behavior of people from different cultural backgrounds. Their results suggest that larger strong tie networks are positively related to OSN network size and photo sharing, with strong tie defined as a person who the participant has known for a long time, has frequent communication with, and positive feelings for. Subrahmanyam et al. [21] shows how young adults use OSNs to strengthen different aspects of their offline connections.

Specifically on self-disclosure, most studies that have compared self-disclosure in online and offline contexts are focused in dyadic interactions [22]. Nonetheless, in a different direction, Emanuel et al. [23] compared how self-disclosure may differ between offline, general online and specific contextual online environments, by asking people to provide different statements in response to the question "Who am I?". Their results suggest that participants were willing to disclose more of their private information in face-to-face settings than within an online space. Additionally, studies have shown that the reason why self-disclosure might be different in offline and online contexts is because of the system's affordances, in this last context, which may influence the goals of self-disclosure and also affect the strategies that users employ when making decisions about what and with whom to disclose site [2, 4, 5, 7, 24].

In our study, we compare offline and online self-disclosure in a one-to-many context, focusing on OSNs for online self-disclosure. Different from previous works, we take into account the level of personalness of the information to be shared, as a determinant factor in the way people share their information in both online and offline environments. We analyze how attitudes regarding self-disclosure change when people migrate from face-to-face settings to OSNs. Thus, understanding users' attitudes towards different pieces of information in online and offline worlds can support research on privacy and on privacy management interface development.

3 Study Design

To collect data about how personal people perceived a piece of information to be and their attitudes towards sharing information in the physical and virtual worlds we chose to conduct a survey. We used Amazon Mechanical Turk to recruit and screen participants for our study. The survey was implemented separately and hosted on a server located at the Federal University of Minas Gerais (UFMG). Participants accessed the survey link from Mechanical Turk and at the end of the survey they received a code that they then had to enter into Mechanical Turk so that they could receive credit for participating in it.

We followed best practice guidelines for using Mechanical Turk described in the literature [25–27]. We couched our screener and questionnaire as a Mechanical Turk Human Intelligence Task (HIT). The HIT was offered to United States Turkers who have proven themselves reliable in their past work (i.e. 95 % or greater HIT approval rate and 50 or greater number of HITs approved). The HIT was framed with a strongly worded statement that we were seeking participants who were Facebook users. We double-checked these characteristics in the screener and respondents who did not have a Facebook account could not continue to complete the questionnaire. Respondents were paid at established rates for Mechanical Turk, which worked out to 50 cents/questionnaire; even if their data was eventually discarded.

The survey, as a Mechanical Turk HIT, took the form of a series of questions that collected participants' demographic information, their use experience in online social networks, their beliefs and attitudes about privacy in general and privacy in Facebook and their perception about online privacy versus offline privacy. At the end, a final question tested the respondent's reading comprehension. Although the survey had a broader focus, in this paper we focus on the analysis regarding users' perceptions and attitudes regarding information disclosure in face-to-face settings and on Facebook.

The HIT was deployed for one month from March to April 2014, but the total number of requested respondents was achieved in just 10 days. As we were interested in identifying privacy issues related to American culture, we discarded data from respondents who reported not being Americans and having been living in the U.S. for five years or less. In addition, we screened the responses based on a three point disqualification test. In other words, there were 5 disqualifying criteria, and if a respondent scored 3 or more points in them, his/her answers were not considered in the analysis. The disqualifying criteria adopted were:

- Respondent answered the reading comprehension question incorrectly;
- Respondent reported using Facebook for longer than they informed they had been using online social networks in general;
- Respondents reported incompatible responses in the question asking with whom they felt comfortable to share information in the physical world (for example, respondents who selected the option nobody, as well as other options that indicated other groups of people, such as family or friends);
- Respondents who reported incompatible responses in related questions. For instance on how many Facebook friends they knew in person and which groups of people they had added as friend on Facebook. So if respondents reported not knowing personally any of their friends on Facebook and reported having added as friends only people they knew personally (e.g. friends or family) their response was considered inconsistent. The same situation also applied to respondents who reported knowing personally every one of their friends on Facebook and reported having added as friends people they did not know personally;
- Respondents who chose inconsistent options as answer to the question about what kind of privacy-related issues they had experienced on Facebook. For instance, if they selected both "never had privacy issues" and another option that described a specific privacy issue.

After ten days, the HIT had been completed by 594 respondents and 581 passed the secondary screening criteria. Respondents took on average 11 min and 20 s to complete the survey, which was sufficient to read and understand the questions.

4   Results

In this section we will present the results derived from quantitative analysis of the data collected in this study. First we describe participants' profiles and then present our analysis of the different levels of "personalness" they can consider a piece of information to be in. Finally we contrast how people share information in face-to-face settings and on Facebook, to probe if they reflect the changes in people's concerns when migrating from the offline to the online world, considering the differences between these two settings.

4.1   Characterizing the Participants

Nine initial questions were aimed at characterizing the study participants. From the screening, we knew the participants were Facebook users. Forty percent of the participants were situated between the ages of 25 and 34 and 21 % were situated between the ages of 35 and 44, and 59 % were female and 41 % male. The majority of participants have bachelor degrees (38 %) or some college education (37 %) and most of them (87 %) do not have background or work in Information Technology. Half of the respondents have already deactivated their accounts on an online social network before and 33 % of them reported that the reason for doing so was related to privacy issues. The majority of the participants have been using Facebook for more than three years (78 %) and access the system very often (71 % of the respondents access it at least once a day, and of these, 51 % are always connected or access it several times a day).

4.2   Information Sharing

Information Personal Degree. In order to find out with whom participants share information they consider the most and the least personal, we asked participants to rate some pieces of information according to how personal they consider them to be, on a four-point scale, ranging from "not personal" to "very personal". Such pieces of information have been chosen based on Facebook's profile elements and on results from an exploratory study [28, 29] in which we asked participants "Who do you consider the closest people with whom you share your personal information? Which type of information do you share?". In this paper, we will call the level into which a piece of information was classified its *personal degree.*

Based on how respondents rated the pieces of information, we created groups according to how personal they are. These groups were obtained through the k-means method [30]. The best group explanation was obtained for 5 clusters. Figure 1 shows the mean response for each category and its 95 % confidence interval, as we can see the categories mean visual separation closely agree with the group classification obtained by the k-means method (represented by the boxes in Fig. 1).

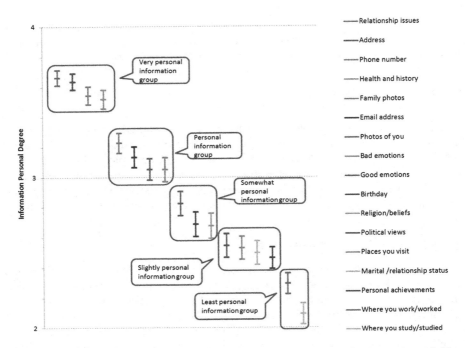

Fig. 1. Information personal degree classification varying on the y axis from not personal (1) to very personal (4) – Notice that each piece of information shown on the right side is presented in the order it was classified by participants.

As shown in Fig. 1, we can distinguish two information groups on the top tier (between the values 3 and 4). Thus, we denominated the top most group (means are closer to value 4) "very personal information group". This group is composed by *relationship issues*, *address*, *phone number* and *health and history*. We denominated the other group within this range "personal information group" which is composed by *family photos*, *email address*, *photos of you* and *bad emotions*.

The other three groups we have identified are located between the values 2 and 3 and they are not so clearly separated from each other as the first two groups. The third group closer to value 3 has been denominated "somewhat personal information group" and is composed by *good emotions*, *birthday* and *religion/beliefs*. We called the next group within this range the "slightly personal group" and it is composed by *political views*, *places you visit*, *marital/relationship status* and *personal achievements*. Finally the last group (means are closer to value 2) was called "least personal information group" and is composed by *where you work/worked in the past* and *where you study/studied in the past*.

The classification is interesting because it indicates that people do not think about the different pieces of information as being equally personal. Therefore, their attitudes towards different pieces of information may change accordingly to how personal that information is perceived to be. Thus, in our survey, participants were asked to indicate which piece of information they felt comfortable sharing with whom in both face-to-face settings and

Facebook. In face-to-face settings, respondents could choose as their responses the groups "family (parents, spouse, siblings, children)", "relatives", "closest friends", "work/school colleagues", "acquaintances", "everybody" or "nobody". In Facebook, the respondents could choose among the groups "friends", "friends and friends of friends", "public", "custom (specific people)" and "groups". We then contrasted the degree they had attributed to each piece of information and to whom they shared it with in the physical world and Facebook.

Sharing in the Physical World. In the physical world, we found that people share information more intensely and in a similar way with family and close friends (see Fig. 2) when compared to other groups. We also notice that the information related to contact (*address*, *phone number* and *email* address) is the most shared, regardless of their personal degree.

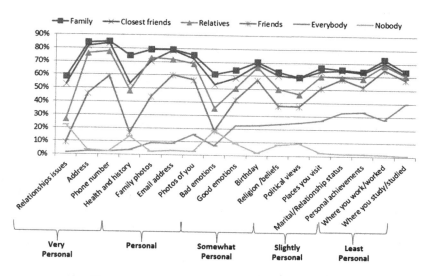

Fig. 2. Sharing information in the physical world

However, if we look at which pieces of information people choose to share with everybody versus nobody, we notice that their personal degree makes a difference. Based on Fig. 2, we notice the most personal information is the less shared group, i.e., more people report not to share it with anybody and less people share it with everybody. However, we can notice some outliers, as *address* and *phone number*, which were rated as very personal information, and that only a few people have reported not to share. Notice that these pieces of information are related to contact and even physical identity, and that for many commercial relations one is asked to inform them.

The other outlier is *bad emotions,* which is in the second level of personal degree – *personal information*, but closer to the group's lower limit. Nonetheless many people reported not sharing it with anybody.

As the personal degree of the information lowers, we notice that people tend to be willing to share the information more publicly, i.e., with everybody.

Sharing on Facebook. In Facebook we found that people mostly do not share (share with nobody) or share their information with friends when compared to other groups of people. As shown in Fig. 3, information in the *most personal group* (*relationship issues, health and history, address*, and *phone number*) tends not to be shared.

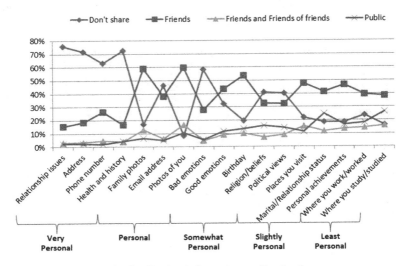

Fig. 3. Sharing information on Facebook

If we analyze people's attitude towards the second personal degree group – *personal information* – we notice that it is not homogenous regarding the pieces of information that comprise the group. *Email address* (the contact/id information in the virtual world) and *bad emotions* people tend not to share. On the other hand, *family photos* and *photos of you* (the other pieces of information classified in the personal group) tend to be among the most shared information, in spite of being considered personal.

The information in the lower three groups of personal degree tends to be more broadly shared. However, looking at Fig. 3 it comes to our attention that *religion/beliefs* and *political views* which are classified as *somewhat* and *slightly personal*, respectively, and many people choose not to share on Facebook.

5   Contrasting Online and Offline Self-disclosure

In comparing the self-disclosure attitudes in online and offline contexts towards the *very personal information group*, we notice the difference towards *address* and *phone number*. In the physical world they are broadly shared, while in Facebook they are among the least shared. This is an indication that people do not want to give access in the physical world to all their friends in the virtual world.

It is interesting to notice that people's attitudes towards *bad emotions* are similar in the physical world and Facebook. In both worlds, people tend to be protective of this piece of information, and treat it as they do the more restricted information, in the very personal group. One possible explanation for this fact is that there can be other factors at play besides its personal degree which might influence the way people share it. For instance, people might take into consideration how sharing a piece of information may affect the image other people have of them, and may not want to be associated to an image of a negative or whining person.

In the physical world, *political views* and *good emotions* come into the top five least shared. Notice that *good emotions* and *political views* are in the *somewhat personal* and *slightly personal information* groups, respectively. Thus, the reasons not to share it with anybody might be related to other aspects and not only to their personal degree. However, when comparing with Facebook, although these pieces of information are not among the most restricted information, people still restrict *political views* and *good emotions* more in Facebook (40 % and 32 % of the respondents respectively do not share them with anybody) than they do in the physical world.

If we go to other side of the spectrum and compare the pieces of information that are most shared publicly in the physical world as well as on Facebook, we can notice that the top four are the same, as shown in Figs. 4 and 5.

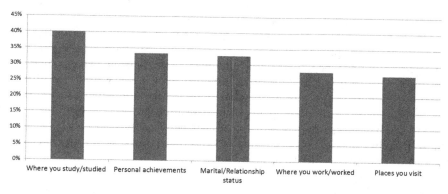

Fig. 4. The five pieces of information most shared publicly in the physical world

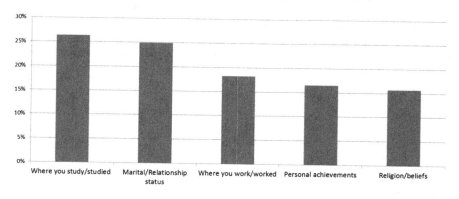

Fig. 5. The five pieces of information most shared publicly on Facebook

Considering the information groups shown earlier in Fig. 1, these pieces of information are on the two lower personal degree groups. The only exception is *religion/ beliefs*, which is among the least restricted piece of information in Facebook and is classified as *somewhat personal*.

It also interesting that comparing Figs. 4 and 5 it is possible to see that in the physical world the number of people who reported sharing the pieces of information as public is much higher than in Facebook.

The data presented indicates that people have different attitudes towards sharing information in the physical world and in Facebook. In short, they share less the information they consider to be more personal, and even with the less personal information, less people are willing to share it publicly.

Also, if we compare the most restricted information in both worlds – i.e., information which more people choose not to share with anyone, we notice that the number of people who choose not to share information is much higher in Facebook than in the physical world.

These differences can probably be explained if we take into consideration the sociological definition of primary and secondary groups.[2] In face-to-face settings, people have different interactions and attitudes with members of their primary and secondary groups. On Facebook, however, people tend to include as friends people they do not have any primary relationships with in the physical world. For instance, when people include people they do not know, or someone who is part of a community, but with whom they do not interact personally, we can say they are including members of secondary groups as friends. The large number of Facebook friends reported by many participants is an indication of this, since people do not have close relationships with hundreds of other people. Thus, in Facebook people tend to share information as they would with secondary groups, limiting the access to information they consider to be more personal.

In order to generate a better comparison of the difference between sharing information in the physical world and online, we created an indicator denominated *level of exposure*. For each piece of information the *level of exposure* indicated if participants shared it more online, more in the physical world, if they shared it consistently in both worlds, or inconsistently – that is with different groups of people. The indicator was calculated by an algorithm that we have created (see Algorithm 1) which compared participants' answers to the questions regarding whom they felt comfortable sharing each piece of information in both worlds.

---

[2] In a sociological view, society is composed by primary and secondary groups [33, 34]. Primary groups refer to small groups in which members have face-to-face relationships that are affective and more intimate, such as with family, close friends or neighbors. Whereas secondary groups refer to broader social categories in which a person is part of a group but does not have a face-to-face relationship, such as professional associations or unions.

```
Let Q_FB and Q_Off be the questions about with whom
participant share information in Facebook and offline,
respectively
for each participant P_i do
  for each piece of information Inf_j do
    Ans_FB ← Answer to Q_FB;
    Ans_Off ← Answer to Q_Off;
    if Ans_FB is "public" then
      if Ans_Off is "everybody" then
        audience_consistent_j +=1;
      else
        audience_online_j +=1
      end-if
    else if Ans_FB is "friend" then
      if Ans_Off is "nobody" then
        audience_online_j +=1;
      else if Ans_Off is "everybody" then
        if friends include unknown people then
          audience_consistent_j +=1
        else
          audience_offline_j +=1
        end-if
      else
        compare people included Ans_Off and Ans_FB
        if Ans_Off includes more than Ans_FB then
          audience_offline_j +=1
        else if Ans_Off includes less than Ans_FB then
          audience_online_j +=1
        else
          audience_consistent_j +=1
        end-if
      end-if
    else if […]
      //compares all the different possibilities
      […]
    end-if
  end-for
end-for
```

Algorithm 1. Partial pseudo code to calculate level of exposure

The results calculated by the algorithm are shown in Fig. 6. The values on the y axis represent the number of respondents and the x axis shows the types of information ordered from the most to the least personal. Notice that for the less personal information participants tend to expose themselves more consistently in both worlds, and even the

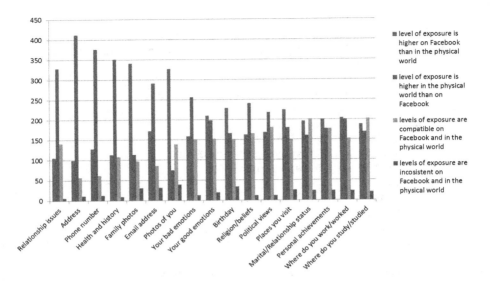

Fig. 6. Participants' exposure level for each piece of information

number of participants who expose themselves more in one world than the other seems to be closer to each other. Regarding the very personal information group and *bad emotion*, as expected, people expose themselves more in the physical world than in Facebook. People also expose their *email address* more offline than online.

It is interesting to notice that *photos* are highly more exposed online than offline. Few people reported not sharing *family photos* or *photos of themselves* with anybody in the physical world (2.8 % and 2.9 %, respectively), and the high majority reported sharing it mainly with friends in Facebook (58.9 % and 59.6 % respectively). This large difference in online exposure is probably a result of people having a broader group of people included as Facebook friends than the groups they reported they would share their photos with in the physical world. In other words, having a higher level of exposure in Facebook indicates that people with whom the participant would not usually share the photo in the physical world are having access to it through Facebook.

The other result worth commenting is *religion/beliefs* and *political views*. Even though *religion/beliefs* was among the pieces of information most shared publicly on Facebook (Fig. 5) and *political views* was among the most restricted in the physical world, they are both more exposed in the physical world than in Facebook.

The data presented indicates that people have different attitudes towards sharing information in the physical world and in Facebook. Also this attitude is not only due to their attitude towards the physical or online worlds, but it changes according to the piece of information and how personal it is considered to be.

The results here, in line with Emanuel et al. [23], suggest that participants felt comfortable sharing more of their personal information face-to-face, as compared to disclosing personal information on Facebook. From a privacy standpoint, the persistency of information published on Facebook, unlike information shared face-to-face, could be a factor explaining reluctance of people to publish private information online [31].

Besides, uncertainty around who may have access to personal information on online context should have led to less self-disclosure [32] and users have adopted self-censorship as self-disclosure risks management strategies on Facebook [2].

6   Final Remarks and Next Steps

In this paper we have set out to investigate two questions: (1) What information do people consider personal and to what degree? (2) With whom do they feel comfortable in sharing which pieces of their information with in the physical and virtual worlds? Based on the data collected through a survey applied to 581 people, we have been able to identify a five level classification of how personal a piece of information can be perceived to be.

Analyzing people's responses regarding with whom they feel comfortable sharing information in the physical and virtual worlds, we were able to identify different attitudes related to different pieces of information or personal degree categories in the physical and virtual worlds.

The results discussed are relevant because they show that in analyzing privacy in the virtual world researchers and developers should not only be taking into consideration if the information is personal or not, but its personal degree could be a relevant factor regarding with whom or how users intend to share it.

It also indicates that Facebook users, taken as a representative of OSNs, do not reproduce in the virtual world the difference between members of their primary and secondary social groups in the physical world. As a result, regarding the information that is considered most personal, people tend to treat all Facebook friends equally as members of a secondary group, with whom they share less information. It could be interesting to investigate deeper if this attitude change is due to new interactive possibilities offered by OSNs, or if it is a limitation in mechanisms provided to users, making it costly (even if possible) for them to create groups of friends with whom they interact differently.

Understanding the different attitudes people have towards different pieces of information can support the design and evaluation of interfaces that allow for a more fine distinction and sharing of different personal degree information. The next steps in this research include a qualitative study that aims at analyzing how different OSNs present and allow users to share the different pieces of information, according to the attitudes discussed in this paper.

This research focused on US users, and we understand that the culture may influence people's view of how personal a piece of information is and their attitudes towards sharing it. Thus, it would be relevant to conduct a similar study with people from different cultures and compare their attitudes to those identified in this paper.

Acknowledgments. Authors thank all the survey participants. Maria Lúcia B. Villela thanks CAPES, and Raquel O. Prates thanks CNPq for the partial support to this research.

References

1. Duggan, M., Ellison, N.B., Lampe, C., Lenhart, A., Madden, M.: Social Media Update 2014. Pew Internet and American Life Project (2015)
2. Vitak, J., Kim, J.: You Can'T block people offline: examining how facebook's affordances shape the disclosure process. In: Proceedings of the CSCW 2014, pp. 461–474. ACM Press, New York, New York, USA (2014)
3. Taddei, S., Contena, B.: Privacy, trust and control: which relationships with online self-disclosure? Comput. Hum. Behav. **29**, 821–826 (2013)
4. Sleeper, M., Balebako, R., Das, S., Mcconahy, A.L., Wiese, J., Cranor, L.F.: The Post that Wasn't: Exploring Self-Censorship on Facebook, 793–802 (2013)
5. Stutzman, F., Gross, R., Acquisti, A.: Silent Listeners: The Evolution of Privacy and Disclosure on Facebook, 7–41 (2012)
6. Nissenbaum, H.: Privacy as contextual integrity. Wash. Law Rev. **79**, 119–158 (2004)
7. Bazarova, N.N., Choi, Y.H.: Self-Disclosure in social media: extending the functional approach to disclosure motivations and characteristics on social network sites. J. Commun. **64**, 635–657 (2014)
8. Wiese, J., Kelley, P.G., Cranor, L.F., Dabbish, L., Hong, J.I., Zimmerman, J.: Are You Close with Me? Are You Nearby? Investigating Social Groups, Closeness, and Willingness to Share, 197–206 (2011)
9. Kolimi, S., Zhu, F., Carpenter, S.: Contexts and sharing/not sharing private information. In: Proceedings of the 50th Annual Southeast Regional Conference on - ACM-SE 2012. 292 (2012)
10. Olson, J.S., Grudin, J., Horvitz, E.: A study of preferences for sharing and privacy. In: CHI 2005 Extended Abstracts on Human Factors in Computing Systems - CHI 2005. 1985 (2005)
11. Consolvo, S., Smith, I.E., Matthews, T., Lamarca, A., Tabert, J., Powledge, P.: Location Disclosure to Social Relations: Why, When, & What People Want to Share. CHI, pp. 81–90 (2005)
12. Bevan, J., Cummings, M., Kubiniec, A., Mogannam, M., Price, M., Todd, R.: How are important life events disclosed on facebook? relationships with likelihood of sharing and privacy. Cyberpsychology, Behav. Soc. Networking **18**, 8–11 (2015)
13. Day, S.: Self-disclosure on Facebook: How much do we really reveal? (2013). http://www.citrenz.ac.nz/jacit/JACIT1701/2013Day_Facebook.html
14. Attrill, A., Jalil, R.: Revealing only the superficial me: exploring categorical self-disclosure online. Comput. Hum. Behav. **27**, 1634–1642 (2011)
15. Gross, R., Acquisti, A.: Information revelation and privacy in online social networks. Proc. WPES **2005**, 71–80 (2005)
16. Wang, Y., Norice, G., Cranor, L.F.: Who is concerned about what? a study of american, chinese and indian users' privacy concerns on social network sites. In: McCune, J.M., Balacheff, B., Perrig, A., Sadeghi, A.-R., Sasse, A., Beres, Y. (eds.) Trust 2011. LNCS, vol. 6740, pp. 146–153. Springer, Heidelberg (2011)
17. Attrill, A.: Sharing only parts of me: selective categorical self-disclosure across internet arenas. Int. J. Internet Sci. **7**, 55–77 (2012)
18. Cranshaw, J., Toch, E., Hong, J., Kittur, A., Sadeh, N.: Bridging the gap between physical location and online social networks. In: Proceedings of the 12th ACM International Conference on Ubiquitous Computing - Ubicomp 2010. 119 (2010)
19. Grieve, R., Indian, M., Witteveen, K., Anne Tolan, G., Marrington, J.: Face-to-face or Facebook: Can social connectedness be derived online? Comput. Hum. Behav. **29**, 604–609 (2013)

20. Rosen, D., Stefanone, M.A., Lackaff, D.: Online and offline social networks: investigating culturally-specific behavior and satisfaction. In: Proceedings of the HICSS 2010, pp. 1–10. IEEE (2010)
21. Subrahmanyam, K., Reich, S.M., Waechter, N., Espinoza, G.: Online and offline social networks: use of social networking sites by emerging adults. J. Appl. Dev. Psychol. **29**, 420–433 (2008)
22. Nguyen, M., Bin, Y.S., Campbell, A.: Comparing online and offline self-disclosure: a systematic review. Cyberpsychology, Behav. Soc. Networking **15**, 103–111 (2012)
23. Emanuel, L., Neil, G.J., Bevan, C., Fraser, D.S., Stevenage, S.V., Whitty, M.T., Jamison-Powell, S.: Who am I? Representing the self offline and in different online contexts. Comput. Hum. Behav. **41**, 146–152 (2014)
24. Sundar, S., Kang, H., Wu, M., Go, E., Zhang, B.: Unlocking the privacy paradox: do cognitive heuristics hold the key? In: CHI 2013 Extended Abstracts …., pp. 811–816 (2013)
25. Marshall, C.C., Shipman, F.M.: Experiences surveying the crowd: reflections on methods, participation, and reliability. In: Proceedings of the 5th Annual ACM Web Science Conference, pp. 234–243. ACM (2013)
26. Jakobsson, M.: Experimenting on Mechanical Turk: 5 How Tos (2009)
27. Downs, J.S., Holbrook, M.B., Sheng, S., Cranor, L.F.: Are your participants gaming the system? In: Proceedings of the 28th International Conference on Human Factors in Computing Systems - CHI 2010, p. 2399. ACM Press, New York, USA (2010)
28. Xavier, S., Villela, M., Prates, R.O., Prates, A.A., Cardoso, A., Prates, M.: Migrando das redes sociais offline para as redes sociais online: O que houve com a privacidade? In: Proceedings of the Brazilian Simposium on Human Factors in Computing Systems (2014)
29. Villela, M.L.B., Xavier, S.I.R., Prates, R.O., Prates, M.O., Prates, A.A.P., Cardoso, A.A.: Moving from offline to online social networks: what happened to people's privacy? A Brazilian Case Study (2015)
30. MacQueen, J.B.: Some methods for classification and analysis of multivariate observations. In: Proceedings of 5th Berkeley Symposium on Mathematical Statistics and Probability, pp. 281–297. University of California Press (1967)
31. Alarcón, R.A., Guerrero, L.A., Pino, J.A.: Temporal blurring: a privacy model for OMS users. In: Ardissono, L., Brna, P., Mitrović, A. (eds.) UM 2005. LNCS (LNAI), vol. 3538, pp. 417–422. Springer, Heidelberg (2005)
32. Barkhuus, L.: The mismeasurement of privacy. In: Proceedings of the 2012 ACM Annual Conference on Human Factors in Computing Systems - CHI 2012, p. 367. ACM Press, New York, USA (2012)
33. Chinoy, E.: Society: An Introduction to Sociology. Random House, NY (1963)
34. Broom, L., Selznick, P.: Sociology – A Text with Adapted Readings. Harper & Row, NY (1968)

Author Index

Adewoyin, Oluwabunmi   111

Baião, Fernanda Araujo   164
Baloian, Nelson   1, 63, 198
Barrientos, Cristopher   210
Biella, Daniel   1
Bordiés, Osmel   45

Cárdenas, Catalina   198
Cardoso, Alexandre A.   232
Chounta, Irene-Angelica   124, 140

Darbinyan, Armen   190
de Vreede, Gert-Jan   28
Dimitriadis, Yannis   45

Egusa, Ryohei   181

Frez, Jonathan   63

Galdames, Patricio   210
Gutierrez-Soto, Claudio   210

Harrer, Andreas   19
Hecking, Tobias   140
Hoppe, H. Ulrich   124, 140

Inagaki, Shigenori   181
Inoue, Tomoo   219

Jansen, Bernard J.   72
Jivanyan, Aram   190

Kamiyama, Shinichi   181
Kienle, Andrea   19
Kuhlen, Torsten W.   86
Kusunoki, Fusako   181

Link, Georg J.P.   28
Liu, Zhe   72
Luther, Wolfram   1, 86

Manukyan, Azat   190
Medina, Esunly   95
Medina, Humberto   95
Meseguer, Roc   95

Mizoguchi, Hiroshi   181
Mohkami, Mohsen   148
Moura, Ednilson Veloso   164

Namatame, Miki   181
Noguchi, Yasuhito   219
Noorian, Zeinab   148

Ochoa, Sergio F.   95

Pino, José A.   63
Prates, Antônio A.P.   232
Prates, Marcos O.   232
Prates, Raquel O.   232

Robra-Bissantz, Susanne   28

Sacher, Daniel   1, 86
Saito, Machi   181
Sakai, Tsugunosuke   181
Santoro, Flávia Maria   164
Schlieker-Steens, Philipp   19
Schlösser, Christian   19
Schreck, Tobias   1
Shipman, Frank   232
Siemon, Dominik   28
Steinert, Laura   124
Sugimoto, Masanori   181

Takeda, Yoshiaki   181
Tamaki, Haruya   181

Vassileva, Julita   111, 148
Villela, Maria L.B.   232

Weyers, Benjamin   1, 86
Wu, Kewen   111

Xavier, Simone I.R.   232

Yamaguchi, Etsuji   181
Yeghiazaryan, Roland   190
Yoshida, Ryuichi   181

Zurita, Gustavo   63, 198

Printed in the United States
By Bookmasters